"*A Cloak of Good Fortune* is a vivid, often funny, and sometimes almost naïve testimony of the author's adventurous childhood during the time of the Khmer Rouge in Cambodia. And this naivety is precisely what makes this book new and unique. Mr. Do does not indulge in history, geopolitics...or philosophy. Instead, he makes us see through his own eyes what daily life was during that time in what was, only a few years earlier, considered a peaceful and welcoming country."

—**Dr. Gilles Germain,** Medecins Sans Frontieres, Caluire, France

"With a prose style that depicts the beauty, scents, and sounds of life in his native Cambodia, Mr. Do illustrates beautifully the quandary of so many immigrants: nostalgia for a lost way of life while also always celebrating the relative safety and promise once out of a war-torn country."

—**Hali Hammer, M.D.,** Professor of Clinical Family and Community Medicine, University of California San Francisco

"Sieu Sean Do takes the reader on an unforgettable, harrowing personal journey, rich with detail and stunning turns of events. Ultimately, Mr. Do's life story stands as an uplifting testament to the resiliency of the human spirit!"

— **Peter H. Hwang, M.D.,** Professor, Stanford University School of Medicine

"In his mesmerizing memoir, Sieu Sean reminds every reader that there is evil in the world, but that if we hold onto the core of our humanity, evil cannot win. These are raw, gut-wrenching truths that unapologetically speak to both our cruel inhumanity and our boundless absolution. A powerful journey!"

— **David Tran, DPM, M.S.,** Surgeon and Educator (Vietnam War refugee)

"Childhood, especially to Cambodian children born after 1960, is a faraway time, one they can neither relive nor restore, and which for each of them has become a mystery to cling onto. Those children who have survived the Khmer Rouge Killing Fields are condemned to live with those memories. Sieu Sean Do was a young child in the 1960s, when all family members and extended family, even the siblings of great-grandparents, existed as one beloved unit. Sieu Sean's memory of childhood is a treasure trove of Cambodian folklore, beliefs, superstitions, traditions, ghosts, goblins, fairies, and witches that enchant the spellbound reader. He writes with a sensitivity somehow devoid of hatred that any survivor might be expected to feel for the inhumanity to man that he witnessed firsthand: first during the reign of terror by the Khmer Rouge in Cambodia in the 1970s.

This is Sieu Sean telling tales from the lips of his ancestors, who provided the saving grace from the terror that would soon victimize him and his family. The story shows his journey from a privileged childhood to a kingdom of terror."

—**Dr. Di Finch**, United Nations Volunteer for Children in Ethiopia

"The stories in *A Cloak of Good Fortune* launch the reader on an amazing journey through mysterious cultures and mythic beliefs. The author's never-ending struggle to survive unrelenting adversity brings the reader from tears to joy. His striking resilience teaches us that love and kindness to others can be the most effective therapy for a survivor to recover from emotional trauma inflicted by the violence of war."

— **Nang Du, M.D.**, Clinical Professor of Psychiatry, UCSF San Mateo North County Medical Chief (Vietnam War refugee)

"*A Cloak of Good Fortune* is a riveting human-interest story—a wondrous journey of delight and survival against all odds. A must read!"

—**Gayle Tang, MSN, R.N.**, Professor Adjunct at City College of San Francisco; Former Senior Executive Director, National Diversity & Inclusion, Kaiser Foundation Health Plan, Inc.

"*A Cloak of Good Fortune*, by Sieu Sean Do, is a moving, heartfelt story of a young boy who survived by relying upon all his senses, only to embrace the anxiety of imminent deportation back into the war zone after his family had finally reached safety across the border with Vietnam...The roots of family devotion run through every story, documenting Do's incredible journey... During chaos and danger, the family still exercised compassion to others and instilled the importance of education as evidenced by their resolve to empower their son, the author, to learn multiple languages under the most extreme conditions. This book exemplifies the family's humble and forgiving nature, and their appreciation for life in the USA today."

—**Lt. Carlos B. Sánchez**, Director of Alameda County's Social Services Agency Program, Integrity Division, and former assistant Chief Investigator for the San Francisco District Attorney's Office

"Prior to reading *A Cloak of Good Fortune*, I had the privilege of meeting Sieu Sean Do and getting to know him through his dedicated work to combat elder abuse and consumer fraud through his work at a government agency. What struck me immediately from when I first met Sieu Sean was his deep dedication to believing in and always fighting for fairness and the humane treatment of all people.

Sieu Sean's memoir is a vivid, deeply personal account of having grown up a happy child until the age of 12 in Cambodia, only to then abruptly—along with his whole family and scores of others—find himself increasingly subjected to the numerous atrocities of war in the form of repeated acts of supposedly justified, socially engineered acts of cruelty and genocide under the Khmer Rouge. However, under such conditions, for a survivor of such atrocities to choose, as Sieu Sean has, to still live with a sense of meaning, a continued sense of joy, and a spiritual belief in the goodness of humankind—and with an appreciation and love for all people in the world—is truly incredible and inspiring."

—**Heidi Li**, family law attorney/advocate & former Director of Elder Abuse Prevention Program at the Institute on Aging

A Cloak of Good Fortune

A Cambodian boy's journey from paradise
through a kingdom of terror...

Sieu Sean Do

HIBISCUS PRESS

The stories in this book reflect the author's recollection of events. Some names, locations, and identifying characteristics have been changed to protect the privacy of those depicted. Dialogue has been recreated from memory.

Information about *A Cloak of Good Fortune* by Sieu Sean Do may be found at www.Sieuseando.com

For copies of A Cloak of Good Fortune by Sieu Sean Do, contact us at:

    Hibiscus Press
    5432 Geary Blvd, Suite 312, San Francisco, CA 94121
    Phone: (628) 256-3673
    Or email: Acloakofgoodfortune@gmail.com

If you are a teacher and would like group copies, please contact us for a discount.

Cover photograph: Saravuth
Name of boy on cover with chicken: Nasynonh
Author photograph: Jason Collom
Book Cover and Interior Design: JM Shubin, (bookalchemist.net)
Copy Editor: Bob Cooper (bob-cooper.com)

ISBN 978-1-7331819-0-7

Library of Congress Control Number 2017914919

First Printing in 2019

This book is dedicated to:

My Grandparents; Father and Mother; Second Mother,
Dr. May Fung Mei Tam; Uncle Phan and
Aunt Kien; Dr. Vuong Lam; Brother Chen;
Sister Mei Juang and Brother Sok;
my children—Udam, William, Hedan, and Samantha;
and finally,
with respect to my mentor, Father Thomas Dunleavy

My only childhood picture

My beloved second mother,
Dr. May Fung Mei Tam

Preface
A Note to the Reader

Forty-four years after my escape from the Khmer Rouge massacres in Cambodia, I decided it was important to recall as fully and completely as possible the facts, details, and emotions of those experiences. I'd locked the memories in a box while rebuilding my new life in America. Too often I have felt it had been a wearying journey, and I thought that recording my memories in a diary might help me recover my soul before it was lost to me forever.

Over time, writing in my diary healed me. The process of recounting and reliving my enigmatic experiences restored my identity—the sense of self that had been forbidden, shattered, scattered, suppressed, denied, distorted, and hidden during my struggles to survive. I came to understand that writing down my recollections restored my health and confidence.

When I thought of myself as a refugee and immigrant trying to make my life better, I found no place that was truly home. I was a tree without roots, and from this realization I understood the plight of other victims coping with the trauma that haunts their lives. Future generations need to hear what happened from those who lived through it. The past must not be forgotten.

When a dark, lonely shadow steals over me, I revisit my life by reading entries in my diary. Even though that can trigger anger, regret, and pain, in time I find relief and a measure of peace. That inner peace continues to reveal new, positive insights that empower the life I am choosing to create, which is reinforced by my certainty in the ultimate good of people and the power of stories to heal people all over the world.

Contents

CAMBODIA

Prologue
A Prophesied Birth

When I was a boy, my Grandma Lo Lian loved telling me about what happened the night before I was born. It was a full moon day in the spring of 1963. On days when the evening moon would be full, Grandma Lo Lian set up a table on the balcony, with candles, fruits, and flowers as an offering to the spirit of Preah Chan Penh Vong, the full moon. She told me she often prayed for the unity of her family to be full and harmonious, like the full moon itself. On those days, she and the rest of the family ate only vegetarian meals, so that everyone's soul would be cleansed.

On just such an evening, the night before my birth, Grandma Lo Lian was standing alone on the balcony. Suddenly, a ball of fire dropped onto the table. In shock, she ran downstairs shouting her youngest son's name, Bun Kheang, and called for the rest of the family to come see the ball of fire that had just landed on the table. They all rushed upstairs onto the balcony, but everything looked normal. Grandma Lo Lian didn't know what to think about what she had witnessed, but she kept insisting she did see the fireball land on the table. She claimed it was a powerful message from the Supreme Being, alerting her to what was to come. She believed it was a good sign, and that it indicated that I was to lead a special life. Everyone looked at each other, wondering what had just happened. Later, whenever Grandma Lo Lian told me that story, I couldn't help but think it was a peculiar sign connected to my birth.

The next day, my mother, a seamstress, was working on her customer's clothing when she suddenly had a strong stomach cramp and pressure in her pelvic area. She knew that my delivery was near. My father immediately called a taxi to take them to Calmette Hospital in Phnom Penh.

As soon as the taxi arrived, the driver ran to the front door and told Papa his car had a flat tire. Apologizing profusely, he suggested that Papa find another ride because he had no spare and it would take at least a couple of hours to get the tire fixed. The whole family was in chaos. My mother's contractions grew stronger, and she kept crying out in pain.

At that moment a well-known midwife, Yei Khout, walked past the house. Spotting my Grandma Lo Lian pacing anxiously at the front door, Yei Khout called out to greet her. Grandma Lo Lian immediately pulled Yei Khout inside and barked, "My daughter is about to give birth. You must deliver the baby!"

The midwife was taken aback. "But I have no equipment with me. Let me run home and get it and come right back." Before leaving, Yei Khout decided to check on Mama. She walked quickly back to Mama's room and, seeing how urgent it was, commanded, "Don't go anywhere, the baby is coming fast!" Then she ran back to her house, fetched her equipment, and returned just in time to take charge of the delivery.

"Wow! This child is coming out in the sac," announced Yei Khout in amazement. Even outside Mama's body, I was still in the amniotic sac. Yei Khout cried excitedly, "You have a clean child! He has been protected by a cloak of good fortune. That's a good omen!"

She explained that a baby born in an amniotic sac is believed to be born without sin. "Such a child will bring great fortune to the parents," she added.

After handing me over to Mama, Yei Khout wrapped the placenta and sac in a bag and gave it to Papa. "Take these and bury them by the river to keep them whole and cool for the rest of this child's life, so he will remain free from sin."

Many years later, Mama told me she had been in so much pain and so exhausted that she didn't really care what the midwife was saying. She just wanted to give birth to a healthy baby.

Not a day goes by when I don't think of that image and that prediction about how

I was born under the cloak of good fortune.

❀

Uncle Bun Khieng died during the Pol Pot regime.

1.
Bun Kathen

As a devout Buddhist, Mama often recounted to me and my siblings the fascinating story of the Buddha's birth. Her way of storytelling was so sweet and informative that it feels like yesterday that she told us.

"Long, long ago," she began, "during the sixth century, in the grove of Lumbini in Nepal, Queen Mahamaya became pregnant. Soon after, a dream came to her in which she spotted a white elephant bearing a white lotus flower, which then magically entered her body. She named her Nepalese prince Siddhartha, which meant one who has accomplished his goal. A week after he was born, his mother Queen Mahamaya died. Shortly after, her sister, Mahaprajapati, was married to King Suddhodana and soon took on the tender role of mother for Siddhartha. She raised him with great care and love. When Siddhartha was still an infant, the king anxiously asked the soothsayers if his son carried any sign of bad luck, which was his way of assuring that the boy wouldn't replace him. The soothsayer cried loudly in amazement and told the king he foresaw that Prince Siddhartha had a special destiny, for he would have a talent for understanding the true nature of the mind. Eventually, the soothsayer confided to the king that his son was fated to lead the world to be free from illusion and suffering.

"Upon hearing it, the king became extremely concerned. He definitely didn't ever want his son to have anything to do with religion or a spiritual path. He only wished that he would become the next king. The king was vehement in his denial and called on a few Hindu priests who had sacred knowledge skills to explain the prophecy of the prince. They all agreed with the prophecy of the soothsayer, saying that the child would leave home to become 'Buddha,' which means 'The Enlightened One,' and that he would save the world from its ignorance and madness.

"This news distressed the king, who wanted to be sure, and sought out another priest for further advice on what might prove to be even more tragic, which was the possibility that the prince would renounce home, family, and responsibility for the sake of a strange spiritual role in life. The sacred priest explained that the only way to prevent the prince from renouncing home was to somehow prevent him from seeing the sacred Four Signs: an old person, a sick person, a dead person, and a monk.

"Over the next many years, until the child prince turned sixteen and became a young man, the king ordered the guards to stay at the gate and make sure such persons would never enter the royal palace. When he reached the age of marriage, the king decided to force his son to take a wife, which would be another way to assure that he wouldn't even want to renounce home. And so Siddhartha married the princess Yashodhara, who felt it was her destiny to please him with music and many dancing girls in his stately home.

"However, when Prince Siddhartha reached his late twenties, he decided to tour his crowded city in his royal carriage. This made the king extremely worried, and he ordered the guards to make sure the roads were clear of "the Four Signs," which proved impossible to prevent. As he saw his city with his own eyes for the first time, one by one, Siddhartha did indeed encounter the four signs, the four stages of man: an old person, a sick person, a corpse, and a monk. "Siddhartha never forgot these encounters and the omen they provided—that life was short and full of suffering. A few years later, he became the father of a young boy, who he felt could easily take over the responsibilities of a king. He decided that he could now safely and responsibly renounce his family and the kingdom. Soon after his moment of clarity, in the dark of night, he secretly left the palace and calmly walked away, passing through the heavy gate that protected his city, and set off alone into the forest. He vowed to never return and instead to pursue his spiritual path, which was to escape the realm of *samsara*, and be released from the wheel of suffering that brings so much pain. Siddhartha walked for weeks and months before reaching Uruvela, a small distant village. There, he found a beautiful tree, under which he sat quietly and calmly for forty-nine days without moving, until he reached his goal. Thousands of years later, that tree is called the Bodhi Tree, in honor of his attaining enlightenment.

I was inspired by the legend of Prince Siddhartha prevailing over materialism and delusion by choosing his own path to spiritual enlightenment. I thought the story was powerful as it contained the life-changing lesson that the way to change ourselves is through the mind.

❀❀❀❀❀

As a child, I often had the good fortune of hearing our ancestral stories from my grandparents. My family and I lived with them in Kampong Speu Province, about fifty kilometers from the capital of Cambodia. Grandma Lo Lian took every opportunity to remind me how selfless her parents were. My Great Grandpa Lo Kim Han and Great Grandma Chea Mi Ung were humble people who had lived in a tree-and-monkey-shrouded peaceful village, Ampe Phnom, since the 1920s, when Cambodia was still a colony of France.

They owned a grocery store and sold palm-fruit sugar cakes (*nom a kao thnaot*) and fish-noodle soup (*somlau nom pajok*). They were seen as being among the village's wealthy merchants. However, they did not pass on their inheritance to their children. They believed children should learn to work hard and make their own fortune, and that good karma would lead them to a better life.

Our family philosophy had its roots in Buddhist spirituality. Grandma Lo Lian told me that her mother, Chea Mi Ung, and her brother, Second Great-Uncle Chea Sun, had a profoundly close relationship due to the path of their practice. They both believed in the need for the cessation of Samsara in order to escape the continuous, suffering-laden cycle of life, death, and rebirth, without beginning or end. But it wasn't only their belief system that they shared. They were devout in their practice of Buddhist rituals that were designed to honor their commitment to seeing each other again in the pure land of bliss, Sukhavati. Their bond was so beautiful that they inspired not only their descendants but many of the villagers.

In Cambodia, followers of Buddhism celebrate a range of religious events. One important ceremony, known as Pchum Ben, takes place in October and lasts for fifteen days as it celebrates the lives of relatives who have died. According to historians, Pchum Ben is the only time over the course of the year in which the gates of hell are open for those spirits who are trapped in the afterworld, to return to the land of the living in search of their living relatives. The favorite places for these spirits to gather is at pagodas, where they wait for their relatives to arrive with offerings of food for the monks. In this spirit of celebration of life in the midst of death, families and friends bring their gifts, chant, ask for forgiveness and repentance for their misdeeds, and otherwise pay respect to their beloved relatives who have passed on.

All Buddhists, regardless of how busy they are, follow a long and complex series of practices, rooted in compassion, that are meant to avoid being cursed by their hungry dead ancestors. Meanwhile, many Cambodian Buddhists also go to pagodas before sunrise to pay respect to those spirits who wander around aimlessly because they have no relatives to pray for them. These selfless people throw rice cakes into the containers around the wall outside the pagodas to feed these hungry ghosts, while others leave offerings of food behind in the fields or on the streets.

Once a year, following Pchum Ben at the end of the Vassa, the three-month Theravada Buddhist rainy season retreat, my Great-Grandpa Lo Kim Han and Great Grandma Chea Mi Ung would send someone to ring a metal bell far and wide, announcing an ancient festival called Bun Kathen. This spectacular public feast lasted several days and featured festive music and opera performances. The main reason for staging it was to honor Buddhist monks for the charitable work they did for the community throughout the year, but it was also put on because everyone loved it. People from the mountains and nearby woods traveled by foot and on ox-drawn carts to join hundreds of local villagers to enjoy chicken curry soup, dried fish with mashed papaya, and roasted chicken. Everyone left with a full belly. My maternal great-grandparents always made sure that the toothless, smiling Buddhist monks who prayed and chanted for peace never left hungry. This hospitality was a natural spiritual asset for community building as well as to cultivate a strong bond with neighbors and friends, if only to prevent any serious problem that might arise down the road.

My Maternal Great-Grandma and Second-Great Uncle Chea Sun, as Buddhists, saw the feast as an opportunity for charity. At the end of the two day event, they would walk the long distance to the monks' monastery to deliver donations of food and new robes. They also distributed food, clothes, and household goods to the destitute and homeless. By doing so, they believed karmic blessings and spiritual merit would accumulate toward their next lives. The festivities gave everyone a brief rest from their anxiety because villagers lived in constant fear of random attacks by a chain gang of fugitives whom they called bandits. The bandits lived as outsiders, stealing and murdering people, then hiding like cowards in the forest.

✿

2.
Bandits

Every generation has its own set of social issues and challenges to face.

I could hardly imagine what it must have been like when people struggled in constant fear while making a living. By then I was about five years old and I had often wondered if this would ever happen to me. Grandma Lo Lian recounted a scary story about the village where Maternal Great-Grandma Chea Mi Ung and Great-Grandpa Lo Kim Han lived. They were terrified of bandits. They said nobody knew when the bandits would strike. The villagers' hearts sank when they heard the robbers loudly approaching from a distance. With torches brazenly spewing sparks and smoke, they threatened to burn down people's homes if the villagers refused to give them dried fish, rice wine, or anything they could gorge on.

Because of the bandits, villagers tried to hide their supplies in the storage spaces beneath their houses. Knowing this, some bandits cunningly dug tunnels under the houses to steal food. The criminals would then retreat to the thick foliage bordering the rice fields, where they drank and ate their spoils. The next morning, villagers would often find the bandits passed out and snoring in the fields.

These bastards were just too lazy to work. They only bullied and preyed upon poor, hardworking villagers who had no way to fight back and defend themselves.

Some villagers refused to give in without a fight. They spent days and nights preparing to strike back when the next attack occurred. They stuck sturdy wooden sticks and sharp bamboo shafts in the ground all around their houses. Others ground hot chilies, mixed them with water, and preserved them in brown clay pots. When the bandits came in the night, villagers filled hollow bamboo tubes with the liquid and, when the invaders got close enough, blew a spray of hot sauce into their eyes.

Other residents armed themselves with sharp makeshift spears fashioned from either bamboo or iron. After some bandits suffered head wounds from the weapons, they began wearing metal headgear for protection. The battles escalated.

Finally, the residents of Ampe Phnom could no longer put up with the thieves. Carrying cleavers, kitchen knives, and spears, they banded together and chased the criminals into the muddy rice fields. The villagers caught and beat the slower bandits who'd been abandoned by their gang. The bruises and gashes on their backs were intended to be a painful reminder for them to never return to our village.

❁

3.
Elephant Tale of
Ampe Phnom

According to Grandma Lo Lian, stray herds of wild elephants occasionally invaded the village where her parents lived. These giant beasts often appeared suddenly and dangerously from the nearby forest and stampeded through the village, smashing the villagers' houses and food storage sheds, devouring everything that was edible. When the attacks erupted, everyone screamed and ran in terror, abandoning their homes and fleeing for their lives.

One time, Grandma Lo Lian told us that a man in Ampe Phnom tried stealing a newborn baby elephant from its mother. The herd of elephants saw the man from a distance and rampaged toward him. The man escaped by climbing to the top of a nearby tree. The angry herd didn't give up and shook the tree to get the man, hitting their tusks against the tree trunk. Some rammed their heads into the tree. Others sprayed river water around the base of the tree and tried to uproot it.

Eventually, the man took off all his clothes and arranged them at the top of the tree, hoping to trick the elephants into believing he was still there after he jumped to another tree, climbed down, and ran for his life. The herd of angry elephants circled the tree for a long time before they finally gave up and took off.

This curious incident became a local folk legend that was passed down by word of mouth through generations with the moral: "Don't mess with wild elephants!"

❀

4.
My Childhood Home

I have sweet memories of my childhood in Kampong Speu town. The houses were built with brick, concrete, wood, and scraps of sheet metal. A giant, oval-shaped bowl sat on a stone base in the center of town, encircled by the main road. People stood on the base and looked over the edge into a flourishing lily pond. Children watched small fish, polliwogs, and water beetles swimming back and forth while others chased dragonflies around the pond. The pond was just across the road from our house. Our four-and-a-half-story home was made of concrete, with an indoor spiral staircase running from the ground floor to the roof. Each level had a balcony filled with potted plants.

Looking to the left of the giant pond from our balconies, we could see the Black Iron Bridge sitting above the Stoeng Prek Thanot River. Beyond the bridge, beautiful thick green vegetation spread across the land. Along the road, people grew fruit trees, such as coconut, banana, papaya, guava, and mango. Cool breezes brought the rich scent of wild fresh jasmines. To me, it seemed we dwelt in a kind of paradise, but that paradise was about to be spoiled by the evil serpent of the Khmer Rouge.

Looking out from the backyard of our home, only twenty meters away, was a tall grey opera house built of solid concrete. Every evening, especially on weekends, the area was filled with people from all over the countryside. They came to watch *lakhorn*, Khmer drama, and to relax and enjoy the local food and drink. Street vendors had stalls out front. The smoke and distinctive pleasant smell of grilled sausage sandwiches permeated the air. Every so often we heard the faint, soothing sound of music vibrating through the neighborhood.

Grandpa Kaing Hak Yi and Mama shared the first floor of the house for their businesses. He sold school supplies, wristwatches, and men's dress shoes. His business name, Kaing Chiep Chheung, was carved into a wooden sign that hung above the entrance. By age sixteen, Mama was already a renowned dressmaker and supervised several seamstresses in her store. Her custom designs captured the interest of the wives of both local and foreign diplomatic officials.

By then, my father was a popular and successful fabrics merchant wholesaler. He made frequent business trips to Vietnam every other week to the warehouse and always came home with a large volume of all sorts of colorful materials in a big truck. Whenever he returned, a crowd of neighbors would gather to watch him and his helpers and cheer as he unloaded his treasures from the back of the truck. Before Papa distributed the fabrics to his retail merchants, he lovingly offered the first choice to Mama, who would select the best fabrics, which she turned into nice clothes for me and my siblings.

There were four children in our family. Brother Chen was one year older than me. I fondly remember him as the brave and fearless one. He was not afraid of climbing the tallest and most dangerous trees in the neighborhood, jumping from branch to branch, tree to tree, like a squirrel. He was tough and strong, and often protected me and my siblings from the older kids in our neighbohorhood who sometimes bullied us. Brother Chen was always full of energy, partly because he was the biggest eater in the family, devouring anything my mother put on his plate. Most importantly, I looked up to him. Looking back now, I realize he was my first hero.

Sister Mei Juang was the third child in the family, and four year younger than me. She was sharp and gifted with a charming smile. Everyone loved her. She had the gift of finding humor in positive and negative situations. I like to think of her grace and kindness as balancing out the irreverence and wildness of her three brothers.

Brother Sok was the youngest of the brood, a year younger than Mei Juang. We regarded him as the most loyal and obedient of all the kids in the family.

Autumn was always the most magical time, when all the trees transformed into brilliant shades of yellow, brown, and orange. Fallen leaves, curled in circles by small whirlwinds, gently swept across the road. When mild breezes carried the fresh smell of rain, Grandma Lo Lian worried and barked, "Put your clothes on and stay out of the rain or you'll catch a bad cold and get sick with fever."

I fondly remember I was about six walking in the rain to school with Brother Chen. Ignoring Grandma Lo Lian's warnings, we ran along in our raincoats, splashing in puddles of rainwater. I laughed as the raindrops tickled my cheeks and dripped down my nose. We loved running under the tall *derm chher teal* (dipterocarpus) trees along the red gravel road, where we tried to catch their winged flying seeds that floated down, spinning in the air like little helicopters. Sometimes we found giant water beetles and took them to raise as pets.

Brother Chen always looked out for me, and he didn't seem afraid of anything. I recall one time on the way home from school, when the Stoeng Prek Thnot River flooded, its waters rose high enough to touch the bottom of the black iron bridge. Brother Chen and his friends stripped down to their underwear in the middle of the bridge and plunged into the fast moving torrent below, shrieking with laughter while they swam to the riverbank. I admired his braveness and wondered if I would ever find the courage to do this.

Life was peaceful in those days. We played and ran around freely. We went to school and returned home without our parents worrying about our safety. During *Chol Chnam Thmey* (Khmer New Year), street vendors sold delicious food, candies, snacks, and beverages of all kinds. In the evening, the grownups and young kids sat out on the sidewalks to play *klah klok* (a traditional betting game) and *chak apong* (a spinning dice game). By candlelight, I saw people laughing loudly, cheering, and patting each other on the back.

One year during the New Year celebration, Maternal Uncle Bun Kheang bought Brother Chen and me a bicycle as a present to share. We were so excited as we took turns riding it around the lily pond. When it was Brother Chen's turn, he pedaled it so fast that he hit a police officer from behind, causing the officer to fall. When the officer threatened to drag Brother Chen and me to his station, I was scared but blurted out, "That was your fault. You blocked our way." He laughed and just shook his head as he walked away.

One hot shimmering afternoon, a group of about twelve tragically sad people, dressed in torn ragged clothing, appeared in our neighborhood. They walked slowly in line with bare feet, wandering from door to door begging for food and water. They were physically exhausted and weak. When our elders spoke to them and asked what happened, they told us that they hadn't eaten for days. Many of our neighbors came out and watched them as if they were aliens from another planet. Among them was a woman holding an infant in her arms against her face with several children at her side. The strangers talked in an odd and unrecognizable accent, so we hardly understood a word of what they were saying.

Mama whispered to me, "They are Khmer Montagnard. They don't usually walk around like this. Something must be happening in their village."

Revealing her spiritual belief in compassion, Mama invited them in to sit on the straw mattress on the floor in her guest room. She brought out a lot of used clothes and *kramas* to give them. She also offered them food and rice to take along with them. A crowd of neighbors formed in front of our house and stared at them with curiosity. I felt sad and wondered what happened to one of the child's eyes, which was bloody, red, and swollen with a yellow discharge. They left our place a couple of hours later, with tears of gratitude filling their eyes. Watching them walk away down the long dirt road leading out of our village, I wondered what would happen to them.

✿

5.
Grandpa Kaing Hak Yi

My Grandpa Kaing Hak Yi was the greatest influence on my early life. He grew up in Jie Yan, a small town in southern China. Born to peasants, he learned to plant and harvest rice at an early age. Although he only attended four years of elementary school, his exceptional skill in mathematical calculations was recognized by a local company, who hired him to work as an accountant at age sixteen.

After many of his family members died from starvation during the war against Japan, Grandpa Kaing Hak Yi was left to fend for himself. According to family legend, he journeyed with other refugees in a small, overcrowded boat from China to Vietnam. One day an astonishing thing happened. A whale erupted through the surface of the water. People were terrified of the boat flipping over. They threw food as far from the boat as possible to lure the whale away. Even after it disappeared beneath the waves, everyone was still frightened, but Grandpa Kaing Hak Yi believed the encounter with the ocean-dwelling beast was a sign of good luck.

Hoping to find a better life, people fled China without a plan or destination. Unexpectedly, a year after arriving in Cambodia, Grandpa Kaing Hak Yi happily stumbled upon his uncle, who was living in the same town. After working at his uncle's local fish market for some time, he saved enough money to open a general store. Reflecting on his own lack of formal education, he often told me that a person who possesses advanced educational degrees does not necessarily possess good business sense.

When he was twenty-seven, Grandpa Kaing Hak Yi met and married Grandma Lo Lian, a native-born Cambodian. In a relatively short time, they had seven children and could afford to build two mansions. Grandma Lo Lian did not speak Chinese and Grandpa Kaing Hak Yi did not speak Cambodian fluently. I always wondered how they communicated with each other without speaking the same language. But I noticed they often gestured their hands in their own version of sign language when they talked to each another.

Even though Grandpa Kaing Hak Yi and I lived together in the same house from when I was born, we didn't become close until I was five. I still picture him today as he was then— a short, skinny, active man in his late forties with wrinkled skin. Years later, I learned that he was loved and respected by everyone in the neighborhood for his wisdom and admired for his generosity and that he never had a bad word for anybody. Whenever he came across beggars, he always gave them money and said, "Here, this should be enough for a meal for you and your family." Long after he left China, he often showed his familial piety by sending packages of clothes and goods back to his relatives in Jie Yang, which was an enormously important gesture in those days that were bereft of many ordinary things we now take for granted.

Grandpa Kaing Hak Yi told me that his generosity always worried and frustrated Grandma Lo Lian. He once complained, "This old lady always whines about my generosity and never understood how I feel." I was troubled that he would say that because I loved both of them very much and did not like to hear one talk badly about the other. He also proclaimed that

Grandma Lo Lian would argue to the point where "she could argue until a dead body stands."

I could hear Grandpa Kaing Hak Yi sigh when he talked about China. He missed his homeland. Several months after he had left home, a messenger came to inform him that his elderly mother missed him very much. A few months later, before Grandpa Kaing Hak Yi could arrange a visit to see her, another messenger arrived. He delivered the sad news that his mother had suffered a heart attack and passed away while she was at the dining table eating her meal. I could sense that he carried countless unforgettable memories such as this one, but I was not mature enough to share my concern.

One evening right after our family had finished supper, there was a citywide blackout. To pass the time, Grandpa Kaing Hak Yi told me a story about his family in China.

"After my niece was born," he said, "her parents choked her with cold ashes. Baby girls were regarded as bad luck, and her father was extremely upset because his child was born female. In China there is an expression, 'Rocks press the fields.' This means that having a daughter as an only child is just as bad luck as owning a field full of rocks where nothing can grow."

I told him I thought it was very sad. I asked him what they did with the body of the baby girl after they killed her.

Suddenly, Grandma Lo Lian interrupted and scolded him, "Stop telling the little boy these things. Nothing good will ever come out of it. You're disturbing his soul."

"It isn't that easy to disturb his soul," he replied. "There's nothing wrong with telling him what people have done in my country." Grandpa Kaing Hak Yi stopped talking after the interruption, probably because Grandma Lo Lian stared daggers at him and because I was visibly shaken by her ominous warning.

Honestly, I wasn't interested in hearing him continue the story. I was too scared and even shocked by what they had done. As I walked back to my bedroom, I looked out the window and saw neighboring houses with kerosene lamps hanging from the ceilings of living rooms. My room had a lamp, and its flame reminded me of the funeral lamp for Grandpa Kaing Hak Yi's dead niece. Terrified, I prayed for sunrise while shivering in my bed. I couldn't help thinking about my three younger cousins, who were all girls. I felt sorry for my Uncle Chui and the Youngest Aunt because their fields must have been full of rocks and their family cursed with bad luck. I wondered if they were going to stuff ashes down all their daughters' throats. Suddenly I thought of my younger sister, Mei Juang, and wondered what my parents thought of her birth. Mama and Papa always bought nice purses and toys for Mei Juang, so I couldn't believe they would do anything bad to her.

Whenever Grandpa Kaing Hak Yi went grocery shopping, I tagged along like we were best friends. He wore long-sleeved white shirts with four chest pockets. "Let's go!" he prompted me while strutting towards Kampong Speu Bazaar, only fifteen minutes from our home. I was always eager to hold his hand, knowing that he was going to spoil me with treats. My favorites were *Skor kroab roub sat* (candy in animal shapes), *nom plae ai* (glutenous rice balls filled with palm sugar), and *nom ka pong* (fried cakes with shrimp and mung bean). The hectic town atmosphere evaporated because being with him made me feel as if we were the only ones on the street. He could never say 'no' to me, and I took advantage of his kindness to get what I wanted.

Every morning before daybreak, local farmers and fishermen would flock to the markets in the bazaar, hoping to sell their goods. I would wander among the stalls, looking for peasants selling baskets of live water beetles, deep-fried crickets stuffed with peanuts, silkworms, and rows of cans filled with white squirming larvae.

There were baskets filled with frogs that climbed on top of each other trying to escape. The vendor would grab each frog, one after another, and chop off its head, peel off the skin, and while blood gushed out, skewer it with a bamboo thread.

"Look Grandpa! Look! They're still jumping, even without heads!" I shrieked, squeezing his hand tightly.

I wondered if Grandpa Kaing Hak Yi's story about the death of his niece affected me. He muttered indifferently, "I'm sure you'll see more amazing things to come. We have a lot of things to do. Let's move on."

My favorite stall sold field crabs. These small crustaceans were stuffed into grindstones and pulverized into paste. Grandpa Kaing Hak Yi said the paste was used in soups. Sometimes, when the little crabs escaped from the holding basket, I snatched them to take home to raise as pets. Mama worried about my pet crabs hiding under the furniture, dying there, and then causing a rancid odor that would attract red ants. Once, after playing with them for a while, I dropped my little pet crabs into the bathroom water tank so they would live longer.

A few months later, I was taking a morning shower by dipping a ladle in the water tank and pouring it over my head. I glanced into the tank and saw a ghastly looking creature floating on the surface. I screamed, "Ah! A ghost!" Seconds later, I realized it was one of the crabs I had dumped into the water tank months earlier and forgotten. It had grown as large as the palm of my hand!

I was so excited about the crab that I couldn't eat lunch. I waited until Mama and Papa napped, and then unplugged the tank's cork, draining all the water. I searched for the critter, but it wasn't there anymore. Then I realized that because it was so frail and soft, it was sucked into the pipes with the rushing water. Mama yelled at me for wasting water, and following the traditional belief in corporal punishment, Papa beat me on my arms and legs with the wooden-dowel handle of a feather duster.

As disgusting as it might sound now, rice field rats were also sold in the marketplace. Mama had told me that people couldn't always tell they were rodents because the vendors chopped off their heads, legs, and tails, and skinned them. That made them resemble round lumps of red meatballs stacked on top of one another.

"Grandpa! Look at that! Look!"

The old lady who sold the rats laughed, "Would you like to try one? It's delicious! You can roast them, fry them, or stew them. Come, buy some!"

I glanced at Grandpa Kaing Hak Yi and waited for his response, but he didn't seem interested. He respectfully declined by shaking his head and smiling at the old lady.

"Come, kid, you can try it another time. Right now, we have to go buy groceries."

Rows of cages lined the way, holding beautiful reddish-brown roosters. The ones not in cages were lying on their side, their feet tied with string so they couldn't run away. Every time we went to the bazaar, I begged Grandpa Kaing Hak Yi to buy me one, because in my circle of friends, possessing a strong, clucking rooster brought power and respect.

I stared at the loud clucking roosters, in awe of their resistance to being tied up. The roosters he bought me never lasted long, because sooner or later my family killed and ate them for special occasions. I couldn't understand how they could do that to my pets as I loved them dearly. It was sad when the roosters were about to get slaughtered. I could tell in their eyes that they seemed to know something bad was about to happen to them. Their heads kept moving around, anxiously searching for some understanding, struggling and flapping their wings, pleading for their lives with furious piercing sounds.

Grandpa Kaing Hak Yi wanted to buy only hens, not roosters. He liked to pick only young hens because old ones don't lay as many eggs. He taught me how to assess the health of young hens and their ability to lay eggs by examining their rear ends. He turned the hen's rear toward me. "This is what you should know about choosing a hen," he would say to me. "First, look at the hen's anus. If it looks pale or dirty, it may be unhealthy." Then he showed me how to feel for an egg.

"That's icky, Grandpa. I don't want to dirty my hands." I stepped back and hid my hands behind my back.

"Come, be brave. Place your finger right here," Grandpa insisted. "Feel here; this is the tip of an egg."

He grabbed my right hand, extended my index finger, and placed it above the hen's anus. Suddenly feces shot out from the hen, soiling my palm. It was so disgusting! I quickly stepped back and tried to shake it off.

The vendor laughed and joked, "The hen must not like you." Then she handed me an old rotten cloth. "Here, you can wipe your hand on this, little boy."

Grandpa Kaing Hak Yi was not discouraged from the task at hand. "Here, try again, young man," he insisted, taking my finger again.

"No, Grandpa, the lady said this hen doesn't like me!"

"It's okay, kid, don't let anything stop you from learning. Hold the hen and try pressing there one more time." He looked at me with reassurance.

"Yes! Yes! Grandpa, I can feel the tip of the egg!" I shouted, as if I had found something remarkable. Nevertheless, I immediately protested, "I don't care about this. I just want a rooster!" I tossed the hen back to him. "Please, Grandpa! Please! I need a new rooster!" I tugged at his sleeve. "Please, Grandpa!"

"Aren't you ashamed of yourself?" he questioned. "What happened to the one I bought you last month? Remember? It defecated all over the house? It's hard to take care of roosters, and they always run away. Your mother will be upset if you bring another one home."

I cried, screamed, and pulled on his arms. "Grandpa! I really want one! I won't leave this place unless you buy me one! I'm going to scream even louder if you don't!"

My loud words drew stares from strangers, causing him to feel uneasy and embarrassed. "Look, you little devil, I'll buy you a rooster as long as you watch it carefully," he grumbled.

"Those birds can peck your eyes out! Are you sure you really want one? How about a hen instead? They can lay eggs."

"No, Grandpa, hens don't have spurs! Roosters have nice long feathers! You can go ahead and buy yourself a hen, but I want a rooster!" I screamed.

"That boy's right!" the merchant chuckled. "Buy this strong, beautiful rooster!"

"An old rooster won't taste good. A hen's better. New Year's Day is just two weeks away," Grandpa said.

"No, I want it for a pet, not for eating! I hate people who eat my pets!"

I didn't understand why everything we bought at the market had to be eaten.

Grandpa Kaing Hak Yi tried to bargain with the rooster merchant, but his Cambodian was so heavily accented that the merchant couldn't understand him. So, I interpreted for him and got my rooster.

We chose the one with the shortest comb. "You don't want a rooster with a long comb since it would bleed easily if it fights with other chickens," Grandpa Kaing Hak Yi said. I felt guilty after blackmailing him, but I was overjoyed while walking home with my new, burgundy-colored, fine-tailed rooster.

When we got home, I let it gorge on handfuls of raw rice. Grandpa Kaing Hak Yi warned that feeding it rice would cause diarrhea. I wondered if what he had said was true, but the rooster seemed to enjoy the meal. However, within a few days I noticed my rooster's poop turned watery soft and white, and it became sluggish and slow. I was so worried that Grandpa Kaing Hak Yi would slaughter it before it got sicker, but fortunately the symptoms lessened and went away a few days later.

Another memory that has stayed with me for many years took place on New Year's Eve, when I was about six years old. My Uncle Bun Kheang and the house helpers brought home dozens of ducks and chickens from the bazaar. They left them on the kitchen floor in a woven bamboo basket. I went over and saw the creatures were cramped together and making distressed grunting sounds while everyone in the family was preoccupied with being thrilled about the upcoming event. That same evening, Uncle Bun Kheang and the house helpers took the rest of the birds to the backyard and slaughtered each of them. They cut their throats until they bled to death, then dunked them in boiling water to clean up their feathers.

At the New Year's dinner, everyone in the family sat around a huge table with abundant dishes of all kinds of food. Using her chopsticks, Mama kept filling my plate with the chicken meat and saying, "Eat this. It tastes delicious. Eat it so you can grow bigger." But I couldn't. I cried and was too upset to eat them. To me, chickens and ducks were friends, not food.

✿

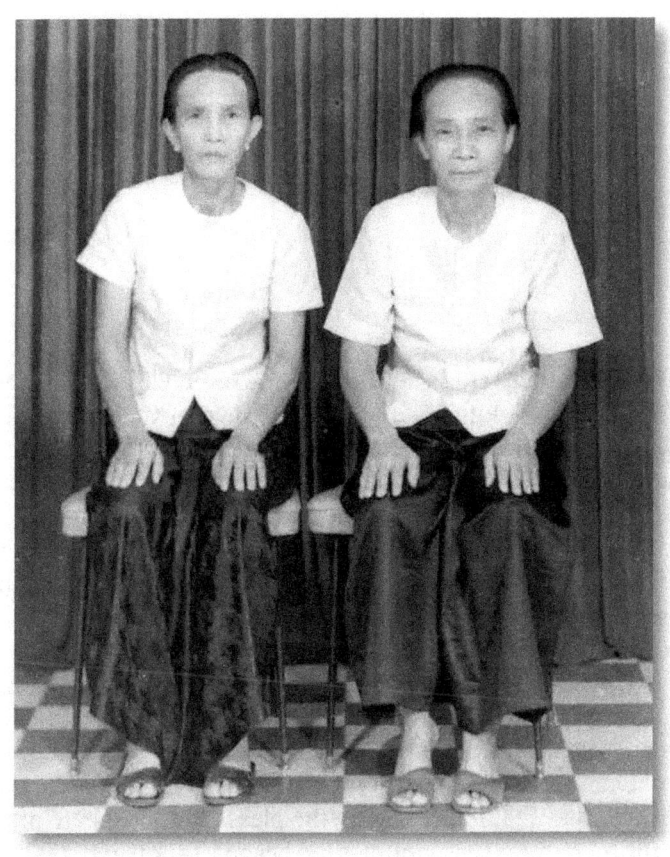

Grandma Lo Lian on the right and her
younger sister Lo Nai Ki

6.
Grandma Lo Lian

Grandma Lo Lian was born in Ampe Phnom, a village about five kilometers from the town of Campong Speu. A beautiful old *wat* was perched on the top of a small hill there, surrounded by a peaceful forest with many giant trees. All year round, Buddhist worshipers made pilgrimages from all over Cambodia to pay their respects to the monk. According to local legend, Ampe Phnom was one of the most remote places in the country. There was an old couple named Ta Am (Grandpa Am) and his wife Yei Penh (Grandma Penh) who originally made it their home. They grew rice crops and tended goats and cattle for a living. Their way of life was timeless, peaceful, and deeply spiritual.

One day, a wise man named Ta So (Grandpa So) walked through the area. Impressed by the pleasant atmosphere of the beautiful natural surroundings, he begged Ta Am and Yei Penh to allow him to use the hill as a place for spiritual meditation. The couple happily accepted his request. They helped him build a hermitage (the current wat) so that Ta So could stay there for his retreat.

Eventually, rumor spread throughout the village that a monk resided on top of the hill. Villagers became curious, and furtively came and snuck a peek while Ta So was practicing his

Buddhist precepts. Subsequently, they regarded him as an indigenous elder or wise man with supernatural powers. They brought food to Ta So and asked him for blessings. From then on, his hermitage was named *Ta Am kveal pope* (Grandpa Am tending goat), and it was regarded as a monastery for Buddhist worshippers to visit and ask for peace and happiness.

Afterwards, it was renamed Ampe Phnom, and villagers sent their children to study with him. Ampe Phnom was also known as Monkey Mountain because it was home to thousands of wild macaques, a monkey species. Visitors could see these creatures hop from tree to tree, skipping and swinging from branch to branch. While leaping about, searching for food, mother monkeys held their little babies securely against their breasts. The monkeys would attack visitors and snatch anything they held in their hands. The locals warned guests to be careful and to keep an eye out for those monkeys.

Chol Chnam Thmey (Khmer New Year) takes place in April. It usually falls around mid-month, right at the end of the harvest, but the date depends on the Buddhist Lunar Calendar.

Grandma often organized trips with our immediate family and relatives to visit the temple. To reach the site, she called for a rickshaw or taxi to drive us up the hill to the temple, where the monks blessed us. She made sure that Brother Chen and I sat next to her so that she could teach us the rules of respecting the monks.

"Sit still! It's sinful to move around while monks chant," Grandma would say impatiently. "Hold your palms together! Pay attention to the monks' chanting, and let them sprinkle sacred water on you. It's good luck for the New Year."

I would sit until my brain turned numb, not understanding a word of what the monks were saying. *"Nek Mo Tak Sak Pherk Cro Vertao An Rang Hat Tao Sam Ma Sam Put,"* the Khmer Buddhist Dharma monks chanted in the ancient language of Pali. The religious service seemed to go on forever, but I stayed because of a deep abiding hope that we would all be blessed because of our prayers.

"Pray harder so that you can be smart at school," Grandma ordered, reminding Brother Chen and me what to pray for. Bored, Brother Chen asked Grandma if he was allowed to ask for ice cream in his prayer. Grandma threatened to pinch his thigh if he continued to say something else so inappropriate in the temple.

One time, our driver waited for us outside and took a nap. He didn't shut his window, and a huge monkey crept into his car, searching for food. The driver and the monkey wrestled furiously until a villager rushed in and opened the car door to free the monkey. The driver was left with many deep, raw claw marks on his face.

When we came outside, Grandma lectured us: "This driver must carry lots of sins. Otherwise, why would this creature attack a pure person?" She added, "He could have stayed in the temple to receive a blessing instead of being attacked by the animal."

Grandma Lo Lian had two sisters, one older and one younger. When she was fifteen years old, her parents relied on her to help with most family duties. Because she was so capable, they gave her greater responsibilities than the rest of her siblings. Grandpa Kaing Hak Yi often said she was an "angst-ridden old lady." Maybe it is because she persistently involved herself in everyone else's business.

On many occasions, I was jolted awake by her sharp voice as she shouted at the household helpers, rousing them to get up and do their chores before daybreak. She also yelled at everyone else in the house. "Get up! Don't sleep until the sun shines on your ass! That's a sign of bad luck, and you won't get anywhere in life!" At other times, Grandma Lo Lian barked with her loud voice, "Can't you just walk silently? Why do you have to let your feet be your head?"

She did not like to hear anyone in the house walking with heavy stamping feet.

It took me a while to realize what she was saying. I thought it was funny when I think back because Cambodian people regard the head as the sacred and most intelligent part of the body. In contrast, feet are regarded as unimportant and dirty. Grandpa Kaing Hak Yi and Grandma Lo Lian were always up before dawn to start the day. They were relatively wealthy, so I thought her words rang true. Grandma Lo Lian took everything she did seriously. She didn't want any of us to bring dishonor to the family.

For the last forty years, I have been haunted by Grandma Lo Lian's determination to teach us to never do anything that would dishonor our family. So much so that never a day has gone by since she passed away that I have not tried to do things that would bring honor to our family, including the writing of this book.

Despite her eccentric temper, Grandma Lo Lian was a kind-hearted person. She often let the household helpers take long annual vacations so they could enjoy longer stays with their families in the rural villages. When they returned, they would bring various kinds of exotic fruit: *pnov phler* (wood apple), *kampin riec* (cotton fruit), *pring* (jambolan plum), *svayo chanti* (cashew apple), *salak* (snake fruit), and *kralanh* (velvet tamarind). To show their gratitude, some brought basketfuls of creepy water beetles or crickets. To welcome them back, my grandparents would treat them to a big feast. They prepared many delicious dishes, including deep-fried bugs from their home villages, served with palm wine. The celebrations lasted late into the night, filling the house with the savory aroma of frying garlic and chilis.

✿

Grandma Lo Lian at cousin Kri's wedding ceremony

7.

Cambodian Folktales

Typically, our whole family sat together for only two meals, one in the afternoon and one in the evening. (In the morning, everyone fixed whatever they wanted, which was usually *borbor*, or porridge.) Often, while we were eating lunch or dinner, Grandma Lo Lian would make us listen to her strange stories. Some would frighten us so much that we remembered them for years.

Now that I look back on those days, I cherish the time before the age of television and the Internet existed. The memories of those valuable stories of my ancestors' native Cambodian folktales enabled me to perceive the essential life morals through our traditional culture. I felt they were one of the most important ways to keep our family and society intact. Here are some of the stories that I remember and love to this day.

Tale of the Dark Cave

Flowing peacefully near Wat Ampe Phnom's main entrance was the Prek Thnout River. Legend has it that a giant tree stood on its shore, and next to the tree was a large cave. Whenever there was a full moon, the local villagers would hear eerie chanting coming from deep within the cave. Once, a man passed by and was curious. He stepped inside. Suddenly he fell into a trance and disappeared into the darkness of the cave.

Days later, many kilometers away, villagers found the man wandering at the other end of the cave. He acted strangely and spoke incoherently. He looked disheveled and had cuts all over his body, as if he had been attacked by a beast. Rumors spread that the man must have been cursed by an evil spirit living in the cave.

Ever since then, every full moon the villagers go and pay their respects to the spirit. They gather at the mouth of the dark cave, burning incense and offering fruit.

Tale of Priya Ap

People in the village were strict about tradition. Grandma Lo Lian was strict about cleanliness. One night, after watching a movie with Uncle Bun Kheang, we returned home very late, reeking of cigarette smoke and sweat. So, she ordered me to go the bathroom to wash off the bad smells. When I refused, she threatened that Priya Ap would find me that night.

She said, "If you don't go clean up yourself right away, Priya Ap will come suck the dirt off your toes and the blood from your body. You'll wake up with bruises all over you!"

Priya Ap is a female ghost. Around her neck hangs a cluster of twisted and tangled bloody intestines wrapped around a baby. She flies around every night searching for sewage to eat. During her search, she licks the sweaty toes from people who exhibit a foul smell.

I ran to the bathroom, quickly grabbing the hose, and sprayed myself from head to toe.

Tale of the Calling of the Dead Spirits

Grandma Lo Lian told us that in the old days, when people fell ill, it was believed they were cursed by evil spirits. Family members would gather flowers, fruit, and poultry, and then summon a *khru khmer* (traditional healer) to their home. The healer would chant and use the items in a ritual service to call upon the dead spirits to help restore the sick person back to health. Over the course of witnessing many healing rituals, Grandma Lo Lian said she learned to recite the spiritual chant for the dead: "*Mlong layo oi, mlong layo my, anapobong naposai onjunng nenghong jol aoi chaap.*" One day, she told me a story of calling dead spirits.

"Once," she said, "a group of curious children from the village were eager to find out what would happen if they recited the chant to summon the dead spirits. One night they went out in the rice field, sat in a circle, and started chanting. Within minutes, an evil dead spirit entered one of the girls' bodies. Trembling convulsively, she shuddered with horror.

"Suddenly, the wind blew wildly through the rice paddy. Two children panicked and ran home, screaming for help. The entire village descended into chaos. A shaman finally had to come to chase off the spirit. He made the children vow to never dare play with the dead spirits again."

Tale of Trey Kranh

During a family dinner, Grandma Lo Lian told us about the village where she once lived. "It was surrounded by rice paddies," she said, "and when the full moon shone down on the village, young and old people scampered through the swampy rice fields to catch a very special fish called *tray kranh* (climbing perch). The fish can live a long life and survive the dry season without water by burying their bodies in the mud. Hooks on their front fins allow them to walk and climb on land. Sometimes the farmers even found them alive in the *daem pothi* (Buddha trees).

"I loved seeing *Trey Kranh* leap from the dark swamps to the shallower rice fields, as if in a playful dance under the moon's bright light. They flipped everywhere in great abundance. We caught them with our bare hands, careful to avoid being pricked by the sharp spines in their fins. We killed them quickly by chomping down on their heads with our teeth. Then we threaded bamboo strips through the gills. Their meat is sweet and delicious, but we had to be careful because of the sharp and tough bones.

"During the fishing season, many villagers suffered infections from accidentally swallowing bones that stuck in their throats. They would call a *Khru Khmer* to perform a ritual ceremony to remove the bone and heal the person by chanting, "*Pa-onh Te deung Ghaco Peu Penh Steung, Che-ung Per Penh Touke Bot Alout Bot Alout Boait Svai Yarch.*" Even when the ceremony was successful, it would take a long time for the person to heal."

I noticed Grandma Lo Lian's eyes had become misty and mournful as she continued in a sad tone: "When I was a teenager, out with some friends in the fields catching *Trey Kranh*, one of my friends excitedly grabbed a fish and tried to bite down on its head, but it slipped between her fingers and down into her throat. Gasping for air, she clutched at her throat, collapsed to the ground, and died right there with her eyes wide open."

Tale of the Spear

On a very dark evening during Moon Festival, a group of us (children, Uncle Bun Kheang, and some household helpers) played hide-and-seek. I grabbed my festival lantern and with a shudder of excitement ran up to the fourth floor and hid under an old, dark wooden bed. Unexpectedly, I found a huge, sharp metal spear covered with dust and entangled with spiderwebs. It was about two meters long and so heavy I could hardly lift it.

The next day, when I told Grandma Lo Lian what I found under the bed, she lectured us. "Don't touch it. It's not a toy. It's mine! When I was fourteen, I used that spear to stab bandits who invaded our home. They didn't work—all they did was travel from village to village robbing people. Those lazy savages! They bullied us and stole our food. Whenever we spied thick smoke in the distance, we knew these bandits were on their way.

"The whole village would stay awake to prepare to battle as many as a hundred invaders at a time. If a villager didn't have what the bandits wanted, they burned down his house. We worked so hard for what little we had. Those heartless bastards cleaned out everything! We had to start over from scratch.

"Even though the spear might not look valuable, it's an important symbol of our family's history."

Tale of Loak-da Chpom Sohk Saw

Grandma Lo Lian bragged to us that she encountered a deity named Loak-da Chpom Sohk Saw (Old Master Bushy White-Hair). She said he would protect us as long as she remembered to include offerings of fruit with her prayers.

"He has long, spongey white hair, with a long white mustache and thick white beard," she claimed. "He is big, strong, and very kind-hearted. If we call upon him for help, he'll come right away to protect our family."

"Have you actually seen him, Grandma?" I asked.

"Well, according to our ancestor, that is how he looked," she whispered. "I can sense him around me when I ask for help."

Early one morning, she brought home a basket of *tearb barung* (soursop) and *chumpu* (rose apple) fruit from the market and asked me to follow her to the altar on the third floor, where she believed Loak-da Chpom Sohk Saw resided. She placed the fruit on his altar, and we knelt and prayed until my knees turned red and hurt. Then we went back downstairs. Later that afternoon, she ordered, "Run upstairs and beg Loak-da Chpom Sohk Saw for the fruit and bring it back to me."

She spoke as if I would encounter him waiting on the altar. The thought of truly seeing him scared me! Uncle Bun Kheang confided to me that he didn't believe in those things. Grandma

Lo Lian often left a stack of green bananas on the altar for days until they ripened. Then she would ask me to go beg Loak-da Chpom Sohk Saw for leftovers.

"Be sure to show respect by using the word 'beg!'" If the leftovers were half-eaten by rats or insects, she chirped cheerfully, "See, this proves Loak-da Chpom Sohk Saw enjoys his fruit!" Grandma Lo Lian always had an answer for everything.

Another time, she asked me to take an offering of crispy fried yams to the third floor.

"Hurry, it's time to take food to Loak-da Chpom Sohk Saw ... he's hungry!" she implored.

Uncle Bun Kheang bumped into me while I was carrying the dish and immediately tagged along. Before we got there, he snatched handfuls of crispy yams, gorged on them, and warned me not to tell Grandma Lo Lian. By the time we reached the altar, the plate was half empty. He quickly dropped to his knees and asked Loak-da Chpom Sohk Saw for forgiveness.

Tale of Phra Mae Thoranee (Goddess of the Earth)

One particularly scary tale Grandma Lo Lian told me and Brother Chen began with a stern look when she said, "Don't ever turn against one who raised you." Then she told the story that reinforced this advice.

"Long long ago there was an old lady who lived with her adult son in a small hut in a rural area. Although she was frail and unsteady, she had to prepare meals for her son every day while he was busy patronizing cockfights.

"The son spent much of his time training the birds to fight, whetting their spurs and exercising them with an aim of winning. Every time his bird lost the battle, he would return home very upset and start cursing his mother under his breath and smashing things in the house. When the tension of hostility escalated and the mother was afraid she might get hurt, she ran and hid herself in a corner.

"Sometimes when the son won a prize at a cockfight, he would bring a group of friends home, where they ate and drank, rejoicing the victory.

"One gusty morning, right after the old lady had finished hand-washing her clothes, her son brusquely appeared in front of her. Pointing to the back of the hut, he commanded, 'Mother, I need you to watch my rooster carefully. I keep it in a bamboo cage behind the hut. I am going out to grab some rice wine and will be right back.'

"The old lady gave a tired heavy sigh, nodding her head in response.

"As she began to wring out her clothes and place them on a bamboo pole to dry, a high wind suddenly rose, blowing the heavy post off the hook. It landed right on top of the bamboo cage and wounded the rooster. The old lady panicked, worrying that the rooster's injury would make her son furious. She immediately picked up the half-dead creature, cradling it in her arms but not knowing what to do. Eventually, it took its last breath.

"When her son returned to find the bird lying dead in his mother's hands, he was shocked. His mouth dropped opened.

"'Mother, what did you do to my precious pet?' he shouted irately. He turned around, taking a scythe from the wall. He walked up to his mother, grabbing a handful of her hair. 'My son, please don't hurt your mother,' the old lady screamed and pleaded.

"'You are so old and useless. You can't even take care of a small thing I asked you to do.' He violently dragged her across the backyard toward the open ground. 'I have to get rid of you,' he barked hysterically.

"His strength overpowered his mother. He raised the scythe up in the air and was about to slash her when a sudden, powerful mass of winds rose up. From underneath the ground, Phra Mae Thorani became visible. The Goddess of the Earth held her long hair with her hands and pointed toward the ground. The earth slowly began to shake and crack, splitting and opening up a giant fissure. The elderly mother was stunned. Speechless, she stepped back and watched her son become fearful. 'Mother, please help me!' he screamed for mercy. The old woman extended her trembling hands, trying to save her son, but the powerful wind swallowed him and plunged him into a giant black hole. Into that hole he disappeared."

These marvelous fables taught me to appreciate life and the living world, and to never do anything that went against the laws of Mother Nature.

❀

Paternal Grandparents, from the right:
Papa Lam Hung, Grandpa Lam Chin , Uncle Van, Great
Grandma, Grandma Kim Hoa, Aunt Lan, and Aunt Cam.

8.
The Giant Pet

In 1958, my Paternal Grandpa Lam Chin and Grandma Kim Hoa were living in Krouch Chhmar District, Tboung Khmum Province, along the Tonle Mekong (Mekong River). Papa's sister (Aunt Cam), her husband (Uncle Van), their children (Cousin Hanh and Cousin Vuong), and various other family members also lived in the same village.

Grandpa Lam Chin was Chinese-Cambodian, whereas my Grandma Kim Hoa was Vietnamese. Many farmers resided along the Mekong, where they grew tobacco, red corn, and cotton. Tropical fruits such as luscious mangos, guavas, papayas, and sugarcane also grew around small, peasant-owned cottages made of bamboo or other woods.

Life was peaceful except during monsoon season (May to October), when rainfall intermittently blankets the region, causing the river to rise and devastate the entire village. Despite the damage, the rich sediments from the flood also created more fertile soil, allowing farmers to grow more abundant crops. Each year, the local farmers must time the harvest of their crops and shelter their livestock before the river floods and washes away everything they depend on for living.

During a sudden downpour on a late autumn afternoon, Paternal Uncle Van rushed out with his machete to save their corn crop. Despite the howling of the wind across the tall bushy field, he caught the sound of a faint, high-pitched wail. Fearing it was a *chhke chachak* (wild dog) or a *chroukaprei* (wild boar), he hesitated a second, then hastened toward the sound, gripping his machete. Uncle Van was stunned to find a baby elephant desperately struggling to break free from a mud hole. Worried that being too close to the baby elephant might anger its mother if she suddenly returned, he quickly climbed a nearby tree to see if he could spot her. The rain continued to fall as the baby elephant's weeping grew weaker. Shouting for help, Uncle Van dashed home.

Shocked at the news, everyone hurried out into the rain. Holding kerosene lamps and calling to their neighbors to join them, they raced toward the baby elephant, still mired in the mud. After several frantic hours using ropes and boards, they finally pulled him out of the sludge. By the time they got him home, it was already past midnight. Grandma Kim Hoa was so excited, she adopted the baby elephant on the spot and named him Somnang, which means lucky. However, she was concerned the poor calf's mother might show up at the cornfield looking for her baby. Grandma Kim Hoa told Uncle Van to keep checking to see if there were signs of the mother's return, but to no avail.

Because she believed Somnang was a divine gift, Grandma Kim Hoa devoted most of her time to taking care of him. She commandeered others to help her feed him and make sure he got enough food. As the days passed, Somnang became popular in the village and was dearly loved by everyone.

In Cambodian society, elders are highly respected by all age groups. Children are taught to respect their elders. When the parents are getting older, it is the children's responsibility to take care of them. Oftentimes, the elders are expected to play an important role in decision-making in the family.

All my life I have tried to respect my elders and live up to their ideals.

✿

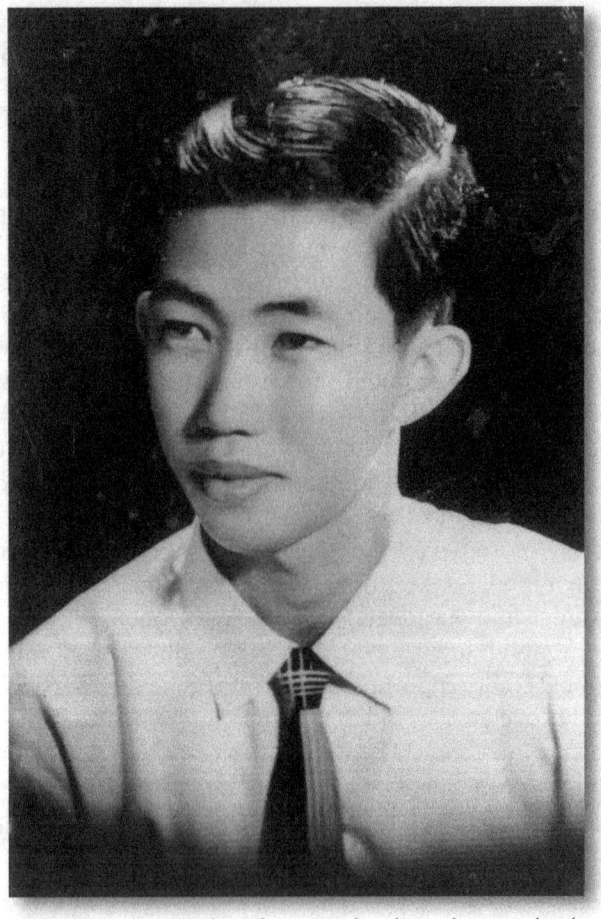

Papa's younger brother Uncle Thai Khieng died
while fighting in the front lines against the Khmer
Rouge

9.
Paternal Grandpa
Lam Chin's Funeral

Most Cambodians practice Theravada Buddhism and believe that ghosts, spirits, and heaven and hell are real. When a person dies, the soul leaves the body to be reborn. Tradition requires family members to perform a special ritual to prevent the deceased soul from getting trapped in limbo. The cycle of life and death never ends.

One day, when I was about five, a messenger from Grandma Kim Hoa delivered an urgent note informing us that Grandpa Lam Chin had suddenly passed away, and we were expected to attend his funeral. By the time we got the message, two days had already passed. So, Papa ran ahead to purchase tickets for a boat trip departing the same night.

We always traveled by boat to their village because the dirt roads took longer. From previous trips, Papa knew that the smell of the boat engine exhaust, pigs, and other livestock on the first deck made Brother Chen and me sick, so he booked tickets for the top deck. That wasn't all. The un-pleasant smoke from cigarettes, the overcrowding, and the nauseating odor of old damp wood and coal made me dizzy and nauseated.

The boat was roughly twenty meters long, with three decks. From our perch, we watched crew members below hoist goods and luggage onto the second deck while others loaded livestock onto the first deck.

As we left the dock, the sky grew darker with the threat of rain. The loud roar of the engine and the sound of the river splashing alongside the boat filled me with mixed emotions—sadness about Grandpa Lam Chin but eagerness to see relatives and Somnang again. Kerosene lamps swung from ceiling hooks and creaked noisily, releasing the pungent smell of burning fuel.

A crew member went around handing rolled-up straw mats to passengers. Mama unrolled ours neatly on the floor and then handed me two boiled eggs she brought from home. Repelled, I said, "No, Mama, I'm too tired right now." As I fell asleep, I envied Brother Chen, who was energetically running back and forth as the boat sailed forward. Papa barked at him impatiently: "You better stand still or go to sleep. Otherwise I'll throw you straight into the river." Cowed by Papa's anger, Brother Chen meekly sat down and crossed his legs.

As I was dozing off, I could sense a melancholic tone in Papa's voice as he shared some recollections.

"During the French Colonial period, when I was eighteen years old, I was known in town as a very strong swimmer. A boat company heard about this and hired me as a crew member to sell tickets and ensure the safety of passengers who sought to cross the river. On a moonless evening, a French inspector was carefully working his way across unsteady wet planks while checking on docked ships. He wore heavy boots and had a backpack slung across his shoulder. A plank shifted, and he fell into the rough torrents of the Mekong.

"Alerted by screams, I leaned over the side of our boat and saw the man desperately flailing his arms, struggling to keep his head above water. I grabbed a rope, handed one end to some crew members, tied the other end around my waist, and jumped into the turbulent river to try to save him. A flurry of bright flashlight beams bounced wildly off the water. Before I could reach him, the raging current pulled him beneath the surface. Poor guy. I wished I could have done something to save him. Many passengers on board were horrified about the drowning."

Papa also shared that when he was about six years old, he caught a pufferfish from the river. He said its skin was rough and spiky and had long lips that were like beaks. It rapidly inflated itself into a ball shape. Curious, he plugged up its lips with one of his palms, but the creature latched onto his hand and tore out a piece of flesh from his palm. Papa's loud piercing scream alarmed the entire village. After that, the villagers gave him a nickname: "Pufferfish boy."

When I was a child, Papa and Mama often liked telling me and my siblings their life stories, so that we might learn to avoid making mistakes in our own lives. That particular night, I thought the stories were very interesting, but I was too sleepy to ask any questions. I put my head next to Mama's chest and heard her heart pulsate. The noises on the boat gradually faded away. I woke up the next morning feeling seasick. The sun beat down heavily on my eyes. Soon the noise and commotion on the boat grew louder as it inched toward the dock. Family members and friends waved to us from the shore.

Papa's sister, Aunt Lan, was waiting between two horse-drawn wagons. Her tired and pallid face managed a smile for us as she remarked, "If it were monsoon season, the boat could sail directly to our village and we wouldn't have to ride in wagons. Everyone is waiting for you guys at home!"

Looking at Brother Chen and me, she then said, "My, the two of you have grown so much. Let's go! We were worried you guys wouldn't make it in time and that we might have to begin the burial ceremony without you."

The wagon driver loaded our bags and drove us from the dock to the village where Grandpa Lam Chin and Grandma Kim Hoa lived. Even though the distance to their house from the dock was less than half a kilometer, it took a long time to get there because the road was harsh and bumpy. As the wagons rolled along, Aunt Lan explained what happened.

"It's sad that he died so unexpectedly," she lamented with quiet tears. "He was riding his motorbike to a wedding party and a reckless driver crashed into him. Mama [Grandma Kim Hoa] begged him to go seek the *Kru Khmer* [herbalist] for help, but Papa [Grandpa Lam Chin] refused, saying, 'There's nothing wrong with me. It's just a scratch on my ankle ...'

"He was so stubborn and chose to stay home with a fever for three days. Now he's dead because of the infection!"

During the wagon journey, I nearly vomited several times from the rocking motion. At Grandma's house, we were greeted with the sad, mourning faces of relatives and neighbors. Everyone was already dressed in white for the funeral. Papa whispered sternly to Brother Chen and me, "Go to your grandma, and don't forget your uncles and aunts."

The countryside neighbors seemed completely foreign to me. Coming from my city life, I was unaccustomed to the culture of the village, despite their cordial hospitality. They spoke to one another in Vietnamese and Cambodian, and I couldn't tell neighbor from family. They treated one another so kindly. Brother Chen and I meandered through the crowd. Suddenly Papa's youngest brother, Uncle Thai Khieng, appeared. He immediately picked me up and placed me on his shoulders.

"Come on, you two, let's go inside. I have a lot to show you!" I had not seen him in so long, I didn't recognize him at first. I thought he looked strange because he shaved his head.

"Do you like my haircut?" he asked. We both shook our heads.

Later, Mama told me that Uncle Thai Khieng had his head shaved to pay respect to Grandpa Lam Chin. At first, Brother Chen and I worried we had to shave our heads, too, but were relieved to hear we didn't. We liked our hair the way it was.

All of the family members and friends gathered in a circle, sitting on a straw mat in the living room. Grandma Kim Hoa led everyone in sharing tales of Grandpa Lam Chin's life while Aunt Lan passed around a mix of cooked bananas and hot, steamy sticky rice served over banana leaves. People broke down in tears as each person recounted memorable stories about Grandpa Lam Chin.

I wasn't quite sure what was going on as I was preoccupied with eating the banana treat and ripe guavas with iced tea. As I was stuffing myself, Mama stared down at me and scolded, "Don't eat too much guava! Watch out, you may get diarrhea!"

"This is only my second one!" I lied.

Later, six Buddhist monks clad in orange robes arrived. We all walked out to Grandpa Lam Chin's casket, which was lying in the backyard and shaded by a canopy of strung-together leaves. The heat was muggy and stifling. In their long-sleeved outfits, everyone was drenched in sweat. Papa's face was wet with trails of sweat trickling down his face.

A rancid odor drifted through the air. It was extremely unpleasant. Flies buzzed around our faces. Mama gently swatted the insects away with her fan. I noticed a white liquid oozing from the coffin, dripping to the ground. I grimaced and tugged at Papa's shirt. "I don't want to be here! I want to leave! This place really smells!"

"*Shhh!* Listen to the monks' chant," Papa demanded. "It's a blessing. The bad odor is a message from your Grandpa. He's happy you're here."

Why doesn't Grandpa have a more pleasant smell, I wondered. I whispered to Mama, "Is Grandpa being punished? He never smelled like this before. He must have done something really bad! Maybe that's why he died so miserably."

Mama pinched my arm, whispering, "Don't you dare say that! I'm going to beat you to death if you say anything like that again!"

I didn't understand why everyone ignored the foul odor and acted as though there was nothing wrong. I hated sitting there in the heat and thought that someone should do something to get rid of the smell.

Agitated though I was with these thoughts, Mama's angry warning kept me quiet for the rest of the ceremony.

After an hour of chanting, the family members lifted the coffin and carefully placed it onto a funeral wagon that carried it to the nearby cemetery. I thought there could not have been a worse time to bury the body, for the scorching sun was at its peak and there was no shade. With the oppressive heat beating down on us, everyone mourned tearfully around the grave.

Mama pulled Brother Chen and me away from the pit, hissing, "Come stand next to me. Don't let your shadows touch the area where your grandpa's body is about to be buried. It will bring you bad luck."

"No, it won't!" I whined. "Grandpa loves us, and we really want to say goodbye to him!"

Mama adamantly refused to let us go back. She held our hands tightly, only letting us watch the funeral proceedings from a distance. As Grandpa Lam Chin's coffin was gradually covered with dirt, Aunt Lan and Uncle Thai Khieng could be heard mourning and crying the loudest. Before we left the cemetery, Grandma Kim Hoa reminded us not to enter any friend's or neighbor's house for forty-nine days. Otherwise we'd be bringing them bad luck.

The change from the melancholy funeral to the lively supper gathering seemed all too strange. People who were crying at the burial were now enjoying their food and chatting merrily to one another. It was as though Grandpa Lam Chin's death had never happened. Then Uncle Chien entered the living room, carrying Grandpa Lam Chin's portrait. He placed it on the altar and burned sticks of incense. As the late afternoon grew darker, Uncle Thai Khieng busily lit candles and hung kerosene lamps on the walls.

Some family members and neighbors gathered in the kitchen to prepare dinner. The odor of cooking spices filled the house. The meal included a huge, caramel-colored, crispy roast pig, brown sticky rice, and thickened, pig-blood chicken porridge with dried shrimp. Dessert was steamed palm-fruit buns with shredded coconut.

As I was about to cross the room to get some buns, I overheard one of Grandma Kim Hoa's neighbors console Aunt Lan. "Your father's spirit still lingers in the house because he is not yet aware that he died. He won't realize this until seven days after his death, when his fingernails start falling off. You shouldn't be too sad. Keep praying hard for him so he can soon reincarnate into a better life."

My goodness, I thought, *she's right. I do sense Grandpa's spirit is still around the house.*

I glanced over at Grandpa Lam Chin's portrait and chills ran up my arms. He was staring right at me, smiling! I thought he was gone. Now it seemed he was still around. But everyone else seemed utterly oblivious. I suddenly didn't feel like eating. I couldn't share these thoughts, fearing Mama and Papa would scold me for talking nonsense, nor did I dare ask about Grandpa Lam Chin's soul.

As the night dragged on, Papa turned to Brother Chen and me and said, "The road this morning was dusty, you're both dirty ... go outside and wash up, then go to bed!"

As we walked down the hall, the wooden floor creaked at every step. Several times I turned around to look behind me, fearing that someone or something was following me. Brother Chen appeared to be very brave and didn't seem bothered by the eerie noises of the old rosewood house. I didn't want to tell him how scared I was. I knew he would tease me. I badly missed the bright city lights.

Carrying a small kerosene lamp, Uncle Thai Khieng led us out to the backyard to a huge clay cistern full of water. I could hardly see anything in the dim light except a small flame surrounded by darkness.

"Can I just skip my wash for tonight?" I begged him.

He didn't pay any attention. He placed the burning lamp on the ground several feet away. "Hurry up!" he cried out in the dark. "I will be back soon. Don't let the mosquitoes bite you." Uncle Thai Khieng's footsteps slowly faded.

Brother Chen and I hurriedly removed our clothes and ladled water onto our bodies. Crickets chirped, strange birds cawed, and frogs croaked loudly. Glancing around, I sensed something familiar. I finally realized we were standing next to the spot where Grandpa Lam Chin's ceremony had taken place that morning. Chills ran down my back. I grabbed my *krama* (towel) and wrapped it tightly around my waist. "Let's get out of here!" I yelled to Brother Chen, and then I ran to the door. As I rushed back into the house, the cries of the nocturnal creatures seemed to grow louder and closer.

I turned the corner at the end of the hallway and ran into Mama and Grandma Kim Hoa. They stared down at my wet, panic-stricken face and naked, trembling body.

"What's wrong?" Mama asked, kneeling to look at me.

"Nothing's wrong," I responded breathlessly, trying to put on a brave façade and act as if nothing had happened. I wanted to prove I was strong and fearless to avoid being mocked by the adults. "I'm done with my bath."

A few minutes later, Brother Chen walked in with the kerosene lamp in his hand as if nothing was bothering him. "Wooh, Mama, Mama," he said excitedly. "I heard lots and lots of crickets chirping in the backyard." He tugged at Mama's arm. "Can we wake up before daybreak and go catch them for a cricket fight?"

Brother Chen and I were told to sleep in the same room with Uncle Thai Khieng. He slept on one bed, and Brother Chen and I shared a bed nestled against the other side of the room. Brother Chen hooked up a mosquito net for us, and then claimed the side of the bed by the wall. I begged him to let me sleep on that side, but he ignored me. I kept picturing Grandpa Lam Chin's spirit and couldn't fall asleep. Throughout the night, I heard a sound like nails scratching the wall—Uncle Thai

Khieng clenching his teeth. Each time, I tried to move closer to Brother Chen, but he kicked me away. Eventually I fell into a deep slumber.

❀❀❀❀❀

The following morning, I woke up to the noise of the house filled with people. Monks were chanting again, and I was told they had to continue for a total of seven days. Because they had started the day Grandpa passed away, we only had to endure another three days of their chanting.

That afternoon, Grandma Kim Hoa, Aunt Lan, Papa, Mama, Brother Chen, and I walked over to visit Uncle Chien. He kept the elephant Somnang in his backyard. Papa and Uncle Chien unlocked the gate door and led Somnang out to the nearby cornfield. As we walked around him, we saw tears in Somnang's eyes. Grandma Kim Hoa said, "It is because he grieves the loss of Grandpa. He misses him and refuses to eat."

After meandering through the field for a while, Mama and Papa made us walk under Somnang three times and put our bare feet in his warm, soggy stools. "Do this so you will stay strong and healthy," they explained. Brother Chen and I took off our slippers and reluctantly obeyed their words. Mama and Papa reminded us that Somnang was a gift from heaven and protected by a fairy. Mama added, "Now if you ever fall off while riding him, you won't be seriously hurt because the fairy will help lift you up."

In front of Grandma Kim Hoa's house was a large, green, and beautiful piece of land where sugarcane, water-melons, sweet potatoes, and yellow bean trees grew. She said Somnang ate a lot. Sometimes, friends and neighbors would donate food to help support him. One time I begged, "Grandma, please find me a baby elephant of my own so I can bring it back home to show my friends." But Papa objected, "It would not fit in our house, and we would have to live on the street." The subject was dropped.

Usually Somnang drank from a small stream running by Grandma Kim Hoa's house. His trunk was like a flexible, thick rubber pipe. During the hot season, he knew how to dig up dry riverbeds to find water. Thirsty livestock would gather to join him. Grandma Kim Hoa was so proud! Sometimes Somnang touched my forehead with the slimy tip of his trunk, and I could feel his cool breath on my face.

When Somnang curled his trunk around my waist and gently lifted me off the ground for the first time, I was scared. I didn't know what he was trying to do, but he gently put me back down. After we got to know him well, Brother Chen and I learned to stand on Somnang's giant toes, clutching his front legs while he slowly walked around the open backyard. We were afraid he might accidentally step on us, but Papa said Somnang was always careful not to hurt the ones he loved.

✿

10.
I Stoned the Witch

Looking back over my life, my childhood continues to haunt me. Much of my past remains a blur to me because I had to endure so much tragedy, but many of my youthful adventures are vivid and return to me on a daily basis. Whether funny or sad, agonizing or ecstatic, I have not been able to forget several events from my mischievous youth that still leave a bittersweet aftertaste. I have a particularly intense feeling of guilt about one event that I am not proud of but feel the need to reveal.

One of my favorite activities as a boy was to sneak barefoot down to the Kampong Speu River for a swim. Wearing only underwear, my friends and I used to wade in the cool, flowing water and caught glass fish, shrimp, and baby crabs with our bamboo baskets. We also dug up clams from the river bottom. Afterwards, we buried them in the hot sand until they were ready to eat.

We heard many horrible stories about goblins, witches, kidnappers, and evil spirits. Because of all the dangers, children were warned not to go to the river alone. Grandma Lo Lian said goblins were ugly, man-like creatures that had legs and arms just like us. Other people said they looked like giant lizards, their bodies emitting rotten odors and their heads bald and slimy. But I was perplexed and wondered about whether everything my grandparents and the villagers said was true.

The goblins, I was told, hid in the deep waters, swam fast, and preyed on children who did not know how to swim. If a person encountered one, he needed to soak in a soapy bath for a long time to get rid of the resulting stench. A coven of witches lived near the river, too. Being young and gullible, I often wondered how much the victims suffered and whether this horrible thing might happen to one of us.

Grandma Lo Lian also warned us, "Spirits of people who died violently are evil and they lurk around the Black Iron Bridge." She terrified us with tales of young children captured by kidnappers who roamed the riverbanks carrying large, empty, brown rice sacks. "They ground up the children and buried their remains beneath the bases of the bridge so their dead spirits stayed to protect it."

When I first heard Grandma Lo Lian's stories, I was, of course scared—even terrified—but at the same time, I loved them, as children all around the world love to be scared. I have always been curious about this and have come to think it is because of the loving safety kids feel when they are out of the story and back to reality. A few years later, when we were living the scariest story imaginable, I sometimes thought about her folktales—and thought they didn't come remotely close to the terror we actually had to face and endure.

Despite all the cautionary tales we'd been told, one afternoon while Papa and Mama napped, a group of us still crept out and ran down to the river. After cautiously meandering through the bushes, we stumbled upon a hut hidden behind thick foliage at the bottom of a hill. We thought we had discovered a witch living downstream from the Black Iron Bridge. The roof was thatched with rotten hay and the bamboo walls were partially covered with crumbling patches of crusted dirt.

We heard a long screech coming from inside. I was extremely nervous as I declared that it must be one of the evil witches who Grandma Lo Lian had warned us about! The eerie sound grew louder as we moved closer. I picked up a rock and threw it through the window opening. A voice cried out, "Ooooooo-oooo-oooooooooh!"

We stared at each other in horror. I urged the others to gather more rocks, and I hurled another one through the window.

"Ooooooo-oooo-oooooooooh!" the voice cried out again.

"See! I told you! There is an evil spirit here. We have to kill it!"

We ran up the hillside to get a clearer view and I shouted, "Get bigger rocks so we can kill it before it's too late!" Then we launched a barrage that collapsed the roof.

"Stone it to death!" I shouted. I felt excited that we had finally banished the evil witch.

Suddenly, an enormous woman charged us from behind. She wildly swung a large stick at us and shouted, "You little motherfuckers! Leave that old lady alone. She's suffering an illness!"

"Run!" I yelled, startled by both her language and her rage. We scattered in different directions. My heart jumped with fear as I realized the "evil witch" we had just attacked was actually a sick old lady.

I dashed home, slinked through the back door, and ran up to the third floor. I climbed onto Grandpa Kaing Hak Yi's thick, dark wooden bed and hid beneath an unfolded mosquito net. I could not remember how long I veiled myself before I was awakened by Grandpa Kaing Hak Yi's voice.

"Wake up, little brother. What are you doing here on my clean bed? Go wash yourself and eat your dinner. Why are you so muddy? Everyone has been wondering where you were." He looked at me with his tender smile.

I rubbed my eyes several times as I tried to find a good response.

"Grandpa, I'm just tired and sleepy."

That whole night, my heart was full of guilt and fright. I worried that a member of the old lady's family might come looking for me.

Many times, walking home from school, I stopped in the middle of the Black Iron Bridge and leaned against the railing, hoping to see the bamboo cottage in the distance. After carrying burning guilt inside me for months, I decided to tell Mama what we had done at the river.

She cursed me for my wrongdoing. She warned that the gods were going to send me to hell as punishment someday. "You know hell? It is a place for bad people. When someone does a bad thing against another, he will be sent to hell. There will be ox heads and horse faces there waiting for you. They take the bad guys and throw them in boiling water or onto burning fires. They carry long sharp knives and will poke you in the back."

Papa stared silently with anger. Then he said he was going to tie me to his bedpost. Thankfully, Grandpa stopped him.

For a while I did not return to the river for fear of more trouble. I still wondered if those goblins, evil spirits, and kidnappers who abducted children were real. I was startled by the hint of violence coming from my own father and the way my parents terrified me with the threat of malevolent spirits. It was a dark omen of things to come.

✿

11.
The Crazy Mother Tale

Every night at bedtime, Mama gathered us together and told stories meant to teach us how to be a good person. Even though my new sibling, Brother Sok, was too young to understand the story, she always included him. This story was about a vacationing mother on a boat with her fifteen-year-old son.

"During the trip," Mama began, "a violent storm wrecked the boat. Everyone was killed, but only the mother and her son survived. They clung to a floating log and made it to a deserted island, where they began looking for food to eat and anything else needed to survive.

"After three years being stranded on the island, and now eighteen years old, the son decided to build a boat to find help, so he could later return and rescue his mother. 'Mother,' he said, 'I promise I will come back to save you before your hair turns grey.' The mother agreed that her son should leave the island to go find help. She was happy and proud that her son was so strong and grown up that he could strike out on his own.

"He chopped down the trunk of a tree and left the island as soon as he finished making it into a small boat. After journeying for several days, a strong wind flipped the boat over, knocking him unconscious. By chance, he floated to shore and was found by a rich family. They took him home and nursed him back to health.

"Gradually, he became one of the family, who had a beautiful daughter. The two of them fell in love and eventually got married. Fearing he would lose the luxurious life he married into, he never told anyone of his mother living alone on a deserted island, waiting for him to return to rescue her. Instead, he told the girl and her family that he was alone in the world and that he had no family at all.

"Several years passed. He was haunted by the guilt of not going back for his mother. But he was afraid to tell the truth because he was ashamed of coming from a poor family. And he was even more ashamed that he did not return immediately to rescue his mother, as he had promised.

"Eventually, he told his wife that he wanted to go sailing and visit an island, giving no explanation. Because she was pleased to just be with her husband, she happily set sail with him in a small boat.

"When they neared the island, they spotted an old woman with long, messy grey hair in a tattered dress. When they landed on shore, she ran toward them, screaming and excitedly waving her arms, calling, 'My son! My son! Are you finally back? I have been waiting for you. You promised me you would come back. Why did it take you so long? I've been so frightened here alone.'

"The wife, terrified, not understanding, began asking her husband, 'Why is this woman calling you 'son?' She's crazy! I'm afraid of her. I want to leave!'

"'You're right, she's crazy. Let's go!'

"Grabbing her son, his mother shook him hysterically, crying 'Why, son? Why did you leave me for so long? You promised you would return to rescue me before my hair turned grey, and look at me now! My hair has been grey for a long time!'

"'Honey,' the wife said, 'this old woman is crazy. She scares me. Come, let's leave! I'm afraid she might hurt us.'

"'Yes, she is crazy. Alright, we will leave.'

"He shoved his mother to the ground, helped his wife get into the boat, and pushed away from the shore.

"Crawling along the wet sand, the mother screamed desperately, crying as she lied on shore, 'Please, son, please don't leave me here alone!' But they both ignored her.

"On their way back home, a violent thunderstorm swept across the ocean. Suddenly, a ferocious bolt of light-ning struck and split the boat in two. The son and his wife both fell into the water, struggling to stay above the waves. Eventually, they drowned."

I know this story well. It sticks in my mind more than any other Mama told us. These stories infused me with the gifts of courage and wisdom, yet enabled me to endure the darkness I went through. It is a major influence on who I turned out to be.

To this day, I have never forgotten the moral of the tale, which is that the sum of a person's actions in the present and previous states of existence can predict his or her future life.

✿

12.
The Move to Phnom Penh

In a belief that he was improving our lives, Papa decided toward the end of 1969 to move us to Phnom Penh. This had always been Mama's dream, too. We moved to the center of the city. Everybody was always in a hurry. I was not used to the noise of so many motorcycles and cars everywhere. People didn't seem to be able to slow down.

It was difficult for me to adjust to city living, which was louder, faster, and vastly more populated than village life. At the time, Phnom Penh had a population of about one hundred fifty thousand, making it one of the largest cities in Southeast Asia.

One day, Brother Vuong came and took me and Brother Chen to explore the city. We went to see the National Museum of Cambodia It was a huge religious space with many Buddhist and Hindu stone statues and sculptures dating back to the tenth and eleventh centuries. Some had a weird, scary look. But Brother Vuong proudly explained that this was the art and culture of our country. We also saw a lot of people from other countries around the world who had come to be inspired by the art. There were so many inter-esting things to see.

Afterwards, he took us to visit his friends at the Royal University of Phnom Penh, which was the oldest and largest school in the country, and the place where Brother Vuong often met his friends. The three of us spent the rest of the afternoon walking around the school.

Meanwhile, Brother Vuong eagerly told me and Brother Chen that someday he wished we could attend this college to study to become doctors if we were doing well in high school. But I wondered if I ever really wanted to study medicine. On the ride home on a cyclo (pedicab), we passed by the National Olympic Stadium. Brother Vuong explained the stadium was built in 1963 by Vann Molyvann, a well-known Cambodian architect, to host the Southeast Asian Peninsular Games, but the games were later cancelled for political reasons. It was now the home of Cambodia's national athletics teams. I admired Brother Vuong, who seemed to have an in-depth knowledge across many topics. That evening when I arrived home, my two calves were sore and achy from walking all day.

At the time, I often missed staying with my Grandpa Kaing Hak Yi and Grandma Lo Lian in their huge house with its many rooms. I also missed running around the neighborhood or going down to the river with my friends. The city had very few trees, and without shade it was much hotter than Kampong Speu. Most people stayed in their houses during the day to escape the oppressive heat, and then came out after sunset when the air was cooler.

Evening streets were jammed with all kinds of motor and foot traffic. Sidewalks were congested with food vendor booths and busy people. Hawkers carrying baskets of French bread pedaled along the street shouting "*Nompong ktaw srouy!*" ("hot crunchy bread!") Streetlights and colorful commercial signs for department stores took turns blinking everywhere you looked.

One evening, Brother Chen and I were thrilled when Papa told us he was taking us to see a movie. He said it was about a giant lizard. I put on my favorite clothes, which Mama had made for me. When we arrived at the theatre, people were pushing and shoving to get in to see the show. As we pressed through the crowd, I grabbed Papa's hand.

I don't remember the name of the movie, only that it was about a giant lizard, which at the time I thought was a real dinosaur. It may very well have been the Japanese *Kaiju* movies, possibly even *Godzilla*, which went on to become a worldwide phenomenon. Whatever movie it was, I recall a lot of enormous, wild reptiles that fought one another, some of them blowing fire out of their mouths. I remember one of them was huge and that it got lost and came to the city. The lizard was angry and destroyed houses and buildings with its breath of fire and killed many innocent people.

After the movie, the three of us walked home in the dark. I was terrified, thinking that the creature would surely come to devour everyone in Phnom Penh. But Papa kept telling me the movie was not real. Brother Chen constantly jumped up and down along the sidewalk and roared, mimicking the giant lizard all the way home.

I held Papa's hand tightly as we passed through the commotion of the city. For an older boy this would have been exciting, but for me it was just noise. I felt as if I was in an alien land and everything was about to topple over on us. After walking a few blocks, Papa waved his hand to call a cyclo to take us home. I was tired and overwhelmed by all the excitement.

Soon after the family moved, Mama enrolled Brother Chen and me in a Chinese school. There they taught us to sing songs praising Chairman Mao. I studied hard and trained myself to be a good singer and dancer. For my effort I was awarded red paper stars, metal red star pins, a copy of Chairman Mao's "*Little Red Book*," and some of his photos from my teacher Liang Mei Ching. I was excited to bring them home to show Mama. She always said, "It is important to know languages, so that we can become international people."

In any event, I heard in Mama's voice that she was full of hope and excitement. We lived several blocks away from Phsa Thmei, the Central Market, which is the largest market in Phnom Penh, with a massive dome twenty-six meters in height. Mama said the building was designed by the famed French architect Jean Desbois and supervised by a fellow French architect, Louis Chauchon. Phnom Penh, once known as the "Pearl of Asia," was considered one of the loveliest French-built cities in the 1920s.

At some point, I became overwhelmed with joy and proud of the fact that I was able to immerse myself in one of the most beautiful cultures in the world, my homeland of Cambodia. And I could sense Mama's excitement when she talked to me and my siblings about our future.

Haunted Apartment Building

We lived in a two-bedroom apartment on the second floor of an old, creepy, three-story building that had five other apartments, two on each floor. Brother Chen and I had to walk past an emergency obstetrics hospital on our way to and from school every day. The exterior wall was covered in blue tiles. At night, the neon lights gave the hospital an eerie blue glow. It sat next to a vacant lot where people dumped trash. Rumor had it that the hospital workers buried stillborn, miscarried, and aborted babies there.

Our building's stairway was dark because the light bulb was always broken, and no one seemed to care about replacing it. It was as if the rest of the residents were not bothered by the dim light. I hated to pass by the apartment that was next to the stairway because the woman's voice that came from it sounded so crazy. I could hear her strange talk and scolding voice every time I walked by her front door.

Sometimes I could hear her screaming in Khmer, "Help me! Help me! Motherfucker, quit hurting me. I'm going to kill you!" Sometimes I heard a wicked laugh—"Ha, ha, ha"—emanating from the apartment. I wasn't the only one who heard these things.

Mama said, "Strange people live in that apartment. Don't worry. We'll move out as soon as we can."

Whenever my parents were gone, my siblings and I huddled together on their bed, against the wall. We wrapped ourselves with blankets for protection, afraid to move until one of them returned home. Something in the apartment felt threatening.

One day, my Uncle Bun Kheang came to visit us. That evening, he took Brother Chen and me to see Bruce Lee's new movie, *The Big Boss*. I was really impressed with the Chinese-American actor's talent for martial arts. We got home very late. I fell asleep the moment I laid on the bed. I was awakened by what felt like claws sticking out from the wall, scratching at my feet. I kept trying to wriggle away, but the claws kept scratching at me. I held my breath and slammed both feet against the wall and they vanished.

I looked around and glimpsed a dark figure in the kitchen, illuminated by a glowing flash of light from behind it. At first, I thought it must be our house helper, Serrunh. But then I heard her snoring in her room on the other side of the kitchen. I rubbed my eyes and looked at the clock on the wall. It was 3 a.m. I was terrified and wondered what I had just seen and if it was still in the house. I was convinced it was a ghost.

Rusty Nail

Mrs. Meng was our neighbor on the third floor of our apartment building. I became good friends with her son, Meng Hong. He told me they were going to move to another part of the city. With Mama's permission, I went to help Meng Hong pack up his stuff, which was strewn across the floor of his messy room. I accidentally stepped on a long rusty nail sticking out from a wooden board. The nail went through my slipper, my heel, and protruded from my ankle. I quickly pulled it out and ran back downstairs to our apartment.

Mama was surprised to see me return so soon. "Oh, I thought you were helping Meng Hong pack. Why are you back so quickly?"

I was afraid to tell her about my injury, fearing she would blame me for being careless. Later that evening, I had chills and fever. As I lay in bed, the pain increased rapidly. My foot was red and swollen.

Thinking that I was getting a bad cold, Mama made me drink a lot of water. Then she noticed me limping to the bathroom before dinner. Grabbing my foot and closely inspecting it, she anxiously started questioning me, "What happened? Why is it red and swollen?"

When I told her about the accident, she rushed me to a nearby clinic. By the time we arrived, the clinic was closed. Mama worried I might die from a tetanus infection. As we were leaving the clinic, we came across an elderly *kru khmer* (herbalist) on the street. She told Mama to catch a live frog and mash it with a lot of chili peppers and salt and press the mixture into my wound. At first Mama hesitated, unsure if it would really work. But because the clinic was closed, she went ahead and applied the prescribed potion to my infected wound. A few days later, a lot of yellow puss drained out, and I had a full recovery.

My Sad Girl Friends

Yen Chung was a tiny, pretty, fair-skinned Chinese girl who lived with her father and stepmother, whom she called Auntie. They lived in the apartment across the hall from Meng Hong. Meng Hong seemed to know a lot about the family and told me that Yen Chung's birth mother had killed herself.

I remember him telling me, "Do you know how her real mother died? One day her mother had a fight with her father, and it upset the mother so much she hanged herself." When

Meng Hong talked about Yen Chung's mother, his lips quivered, his eyes moved up and down, and his face turned blue, as if the woman's spirit was appearing in front of him. I wished he hadn't told me any of this.

Yen Chung and I were elementary school classmates, and we studied together when her stepmother was not home. No wonder she always looked so sad. She never told me what had happened to her birth mother.

Her stepmother was very chubby and quiet. She seldom spoke to anyone. Once, Yen Chung told me her stepmother warned her not to say anything to anyone. I could feel the things I saw in Yen Chung's eyes and sensed the untied strings in her life.

Even though her circumstance was sad, she was sweet and kind. I never asked her about her birth mother because I was afraid it would make her feel even sadder.

❀❀❀❀❀

Another favorite friend who lived in our apartment building was named Ma Ly. She was tall and skinny. She had a round face and nice-looking curly hair.

We met because her mother often brought her along when calling on Mama, who made clothing for both of them. When they visited, Ma Ly and I used to paint and draw together. We became good friends. She was always happy and smiling even though, she confided, her mother angered easily and was often very mean to her—physically.

After all of these times, I began to realized that behind the façade of peacefulness, there was a great deal of "unspoken" violence in the lives of families.

One afternoon, Ma Ly came by and showed me that she had some money. She wanted me to sneak out with her and buy some candy at a nearby shop. We bought a lot of candy and ate all of it. A few days later, I ran into Ma Ly on the stairway. She didn't smile like she usually did. Instead she turned her face away, as if to hide from me. I noticed her cheek was red and swollen.

I asked, "What happened, Ma Ly?"

She raised her dress up to show me that her thighs were covered with bruises and welts. She whispered, "My mother got very upset and punished me for spending all my money on our candy."

I felt so bad. I told her to wait a second. I ran into my apartment and smashed my clay piggy bank. I dashed back to Ma Ly and handed her all the money. "Take it. This is my savings from New Year's Eve, and I want you to have it."

She gave me a beautiful smile. Later that evening, I told Mama about Ma Ly's injuries. She was very upset, and the next day she went to talk to Ma Ly's mother. A few weeks later, her family moved without saying goodbye. I didn't know what Mama had said, but I never saw Ma Ly again.

Cutting Glass

One early evening, an unforgettably horrific moment occurred right after dinner, when a sudden outage in the neighborhood left the whole city in the dark. Papa had not yet returned from work, and Mama continued sewing under the kerosene lamp on the dinner table by the kitchen.

Excited by the dramatic change in atmosphere, Brother Chen suggested we play hide-and-seek with flashlights. So, we called Mei Juang and Sok, my two younger siblings, to join the game. Mei Juang was chosen as the seeker, required to close her eyes and stand still at the base while the rest of us ran and hid, all the time laughing merrily but also screaming in fear of the dark.

Brother Chen was the next seeker. He began to sing a song while the rest of us scattered throughout the house to conceal ourselves. I ran as quickly as I could toward the living room window, which was about a meter above the floor. Behind the curtain, I grabbed the window bars between the glass panes and rapidly climbed as high as I could. When my head almost reached the ceiling, I was surprised by a laughing voice: "I get you. Ha-ha, I get you this time." Oddly, the voice was strange, unrecognizable. Suddenly, someone grabbed my feet, then pinched the tendons behind my ankles, triggering me to weaken my grip on the bars. As I was dragged downward, I screamed helplessly at the top of my lungs, "Stop, it hurts! Don't do it!"

Terrified, I stared down. And in the darkness, I glimpsed a blank white shadow on the periphery of my vision. It stared at me from the wall, near the balcony. I fought hard to keep my grip on the bars, trying to keep from falling off. But the pull on my ankles strengthened. I lost control and fell backward, bumping roughly over the bars and breaking every glass pane. I crashed on what I only later discovered was a folding ironing board. Shattered glass rained down on me and the floor.

The next thing I heard was the scream of Brother Chen. He trained the flashlight on me and shouted in alarm, "You're bleeding! You're cut by the glass. What happened?" Confused, I tried to recapture the events. Feeling a piercing pain in my right arm, I shrieked when Brother Chen's flash-light exposed a river of blood gushing onto the right side of my body. It also seemed as if razors had sliced across my thighs. I began to weep, fearing I was about to die.

Mama dashed over with her kerosene lamp, panting anxiously. I sensed the concern in her voice when she furiously demanded of everyone, "All of you stay away and stand still where you are. You don't want to get any of this glass in your foot."

Overwrought yet determined, she quickly gathered up the larger shards, then grabbed a broom and dustpan and finished sweeping up the rest of the glass. Finally, she could safely reach over to me.

As she drew close, I could hear her breathing heavily, frantic with worry. She bent down and carefully checked on my bleeding.

She quickly cleansed the cut on my arm with alcohol to sterilize the wound. "There's something lodged in the center of your arm," she said. With her fingernails, she dug out a one-inch long shard of glass. I was in extreme torment. It was one of the most painful experiences I had ever endured. I clenched my teeth and wept miserably.

"You are so lucky. You could have lost your arm. These glass shards could have cut your throat or your intestines!" she shouted.

After she stopped my bleeding and wrapped my arm with gauze and tape, she made sure she had swept all the glass from the floor. Once she assured herself that everything was in order, she became angry again, whirling around and barking at all of us children, "All of you go to bed now, before your father gets home and gets so mad he'll want to kill you. He won't be happy to see the way you look."

I fought hard to fall asleep that night, but I was too tired and sore. I hid myself under the blanket, hoping that my worries would disappear. When I finally did fall asleep, I dreamed that I was dreaming while trying to wake up, only my eyes were too heavy. This state between wakefulness and sleep was somehow very scary. I could not shake the feeling that there was something foreign inhabiting this house, something constantly watching me. I could not explain what had happened to me: the creepy laughing voice and the hands that grabbed my legs, pulling me off my perch. I was not even sure that I should dare to try to under-stand what happened.

Every now and then, whenever I look at the scar on my arm, the memory of that eerie and unexplainable event comes back to me.

❀

13.
Somnang the Hero

Although living in the city meant spending less time with our grandparents, we made sure to keep in touch. I often asked my cousin Vuong to ask his mother, Aunt Kam, who lived with Grandma, how Somnang the Asian elephant was getting along.

Everyone in the village dearly loved Somnang. They depended on his help to remove tree trunks from the fields or to lift heavy objects. After the harvest, Aunt Kam loaded Somnang with bundles of sugarcane and corn. Then she rode Somnang from village to village, exchanging the cargo for household goods. She always left before daybreak and did not return until very late. Our family was always excited to receive a letter from Grandma Kim Hoa sharing news about Somnang.

Early one evening on the way home from a trading trip, Aunt Kam and Somnang encountered a wild bull elephant emerging from the jungle that suddenly attacked them. Somnang abruptly lurched forward, throwing Aunt Kam off balance. She grabbed at a tree branch, but she missed and fell off Somnang and landed on a knoll at the side of the road.

The two elephants threw themselves against each other in brutal combat, filling the air with a massive dust cloud. The bull kept charging the knoll where Aunt Kam had sought refuge until Somnang wildly spun back and forth, protecting her. Finally, too wounded and incapacitated to continue the battle, the bull elephant gave up and lumbered off into the jungle. Aunt Kam's entire body shook, and she told us later that it was as if her soul perched on top of her hair and was about to leave her body.

Arriving home hysterical, she struggled to recount Somnang's fight to save her life. As word quickly spread through-out the village, Grandma Kim Hoa's yard filled with neighbors. Everyone was shocked to see Somnang severely wounded. He gasped for air and slowly collapsed. There was concern for Somnang's condition, but they also worried the wild elephant might still be in the area, so they lit lanterns to illuminate the entire village.

Somnang never recovered and passed away a few weeks later.

❀❀❀❀❀

The death of our beloved elephant left Grandma Kim Hoa feeling terrible. It was very distressing for the entire family. During lulls in the growing political conflict between Marshal Lon Nol and Khmer Rouge, and when the road was safe to travel, Grandma Kim Hoa came to visit us in Phnom Penh. She brought baskets of guava, corn, dried salted fish, sweet potatoes, and "fruit grenades" (pomegranates). There were so many that Mama shared them with friends and neighbors so they wouldn't spoil and go to waste.

Whenever she spoke of Somnang, Grandma Kim Hoa burst into tears. Over time, she became obsessed with death. If Brother Chen and I argued, she pulled us together and lamented, "Care for and love one another, as you may not see each other again as you grow older."

During those visits, she often shared odd, colorful stories from her village. One afternoon she told us about her neighbor's son, who went to sleep and never woke up.

"When a person is asleep," she said, "the individual's soul leaves the body and only comes back when the individual is about to wake up."

Now that she had our attention, she continued. "A neighbor's son meant to play a trick on his younger brother by painting a mask on his face while the boy slept. But the boy's soul was unable to recognize his body because of the mask. So the soul continued to search for the right owner and wandered farther and farther away until it was unable to find its way back. The boy never awoke from his sleep."

I knew Grandma Kim Hoa loved us and just was trying to entertain us, but the story creeped me out and gave me nightmares.

✿

4.
Moving Out

In Cambodia, most Khmer people believe that ghosts exist. Many claim to have even seen at least one. It is common to hear people talk about sorcery or tell frightening ghost stories everywhere in Cambodia. Many accept as fact that the soul or spirit of a dead person could appear to the living and roam around on the streets or lurk in a house. Commonly, we would hear our elders warn younger people, "*Prayt Khmaochlong*," or "Watch out for haunted ghost." Or they might say, "*Prayt Khmaoch chaul*," meaning "Watch out for a ghost leaping into your body."

Good fate and bad fate are routinely practiced in our daily living. Cambodians believe that if the twist of fate is good, they might feel healthy and lucky. Anything they do will be successful. On the other hand, when the twist of fate is bad, they might get sick and suffer from disease, and will fail without success. They call this "bad fate" or "being cursed by a ghost."

After a year of living in Phnom Penh, in the inauspicious month of November 1971, my family moved from the apartment into our own three-story house in a better neigh-borhood, bringing us closer to Phsa Thmei. Mama declared emphatically that the location was the right spot for her business, as she could feel the energy harmonize with the surrounding French architecture. A row of about eighteen handsome, single-family cement houses built in different styles were lined up in parallel fashion between Calmette Street and Reu Pasteur. Our home was the fourth one in the row. The front door was facing a family-owned bicycle shop, and the back door was facing a big toy shop. In the first house on the right lived my friend Kien and his family. Nearby, his parents ran a little restaurant where they served lemongrass barbecue pork chops, rice, and all kind of alcoholic and other beverages. The aroma curled up from their kitchen, spreading through our neighborhood day and night. The corner was always filled with noise and laughter.

On the far end to the right was the separate house of Madam Dominique, lodging in a large structure with an iron gate and surrounded by a tall fence. She was a sweet, tall woman with a full head of short, shining, silver hair with strong cheekbones. She had a poodle with very long legs and fed him ice cream. Whenever she passed in front of my house, she would engage a conversation in French with me, speaking in a very loud and happy voice.

A block away to the left of our house was a bookshop where the owner sold and rented all kind of comic books, fairytales, and international graphic historical novels. Whenever we visited the bookshop, Mama would let me and Brother Chen choose the books we liked. She then made us read aloud next to her while she was doing her sewing work. I really enjoyed sharing those amazing stories together with Mama, such as an Arab folktale, the story of Ali Colia, a Baghdad merchant. I also adored the legend of King Arthur, and admired Chinese history books, such as the *Romance of the Three Kingdoms*. My favorite Cambodian folktale was *Krapeu Athon* (Crocodile Athon). Although it has been more than forty years and my memory could be nebulous, this particular story has lived with me all these years.

Once upon a time there was a famous monk who lived in the city of Udong in Kratie Province. He raised a scholar crocodile named Athon. One day the princess of the Udong capital city in Kandal province fell very ill. The king went all over the place looking for a faith healer, but no one could cure the disease of the princess. After learning there was a monk of high prestige in Kratie Province, the king urgently requested the monk travel by boat across the Mekong River to get to the palace to give treatment to his daughter. He did, and eventually, the princess returned to a normal state of health, but the king still demanded that the monk stay longer in the palace to make sure the princess would be safe. Meanwhile, Athon missed his master sorely due to his long absence. For this reason, he swam across the river to Kandal Province and sat at the shore, waiting to fetch his respectful master. On the way home, while navigating across the Mekong River, Athon had his master stand on his back. As they were about to pass through the Sopor Kalei Mountains, they encountered a wild crocodile that blocked the road and stopped them from going across.

Ultimately, Athon and the wild beast engaged in combat. But to protect his master from getting hurt during the fierce battle, Athon suddenly opened his large jaws and swallowed his master to keep him safe inside his belly. Eventually he defeated the enemy and moved on.

Immediately after he returned home from the long and exhausting journey, Athon breathlessly spat out his master, only to find him no longer alive. He became extremely upset as he blamed himself for killing his master. And then many people blamed him for immorally causing the death of his master. Athon started to recall the past and blamed the royal family, vowing to take revenge for the loss of his master. He swam back to Kandal Province, waiting at the shore for the princess to show up. Before the sun went down, he spotted the princess with a group of servants going down to the river to take a bath. He sped up and snapped the princess and swallowed her whole.

Everyone in the water was in shock. They cried and screamed chaotically for help. Athon then ran away and hid himself among the bushes. The king became very worried and immediately ordered the royal fortune teller to track down the location where Athon hid. The royal guards eventually found Athon and killed him at the scene.

As kid, I used to feel I was part of every story I read as I saw that the world around me was full of magic and goodness. Along Calmette Street and Rue Pasteur were all kind of big and small shops where people sold almost everything, such as fabric materials, dresses, suits, jewelry, imported exotic fruits, dried fish, and so on.

Mama liked to purchase her fabric from one of these shops, where she found all kinds of the colorful and flower-decorated materials that she liked. The owner of the shop was from India. Ultimately, they became best friends. Mama made me and my siblings call her ChaaChee Alia (Auntie Alia). ChaaChee Alia wore a red dot between her eyebrows, which I was always curious about. One day, she pointed to her forehead and said, "This is Bindi." She asked me and my siblings to repeat after her: "Bindi." I thought her friendly gesture was funny. I also liked to see her when she smiled because she had beautiful straight teeth. Also, whenever we were at her shop, she would bribe me and my siblings with delicious spicy cookies.

A few blocks to the right of where we lived was Mo-nivong Boulevard. Papa explained to us that the boulevard that cut across Preah Norodom Boulevard near the center of the city had been named after Sisowath Monivong, who was King of Cambodia when it was a French protectorate from 1927 to 1941. He was also the grandfather of King Norodom Sihanouk, who was the great-grandfather of the current king, Norodom Sihamoni.

Soon after moving into our new home, the peak of fish harvesting season welcomed us. We saw friends and neigh-bors chatted among themselves excitedly about the fishery season. It was like another special day of celebration.

One evening, right after dinner, Mama brought me and Brother Chen with her to Phsa Thmei to shop for freshly caught fish. While the three of us were heading towards Phsa Thmei, Mama told to us in her delighted manner, "We should be very proud that we have Tonle Sap, the largest natural freshwater lake in Southeast Asia."

She smiled at me and Brother Chen and haughtily added, "The lake is connected to the Mekong River, which is also one of the longest rivers in the world. Cambodian people rely on these fisheries, which are our natural main source of livelihood."

From our home to Phsa Thmei took us less than five minutes to walk. The streets were full of excited crowds. Food carts trundled along the roads. Street food vendors sold everything, such as sun-baked freshwater clams, hot boiled peanuts, bamboo sticky rice with black beans, crispy fried chive cakes and French bread topped with delicious fried shrimp. Meanwhile, farmers set up straw mats along the street with all kind of tropical fruits. The market area was transformed into an adventurous festival camp where hundreds and hundreds of baskets of all kinds of fresh seafood was sold on the grounds around the market, lit by candles, oil lamps, and kerosene lamps. A fresh fishy odor pervaded the town. Brother Chen and I held Mama's hand as we meandered through the crowd, joyfully watching Phsa Thmei light up in the darkness before everyone's eyes. Mama got herself a bag of freshly fish, and we returned home very late. The next day, she made our favorite Cambodian steamed fish, amok, in a savory lemongrass, chili, coconut milk, and curry. She also shared her cooking with our neighbors.

Soon, Mama became a well known and respected seamstress, with a thriving business on the first floor, where she spent most of the day hunched over her sewing machine. We slept on the second floor, and on the third floor we raised chickens and ducks. Every morning, Brother Chen and I ran upstairs to collect eggs for meals.

I recall during the process of moving from our apartment that I was really excited thinking that I would no longer have to endure the eerie feeling in this apartment, but Papa ordered me to stay and watch over our belongings while they moved things to the new house. He warned me not to open the door for any stranger. Soon, everyone was gone. The half-empty apartment suddenly became weird. I sensed something bad around me but couldn't tell what it was.

I looked around before carefully stepping backward until I reached the door to the balcony and pushed it open. I turned and leaned over the rail. I looked down at the street activity, trying to ignore my growing fear. Suddenly, I heard the sound of a stack of dishes dropping on the kitchen floor and smashing into pieces.

I was too scared to go check how much breakage had occurred. I worried that Mama and Papa would blame me for breaking them. As soon as they walked in, I told them it wasn't my fault—that I had nothing to do with the dishes breaking. I said I had been standing on the balcony ever since they left.

We all went into the kitchen, and I was shocked to see everything was normal. There were no broken dishes. I didn't know what to think.

Soon after, while we were eating our first lunch in our new home, Meng Hong's mother unexpectedly rushed in through our open door. Excited, she asked if she could tell us something she had seen in our old apartment, back when we lived there.

She said, "It was so strange and scary, I didn't know if it was alright to tell you."

We stopped eating lunch and looked at Mrs. Meng. Her pale lips were quivering. She sat in a chair and held her legs tight against her chest.

"When we lived on the third floor above your apartment," she went on, "I often saw a naked, chubby woman walking back and forth down below, on your balcony. Sometimes a skinny girl with long, dark hair dressed in white was sitting by your kitchen window. A young boy ran around, too, until he disappeared. I only saw them in the early evening, just before sunset. I kept rubbing my eyes in disbelief and didn't know how to explain these sightings. The chubby lady stared at me once, and I swore I would never look down at your balcony again."

Mrs. Meng's body trembled as she continued. "I asked myself who these people were. I was so worried about you and your children. I was so glad when you moved out."

Finally, she wished us good luck in our new home and abruptly left, without looking back. That night we all jumped into bed and squeezed together under the covers. We could never forget what Mrs. Meng told us.

Without being melodramatic, and in her own matter-of-fact way, she was certain that we had lived with a family of ghosts. ✿

15.
Little Curly Beak

Shortly after settling into our new home, I spotted a nearby shop that bred and sold baby ducks. I loved stopping there on my way home from school to peek through the window and watch workers select eggs from a large, full basket. They examined each one by holding it up against a bright, bold light. It was amazing to watch ducklings slowly peck their way out of their shells, but it shocked and saddened me to see workers rip the baby ducklings from their shells and roughly toss them onto a large, flat tray to be shipped out later.

One evening, I went to the shop after it had already closed. From an open trash can I heard a faint, raspy peep. Curious, I looked inside and was disgusted at the dead baby birds mixed with broken, slimy, bloody eggshells. In the dim light, an icy chill ran through my body as I searched with my hands, feeling for the source of the noise.

In the sticky, gunky mucus, my fingers found a tiny duckling with its upper beak grotesquely twisted away from the lower one. I couldn't believe people dumped this living thing in the trash while it was still full of life.

The little creature trembled and struggled to breathe. Bubbles came out of its nostrils. In my palm, its chirping softened. It rested its head, closing its eyes as if about to die. Without hesitating, I clasped him to my chest and ran home.

As soon as I set foot in the house, I yelled, "Mama, Mama, look—I found a little duckling with a crooked beak."

The moment Mama set eyes on the little one, she anxiously asked, "Where on earth did you find this poor little ugly thing? I've never seen this before."

"I found it in a trash can, Mama. I promise I'll do my best to take care of it."

Smiling at my entreaty, Mama helped me clean him up. We then spoon-fed the little creature some rice porridge. Because his beak was crooked, it could not eat effectively, so every day, Brother Chen and I took turns feeding it to make sure it got enough food.

I decided to name it "Curly Beak." Over the next few days, a close neighbor, Y Hui, would give us some duckweed to feed it. The days turned into weeks, and my pet duck, Curly Beak, grew stronger. Eventually, being curious boys, we figured out the duckling was a male. He became an important part of my life. Whenever he spotted me, he would cock his head, flutter his wings, and run towards me. He would hop into my arms, beg for food, and follow me every-where. To see him grow strong and happy, my day simply overflowed with joy.

Often, people in the neighborhood starred pitifully at him because of his deformity in appearance. Kids made fun of him and called him "Little Ugly Monster."

Their treatment of my beautiful Curly Beak was a rude awakening, revealing the cruelty of people that was often just below the surface.

"Stop calling him names!" I shouted, but to no avail. The more I pleaded, the more they cursed. I got upset over their criticism and felt it was unfair for Curly Beak to be treated with disdain. Perhaps because of my Buddhist background, I grew up believing that all animals, despite their physical differences, should be protected from inhumane treatment or suffering.

It brought back my memories of what Grandma Lo Lien had often reminded me and Brother Chen about—the central Buddhist precept, "Be generous to all living beings. And strive to free them from sufferings."

Sadly, a year later, Curly Beak suddenly stopped eating and developed severe diarrhea. He acted lethargic and breathed heavily. Mama told us to leave him alone to die in peace, but Curly Beak insisted on resting on the floor beside me. Despite our efforts to save him, Mama said he suffered from an incurable disease.

When he died, we carefully wrapped him in a soft white cloth from Mama's store and buried him inside a giant flower-pot. Even today, Curly Beak's presence still lingers in my heart, with sweet and bitter memories.

The Curly Beak incident taught me the value of revering all life.

❀

16.
Cousin Brother Vuong

When he was seventeen, Cousin Vuong left his home in Krouch Chhmar District to pursue his education in Phnom Penh. More than a decade passed before he was able to return home to visit his family. Mama and Papa had him come live with us in the large house. Traditionally, when a close relative moves in, he's treated as immediate family. Cousin Vuong then became Brother Vuong and was considered our eldest sibling. He was tall, strong, and very handsome.

With another two years of medical school before graduating to become a doctor, Brother Vuong studied very hard and was grateful to Mama and Papa for their support. He promised he would always bring honor to the family. I admired his intelligence and determination.

At his medical school graduation, Brother Vuong's ranking was declared the highest in the nation. As news of his accomplishment spread, many young women came to our house looking for him. They brought fruit and other gifts, asking Mama to pass them on to him. After obtaining his medical degree he could finally relax, and he spent more time with me and my siblings. When he wasn't helping us with our studies, Brother Vuong worked at a local hospital and became our family doctor, treating us at home. But the collective joy we all felt about his accomplishments was cut short a few months later.

The civil war, which had been brewing for years in my beloved homeland, had begun. Although Cambodia had been ravaged by war before, there was no way of knowing how horrible it would be.

❀

17.
Learning Other Languages

Civil war broke out in Cambodia. I cannot remember date and times. From the first moment of chaos in my neighborhood, suddenly my world was upside down. Although it had been building for years, the suddenness took nearly everyone by surprise. Because I was a young boy, I didn't know exactly what or how it happened. But I could tell that our lives had irrevocably changed, so I was confused and scared.

One day, I overheard older adults in the neighborhood who had gathered, whispering cautiously about General Lon Nol, who led the coup against Cambodian Prince Norodom Sihanouk. Violence had randomly erupted one day on the streets of the city, and then on another day, I heard that a Communist leader, Pol Pot, who had fought to bring to the country a revolutionary change, might soon cause Cambodia to fall to Communism. Although I did not understand what that meant, Mama explained that a certain political party, which she would not name, was fomenting revolution to force everyone to become economically equal. That meant the end of private property, a change that would severely impact our own lives very soon.

From one day to the next, I no longer felt I knew what was going on. Things suddenly were very different and dangerous at school. The teachers looked extremely concerned, banning any mention of Chairman Mao. For the first time, we saw adults gathering on the street to heatedly discuss the political issues that were critically changing our future.

I felt anxious, as I could sense something bad was about to happen.

Instead of joy and laughter, the air was full of tension and confusion. Papa told me that the Chinese school was closing. I was bewildered because everyone seemed very worried, but afraid to discuss what was happening. To a kid, that can be terrifying. One of the traumatic changes that told me our world was changing, and not for the better, was that just about every day we heard random gunfire.

In early Septemeber 1974, I was walking through the neighborhood and spotted Kien's mother, who sold barbecue pork chop rice at the corner, excitedly rushing out of her store in fear, crying out loudly, "A soldier just ate a dish of my barbecue pork chop and drank a glass of wine, and when he was finished, he said he didn't have money to pay for the meal. Instead, he slammed a gun on the table and threatened to hurl the grenade that he held in his lap into my barbecue oven if I insisted on him paying."

Her voice choked with emotion. Tears filled her eyes as she continued. "How could this be, but I need to make a living."

A crowd of neighbors watched in sympathy as she moaned, but there was nothing any of us could do. Hearing about the soldier's cruel treatment of Kien made us all feel terrible for her, but also concerned for our own safety.

Soon after we moved to our new house, the government outlawed Chinese schools and prohibited the study of the Chinese language. So, Mama enrolled us in Sala Watt Khoh, a Cambodian school that held classes three days a week. I recall that one of my favorite Cambodian teachers was *Nakrou* (Teacher) Jaye Chem. She was small of stature and frail, in her mid-forties, and kind and friendly, with square-shaped hair. I remember she always had a smile on her face. She reminded us students to treat one another politely and commanded us to respect our elders, especially our grandparents and parents. During class, she would make us students take turns sharing during discussions and think about how much parents sacrificed for their children. She also emphasized that we should help our parents do household chores so they could be proud of us.

At home, Mama didn't feel it was safe for us to run free outside in the streets, which compelled her to place us in a nearby French school for the other two days. Her long-term goal was to send all of us to France for a university education.

To prepare us, she did an extraordinary thing, considering the dire times. She hired a French tutor to come to our house two evenings a week. Mama also arranged for our former Chinese teacher, Liang Mei Ching, to come to our house two other evenings a week to secretly continue our Chinese study on the third floor. Mama was very cautious. She covered every inch of all the windows with dark, thick cotton curtains to suppress the sounds and light, so that no one could hear or see from the outside. For each of our language sessions, our teacher had to be stealthy so that no one would notice, so she snuck in through the back entrance and then climbed the back stairs to reach the attic. There, our classes were held surreptitiously, illuminated by vegetable oil lamps and candles. Our lesson would last from 7 p.m. to 10 p.m., which was late for all of us. Sometimes, Mama would sit in a corner doing her handstitches while we were studying so she could make sure me and my brother behaved.

Going to different schools was a tiring experience, but this was how I grew up rapidly, stretched my horizons, and learned the languages that later saved my life.

❀

8.
Civil War

Life changed with the rise of the Cambodian Communist Party, which became known as the Khmer Rouge. It was all a blur to me. The movement began in the remote countryside, but they soon laid siege to Phnom Penh. First, the soldiers blockaded all roads, cutting off the entire city's food supply. The shortages caused the price of all goods to spiral out of control. Neighbors, friends, and everyone in the city were anxious and panicked that they would run out of food. On the rampant black market, prices were even more exorbitant than usual. We had been accus-tomed to Mama mixing rice with sweet potatoes. Now, she was afraid that we might run out of food, so she prepared only porridge for our meals because it didn't use as much rice. More and more of us who dwelled in the capital were worried about starvation because if the roads remained closed for much longer, we would be reduced to eating anything we could find to survive.

For a long time, we heard nothing from Grandma Kim Hoa. Papa was very worried about her and remained upset for a long time. It somewhat lifted our spirits that Papa's sister, Aunt Lan, moved to Phnom Penh, together with her husband and her children, in 1973. Her husband later served as a government official in the Department of Security. Papa's brother, Uncle Thai Khieng, had also moved to Phnom Penh and married. Having Aunt Lan move in with us eased the disruption by proving we weren't alone, showing us that we had close relatives living nearby in the city. Still, we missed Grandma and worried about her.

Suddenly, Aunt Lan fell seriously ill. I noticed her lower belly grew bigger than unusual even though her weight stayed the same. One day she came by our house with her daughter Ni and her son Rith to fetch me to go out for lunch at a noodle house. They were around my age. Afterwards, we all went to a portrait studio. She made me take pictures of her together with her two children. The three of us were smiling and looked happy in the pictures. As soon as we were finished, Aunt Lan began to share that she was recently diagnosed with a big growth of tumor somewhere in her lower belly and that she was going to have an operation in the next couple of days.

She pulled me aside and said with a brave smile, "I have trust in you."

I could sense a trace of sorrow in her voice as she added, "Just in case I die during the operation, these pictures will ensure that you and my children remain intact."

There's nothing good that can ever come out of the death of someone we love. Her unexpected news suddenly struck me. I wonder how her two children would react about what she had just said to me. But I smiled at her to hide my agony. Fortunately, the surgery went well, and what they found in her belly was benign. Hearing the news, I breathed a sigh of relief.

On Rue Pasteur, in the neighborhood where we lived, people had migrated from different places, and many of my friends spoke different languages, such as Cambodian, Chow Chownese, Fujianese, Hainanese, Cantonese, and Man-darin. When kids played together, they sometimes did not understand one another. I became quite busy playing the interpreter.

One afternoon right after school, my Cambodian class-mate Chap Ly, who was known in school as a talented and exceptionally good artist, invited me to his house to give me some of his attractive drawings. This was an offer I could not resist. Chap Ly lived in an alley behind the Kim Hong Cinema, not very far from school. On our way to his house, we were both completely absorbed in our conversation and laughter. But as we passed by the theatre, we were startled by a massive explosion from inside the building.

Dark smoke billowed out, and with it came the sharp smell of burning. I was stunned to witness a panicked, screaming crowd stampede out of the exit. I looked toward Chap Ly, his face pale and recoiling with shock. Alarmed voices repeatedly shouted for everyone to get down on the ground to avoid getting struck by any fragments of further bombs. Shortly after, more people rushed out of the building, some carrying bloody, wounded, and dead bodies, while others kept screaming in terror. Chap Ly and I were still in a state of fright, but we jumped to our feet and silently ran straight to our homes. The moment I stepped into the house, Mama hugged me tight and gave me a worried look, relieved that I had not been in the fire.

Oftentimes, Mama panicked if she couldn't find me or my siblings at home. The thought of bombs peppering our neighborhood was enough for her to forbid us from wandering the streets. So, after school I would gather my friends to play jump rope, soccer, and badminton in front of our house under Mama's protective eye.

We were also serious runners. My friends and I loved to run as fast as we could on the dirt paths around the house while a group of kids from the neighborhood cheered us at the finish line. Eventually, I built up a reputation for being the fastest runner in the neighborhood. Whenever the race took place, the whole quarter would turn into a lively, dynamic event.

Our lives improved for a while, and I began to have some hope that the conflict was over.

But then came the hordes of homeless migrants from different provinces. All over the city, they wandered aimlessly with their belongings on their shoulders. The Phsa Thmei, or Central Market area, became a public shelter. We saw smoke and fire from the homeless cooking on the street. Sometimes, Mama and I passed by during our grocery shopping. Curious, we stopped and talked to them on the street and learned that many had fled violence in their hometowns in Kompong Cham, Svay Rieng, Kompong Chhnang, and Kratie, the provinces that were taken by Khmer Rouge forces.

Many adult neighbors frequently grouped together and talked about the war and its effect on our lives. More than once, I recall, Mama would whisper helplessly, "I don't know what is happening to the world. I wonder what Cambodia will be like ten years from now."

Our sullen faces revealed how worried we all were. Life everywhere was becoming unsafe, even dangerous. Most of the roads in the provinces, as primitive as they were, had been blocked and closed. Peasants and farmers were not able to sell or trade their harvests. The price of rice and other food sky-rocketed. Even when we had money, no one had anything to sell.

In October 1974, one early morning while the city was under a curfew, we heard a loud explosion nearby. The Phsa Thmei was shut down whenever a bomb had gone off in the crowded area. This provoked a large, angry, and rowdy crowd of homeless and hungry street people to go berserk, smashing windows, climbing fences, and breaking into the Phsa Thmei to plunder anything they could. The area turned into a monstrous scene. My heart pounding, I stood at the street corner watching the whole area fall apart. When I ran home to tell Mama what I saw, she scolded me for not staying in one place because she had been looking all over for me.

Unexpectedly, Mama's cousin, Aunt Pieng, and her sister, Aunt Kim, dashed into our house, hysterical. Aunt Pieng owned a store in the Phsa Thmei and now wept grievously as she reported, "I work so hard in my life, and now everything is gone." Aunt Pieng wanted to go to her store to assess the damage, but Mama restrained her for fear of the dangerous mob. It was not easy when we saw our loved one losing her valuable heirlooms and we cried bitterly.

That same evening, Mrs. Lang, a good friend of Mama's who had lived in Kampong Speu at the same time as we did, unexpectedly appeared at our house while we were eating. Her clothes were torn. Her hair was disheveled, and she was crying miserably. Her voice was full of anxiety as she said that during the past several weeks the area was abruptly broken by the heavy, thudding sound of the explosions. Bombs constantly went off. The entire region was in a state of mad confusion as fighting was abruptly and frequently broken by the heavy, thudding sound of the bombs. In the chaos, she witnessed different wave of troops who spoke English and others who spoke Vietnamese or Cambodian. They had invaded the whole town. There were also robbers who raped young women, and shot and killed any woman who didn't hand over her jewelry. Mrs. Lang shook as she related what had happened. She said when the robbers knocked at her front door, she ran to tell her fourteen-year-old daughter to run out the back door to keep from being raped.

She never saw her daughter again.

As the residents abandoned the town, many houses were set on fire by looters or soldiers. Eventually, Mrs. Lang left as well. During her escape, on the way from Kampong Speu to Phnom Penh, she came across Grandpa Kaing Hak Yi in the woods, but she had no idea where he was going.

As we listened to her words, which she spoke between gasps for air while leaning against her chair, we surrounded her, feeling sadness and fear. Worried that Mrs. Lang was going to collapse, Mama kept rubbing her chest. Hearing her news, I could not swallow my food. My whole body went numb. We all wondered where Grandpa Kaing Hak Yi was.

Mama tried to comfort her with a glass of cold water. Mama tried to keep her with us for dinner, but Mrs. Lang gratefully declined and left a couple of hours later. We spent several days worried and anxious about Grandpa Kaing Hak Yi When he finally found us, I could hardly recognize him with his face and clothes so covered with mud.

Grandpa Kaing Hak Yi explained, "Your Grandma and everybody were all gone. The whole town was empty. Hiding inside the house, I could only hear gunfire. Suddenly two young robbers, acting as if they were under an evil enchant-ment, tore down the door and broke in as if they were losing their sanity."

He continued, "They tried to break the safety deposit box and kept banging on its lock with an ax. When they failed, one of them pushed his rifle into my chest and took a key from my pocket, shouting at me to open it. They grabbed all the jewelry from it and told me to leave the house or else they would shoot me. Everything happened in a matter of minutes. I had no time to take anything with me."

Grandpa Kaing Hak Yi spent four days in the woods with-out food. He was forced to drink water from the puddles in the rice fields. Hearing what happened to him, we were all the more relieved to have him with us again, safe and sound.

We discovered later that Grandma Lo Lian had already arrived in the city, but she no longer wanted to live with Grandpa Kaing Hak Yi She instead chose to stay with her young-est daughter, my Youngest Aunt Ung Chu. Once, Mama told me Aunt Ung Chu didn't have a good fate in life, so she married the wrong man, who didn't seem to care much about her and Grandma Lo Lian. Nevertheless, Grandma Lo Lian wanted to live with her in order to watch over her and make sure her husband didn't abuse her.

I recall one time when Mama's oldest sister, Aunt Kien, my Eldest Aunt, took Youngest Aunt Ung Chu to see a famous voodoo doctor in the countryside. I went there with them in a taxi. The road was bumpy, and it took us forever to arrive at his place. A middle aged man with long, thin white hair came out from the hut to welcome them. As they both walked into the hut, Aunt Kien told me to stay outside because they were going to discuss something that a child should not hear. But I was so curious, I took a risk and eavesdropped on them.

Aunt Ung Chu was begging the old man to help her. "Bring this little voodoo doll home and hide it under your husband's pillow. Soon you'll see your husband in love with you again. And he'll listen to anything you say," the old man told her.

I was puzzled and tried to understand what it was all about. In the car on the way back home, I was quiet. I peeked at Aunt Ung Chu's face and noticed she was much happier than before. However, when I next visited, I saw her arguing with her husband and fighting with him about money. Nothing seemed to have changed.

More often than I want to admit, I heard Aunt Ung Chu crying in her room. Sometimes I heard Grandma try to comfort her by reverting to her traditional belief in karma, saying, "This is your sin that you are bearing. You must have owed his debt from your past life, and now you ought to pay him back." My feelings were mixed, and I wondered if the argument between Aunt Ung Chu and her husband had anything to do with her previous life.

✿

19.
Stray Cats and Dogs

By the end of 1974, we began to see abandoned pet dogs and cats wandering around the neighborhood, searching for food in the garbage. People did not seem to pay any attention to them or care much for them. During this period, between peace and war, we frequently saw trucks driving through our neighborhood in the early morning, loaded with many dogs. From our window, we heard their whining and whimpering. One time, Brother Chen and I found a very large, young brown dog that had wandered into the back of our house. After we fed him leftover food, he refused to leave, so we let him stay in the kitchen. We begged Mama to let the dog stay with us for a while. However, it was hard to take care of a huge dog where we lived. Nonetheless, Mama didn't want him on the street, fearing that starving people might kill him for food. Several days later, Papa took the dog to a nearby pagoda and left him with the monks, who he knew would take good care of him.

One evening, a pitiful group of stray cats showed up in our neighborhood. Mama and Grandpa Kaing Hak Yi were concerned the cats might be starving. They told Brother Chen and me to leave food out behind our house for them. Rumor was that people came to the neighborhood to catch the dogs and cats for food.

Later, I decided to let more than a dozen of the cats into our house and sheltered them overnight on the first floor, without letting Papa and Mama know, believing that the cats would be safer. I hid several of them under the giant redwood armoire in our living room.

During the night, the strays howled, growled, hissed, and made other strange noises as they chased one another throughout the house. Papa was furious at having his sleep disturbed in the middle of the night, so he stormed down and opened the door to herd them out. They rushed out to join the innumerable cats and dogs roaming the streets, pets abandoned by the many people who could no longer afford to take care of them.

A few days after Papa demanded we let go of all of our stray cats, Brother Chen and I returned home after school and sat down in the living room to toss colored marbles to each other. Those we failed to catch rolled all over the floor, one of them running under the armoire. While gathering them all up, I poked under the armoire with a stick and felt something soft. It suddenly moved. Investigating with a flashlight, I discovered a cat curled up against the wall.

Brother Chen and I tried everything to lure her to come out, but she refused. Her tail puffed up and her fur bristled from fright. "Grandpa, Grandpa, come over here!" I shouted excitedly. Grandpa Kaing Hak Yi didn't seem that interested. But knowing something about cats, he came over to help. He took a look and informed us it was a female.

Concerned that the cat was starving to death, I ran into the kitchen to find her some food. I snatched some thin slices of raw fish from right under Mama's nose. She had laid them on the chopping board but was enjoying her cooking so much, I thought she didn't notice when I snuck out the kitchen door with them. Then, while I was excitedly tossing the raw fish to the cat, Mama grabbed my ear from behind and howled, "What have you done with the raw fish? It'll stink up the whole house if you leave it around." But when she bent down to look around and spied the little creature under the armoire, her whole face lit up with a smile.

Grandpa Kaing Hak Yi noted that it was a tricolored cat, which he told Mama was a good-luck sign that would bring fortune to our family. Whether Mama really believed him or not, Grandpa Kaing Hak Yi saying it made her even happier. We decided to name the cat "Tricolor," and from that day on she became part of our family. She was lively, playful, and constantly whirled about the house. She would rub her face against my legs, nuzzle up against my hand, or cuddle up in my lap. Life was sweet.

Considering how life had deteriorated over the previous months, the next few weeks passed in relative joy. That is, until Tricolor suddenly went missing. Brother Chen and I frantically went from door to door in the neighborhood searching for her. An overwhelming fear began to grow inside me that I might lose something that meant the world to me. Brother Chen and I talked to all the residents in the wider area, refusing to give up hope of finding her.

A constant faint meowing took residence in my head. I was emotionally devastated. I couldn't concentrate at school and couldn't sleep well at night. I had a bad dream about Tricolor being snatched up from the street and skinned by a hungry homeless person. When I told Mama about it, she was concerned for my mental well-being.

One day, after weeks of falling deeper and deeper into depression over the loss of Tricolor, I was startled to hear Grandpa calling loudly from upstairs, "Come quickly and see; Tricolor returns home! Tricolor returns home!" I almost tripped and fell as I rushed upstairs. She was curled at the corner of Grandpa Kaing Hak Yi's bed, as if nothing had happened. My heart felt like it had leapt out of my chest when I saw she had returned safely home. "She looks larger than before," I whispered out loud. She laid on her back with her legs spread outwards, whirling and meowing as if trying to tell us something.

The following morning, Grandpa Kaing Hak Yi picked her up and took a closer look at her belly and nipples, and grandly announced that Tricolor was pregnant. I shouted excitedly, "Really? Is that true, Grandpa?"

Assuming we were going to have many kittens in the house to play with, Brother Chen and I enthusiastically began gathering thick cardboard boxes to build a cat house for Tricolor's shelter. Weeks slowly went by, her stomach steadily growing larger. Then one early afternoon, I witnessed Tricolor giving birth in the brown paper box that Brother Chen and I had built.

In spite of my excitement, I was also terrified, since I had never seen anything like that before. The kittens came out slowly, one after another. Each was covered with slimy and bloody mucus, which Tricolor licked away from their mouths and noses. There were four of them. Although Grandpa Kaing Hak Yi warned us to leave the mother alone because she needed her privacy, Brother Chen and I constantly and noisily ran up and down the stairs to check on mother and kittens to make sure they were fine.

A week or two after the births, I returned from school around 4 p.m. Running straight upstairs to check on the cats, I was astonished to find only two little creatures in the box, continually crawling about and meowing in great distress. Frantic about the whereabouts of the two missing kittens and their mother, I spotted Tricolor slinking over the balcony railing, stealthily returning for her remaining two kittens. She hopped into the box, laying down to comfort the two kittens by licking them.

But in a split second, I shuddered to see Tricolor carry one of them by the neck out of the house and down the balcony. I shouted out in despair, "No, what are you doing, Tricolor? Where are you taking your baby? This is your home here." I inched forward hesitantly, stretching my hands out to block her exit, taking care to prevent them from falling off the balcony as they tried to avoid me.

Coming out of nowhere, Grandpa Kaing Hak Yi's calm voice suddenly alerted me, "Young man, she's moving. Cats deserve to be given their freedom. If you really love them, you will let them go free. You can't force them to stay. Let her be happy in her new home."

Try as I might to convince him that I would take good care of the cats and make them happy, I eventually yielded to Grandpa Kaing Hak Yi's wisdom.

I began to understand that I had to learn to let go of my attachment to my cats. I was not only saddened by the prospect of losing them, I also felt guilty, believing that Brother Chen and I must have done something wrong to have caused the mother cat to move her kittens away from us. I missed them terribly. It was one of the most devastating things that had ever happened to me. On the other hand, Brother Chen didn't seem bothered much.

I could only imagine how difficult it would be for those individuals in Phnom Penh who had to muddle through their pain when members of their families died or went missing.

Being so young, we knew that life all around us was changing, but had no way of knowing how radically and dangerously the changes enforced by the Communist Party extremists were going to be.

❀

20.
The Arrival of the Khmer Rouge

In the spring of 1973, the Cambodian government began to draft all adult males from ages seventeen through forty into the army to defend the country. I overheard some neighbors talking and saying that the Communist Party was trying to rule Cambodia and establish its own goverment. To escape being drafted, Papa had to leave us behind and go to the Gem Mountains in the town of Pailin, in Battambang Province. He bought land and hired workers to mine rubies to earn money to support us. He lived there for two years.

At home, Mama and Grandpa Kaing Hak Yi often talked about the need to save food and stock extra rice, other dried food, and fuel. If the city was placed under curfew and the stores were closed, we would have supplies to survive for at least six months. Whenever Brother Chen and I went out to help Mama buy fuel at the gas station, we stood in line for many hours. Meanwhile, Mama supported the family by making clothes for her customers. Many of them had relatives abroad who loved her designs and ordered lots of clothing to take back home.

In January 1975, Papa came home from the Gem Mountains to celebrate New Year's with us. But after the celebrations, a road closure prevented him from returning to the Gem Mountains.

A month before the Khmer Rouge stormed into Phnom Penh, television news and radio network relentlessly broadcasted stories about people who managed to flee territory seized by the Khmer Rouge. Slowly, by way of the television and radio news, and stragglers who had returned to the city, we learned the startling truth that a huge part of the country was already ruled by the Communist Party.

I recall a young woman was interviewed on television with a worried look on her face and a body that was shaking as she shared. While she was visiting her hometown in Tboung Khmum Province, she somehow got trapped inside Khmer Rouge territory. She described in agonizing detail the brutality of how the soldiers mistreated their own people in the village.

She shared in a terrified voice, "One late afternoon while I was in the river taking a bath, I saw a banana tree trunk floated by. On the spur of the moment I grabbed hold of it and rafted with the stream, drifting along the Mekong River. I never believed I would make it here. I had a terrible fear of water and drowning, and I didn't know how to swim. Somehow I managed to get the hell out of there."

Watching her tell her horrifying story on the news was inspiring. We were excited for her as she was able to defy the odds in her successful escape. I could imagine myself in her situation. I suddenly had a feeling as though the entire city was slowly eaten alive by many frightening Godzillas.

Two days before, on April 17, 1975, the Khmer Rouge had invaded the city. That day, Aunt Kien's father-in-law, Grandpa Thia, unexpectedly showed up at our house. Wearing a light brown shirt, short pants, and slippers, he was sweating and nervous. He told us the town of Number Six Kilometer had turned as empty as a ghost town. People were evacuated due to the constant bomb explosions.

Grandpa Thia anxiously asked Mama how to get to Eldest Aunt Kien's place. He had not been to the city since Eldest Aunt Kien was wounded in her elbow by shell fragments and was admitted to the hospital in Phnom Penh. Mama was worried Grandpa Thia would get lost if he went by himself, because he could not speak fluent Cambodian. Without any other options, she called a cyclo to take Grandpa Thia to Eldest Aunt's place. Mama asked me to accompany him and make sure he would arrive safely. Mama paid the cyclo man for a roundtrip and instructed him to bring me back home.

On the way to visiting Aunt Kien, we heard machine gun fire echoing across the streets of the city. All the stores were closed. We saw two helicopters hovering in the air above us. After dropping off Grandpa Thia at Aunt Kien's, the cyclo driver changed his mind. Afraid of all the gunfire in the city, he refused to take me back home. Meanwhile, the sound of the machine-gun fire grew louder. People were scattering and running all over, trying to avoid getting shot. Without transportation, I decided to run back. I eventually arrived home safely, much to Mama's relief. Our neighborhood quickly filled with the constant wails of sirens. Everyone was required to remain indoors.

In the neighborhood, we heard bombs explode every day. Sometimes I ran up to the third floor or climbed to the top of the roof. From the distance, I saw aircraft drop countless long, dark objects, one after another. I was curious what they were. After I told her, Mama was scared to death.

I recall one time, Brother Chen and I were walking home from school and noticed that our faces and bodies were blackened with dark, sticky, sooty raindrops. When we got home, Mama was upset and worried that we had been ex-posed to "poisonous air"—radiation. She made us take a long bath to ensure we washed away all the stink.

Soon after, the gunfire that we had been hearing in the distance reached our own neighborhood. The war had come home, and we became worried about our safety. Our neighbors began talking about the rise of Communism and that their leader, the dreaded Pol Pot, was getting closer to the city.

Rumors spread not to eat certain products made in America, such as imported rice or grain. We were told that products from foreigners were sprayed with poison that could harm our bodies and even cause paralysis. People gathered food supplies and kept them at home, just in case war broke out and the city was put under curfew. We often heard the clicking sounds of shells nearby before they dropped and hit houses in our neighborhood, killing many people.

❦❦❦❦❦

Forty-plus years later, I am still haunted by the day when our world changed forever. The self-proclaimed revolutionary soldiers appeared throughout the city. I ran out to the street with friends and neighbors, watching them march through the city and into our neighborhood. They were dressed in black pajama-like shirts, pants, and rubber sandals made from tires, and had *krama* wrapped around their head or waist. It was the first time I saw soldiers who dressed like this. The whole scene was too strange. Most of them were teenagers, kids barely older than me and my brothers. Each one of them carried a large weapon. They appeared threatening, with a distrustful look in their eyes as if they had been drugged.

"How could this be?" I overheard some adults say. "Their pubic hair can't have grown out yet!" It was an odd thing to say, I thought, but I realized they were expressing their deep concern.

As they marched down the street, I followed, raising my hands, clapping, and shouting cheerfully to welcome them. "*Seripheap!*" (Freedom!) some of them cried out in French. "*La Paix! La Paix!*" ("Peace! Peace!")

I was moved by the crowd, as this was the first time I had ever seen people shouting together to welcome the freedom they had been yearning for.

But something was seriously wrong. The soldiers wore a fierce look of hatred on their faces. What was not just strange but painful was that they weren't foreigners, enemies from elsewhere—they were our fellow Cambodians.

A few hours later, they unexpectedly spread through our neighborhood, going house to house, shouting, roaring from their loudspeakers, "Get out of the house—immediately! The Americans are coming and they're going to drop bombs!"

A young Khmer Rouge soldier banged on our door loudly. "Leave the house right away!" he shouted. My knees felt weak and I could barely make myself walk. My heart was racing. I had never seen or felt anything like this before. I saw Papa, Mama, Grandpa, and Brother Vuong rushing back and forth in the house, grabbing things and throwing them into packs. Sister Mei Juang and Brother Sok, who were eight and seven at the time, were also nervously pacing, looking worried because they had no way of knowing what was going on.

The teenage Khmer Rouge soldier screamed at our door, "Get out of the house, hurry up! Get out of the house right away, no need to take anything with you! You can return home in three days. The Americans are going to drop bombs!"

While I was rushing to shut the door, Brother Vuong was trying to put a lock on it, but he was stopped by another young Khmer Rouge soldier who poked a large weapon through the door at Brother Vuong's chest. "Don't lock the door!" he warned. "If you do, I am going to shoot you!" He then pointed the weapon at my belly. I was in shock and leaned against Brother Vuong's body for support. He dropped the big, heavy, black lock to the floor and raised his two hands up in the air as a sign of surrender. Quickly we stepped back, leaving the door open.

"*Please,* I want to take some of our pet hens with us," I begged to Grandpa Kaing Hak Yi before racing upstairs. "I don't feel safe leaving them alone in the house."

However, there were too many hens. I didn't know what to do, so I decided to carry only two with me, the grey and the white, both my friends for several years. By the time I brought them downstairs and was rushing around trying to get ready to leave home, the hens had become too heavy for me to carry. Deeply saddened, I knew I had to let them go. I put plenty of food in the cage for them, hoping they wouldn't starve. Even the hens seemed to know something was wrong, as they restlessly jumped back and forth in the cage.

Khmer Rouge voices could be heard all over the neighborhood, running amok, shouting repeatedly, "Get out of your house, the Americans' airplanes are going to drop bombs! No need to take anything with you. No need to lock the door. Leave now! You all can return in three days."

Simultaneously, we heard gunfire throughout the neighborhood, accompanied by people screaming and begging for their lives.

Their aggressive behavior made me think of stray herds of wild creatures being unleashed on the rest of the country to devour bloody shreds of human flesh.

"Something doesn't sound right," said Grandpa, now more suspicious than ever about the Khmer Rouge. Looking back, I suspect now that he must have been thinking about Uncle Tai Khieng, who had recently been drafted into the army to serve with front-line troops fighting against the Khmer Rouge.

We were pointed in the direction where the crowd was going but had no idea where that was or what was waiting for us. On the road, I overheard people talking about abolishing money.

Afraid for our lives, we followed the crowd, hoping to return home in three days. Our belongings and everything else we owned were left behind, including our family pictures and my childhood photos in Grandma Kim Hoa's hometown playing with Somnang. Our memories—our *souvenirs*, as the French call them—were suddenly gone. We set off for the unknown.

Walking with us were some of our neighbors, including our good friends Chuan Che and Heng Ngoc Cam and their families. Chuan Che was the second youngest in her family. She had four siblings, three older sisters, and one younger brother. They were all young teachers of English in a private school in Phnom Penh. Her oldest sister, Shioa, who was married a year before to a smart rich man, had recently announced her pregnancy. Her parents were very excited to become grandparents. Heng Ngoc Cam was my age and a good friend of mine. We went to Cambodian school together. She was upset and in tears because her old slippers broke just as she started on the road, so she was now walking in her bare feet under the hot sun. With Mama's permission, I gave her my extra pair of new sandals that I had brought along with me, earning her deep gratitude.

Heng Ngoc Cam's mother had no such remedy for the desperate tears she was shedding because she forgot to bring her valuable jewelry with her. Papa, Mama, and other neighbors took turns helping to "scrape the wind out of her body," as her constant, piercing cries made us think she was ill. To scrape the wind out of the body is a belief in the traditional practice of Cambodian "*kors kha-yal*," to cure illnesses and restore the body to health. It involves rubbing the skin with a metal coin so vigorously that it can leave red marks and bruises.

Caught in the madness of the confused and hysterical crowd, people desperately searched for their loved ones. There were constant, frightened screams as they called out their loved ones' names. Young children looking for their parents cried from fear. The sick and elderly were carried by their loved ones. A woman was walking with her newborn baby in her arms, blood dripping from her clothes. Wounded patients and soldiers were lying or crawling along the roadside. As we moved forward, the desperate and famished people broke into empty houses along the road, rushing into them seeking food. Hysteria was everywhere. I could not believe my own eyes.

❀❀❀❀❀

As night approached, the crying and screaming grew louder. The entire city of two and a half million people was being evacuated overnight. Everyone was forced to leave the city and go into the countryside because the Americans were going to bomb the city. That was what the Khmer Rouge said. My fellow Cambodians were forced at gunpoint to leave their possessions behind, which created absolute chaos. I heard people crying and worrying about the children and elderly parents they left behind, hidden inside their homes and never to be seen again. No one realized that there would be no hope of returning. Many desperately tried to return home a few days later, as they had been promised. But the Khmer Rouge soldiers blocked the way and lifted their rifles. They threatened everyone, shooting off their machine guns loudly in the air, commanding us to keep moving forward on foot and warning us to never return. Grandpa Kaing Hak Yi kept mumbling that he could not believe how such a thing could happen. Mama said the whole thing looked just like a bad curse. I thought a convulsion, a horrible madness, had come over my country.

We passed by a large mansion, where we finally found shade under a small tree and rested for several hours. As we recuperated, we saw people rush into the mansion and come back out gleefully carrying armloads of goods. The turmoil was terrifying.

Suddenly Brother Vuong told me to go with him into the mansion to find a bedsheet to ward off the damp morning dew beneath us. I looked at Papa, who was reluctant to give us permission. We both ran in anyway. When Brother Vuong and I entered the mansion, we saw people rampaging throughout the house. Broken objects were scattered all over the floor. There was total confusion as people pushed and grabbed anything they could use.

To avoid getting lost, I closely followed Brother Vuong as he dashed into one of the bedrooms. Surprisingly, no one was there. Brother Vuong and I immediately approached the bed and excitedly ripped the shiny green sheet from it. I was terrified to discover a dead woman with long, messy hair and wide-open eyes. Blood was all over her pillow. A small handgun lay next to her neck.

"Let's get out of here!" I shouted at Brother Vuong.

He quickly covered up the dead woman and we left the room. As we ran from the mansion, we passed a swimming pool. I noticed another dead body floating in the pool. When we got to the gate, I saw a dark brown book left on the ground. Grabbing it without hesitation, I read on the cover, *How to Breathe Fresh Air.* I left the mansion without looking back. For days, my body shivered whenever I thought about the dead woman with her open, lifeless eyes staring into space.

The millions of people living in the suburbs of Phnom Penh did not know what to do. Waiting to return home, we lived on the street for about two months, scavenging like wild animals. People continually cried out in fear, pain, and grief. Far away over the city, we saw explosive fires and dark smoke.

Meanwhile, we were all worried about Aunt Kien, Grandpa Kaing Hak Yi's oldest daughter, who was still in the hospital for her elbow injury. I recalled Mama taking me and Brother Chen to visit her in the hospital. Sometime in January 1975, in the town of Number Six Kilometers, Aunt Kien had been sitting at her sewing machine in her living room, making clothes for her children, when a bomb burst close by, blasting shrapnel through her window that struck her left elbow. Hun, her seventeen-year-old daughter, was in the front yard. Hearing her mother cry for help, Hun dashed into the house and found her on the floor with blood splattered all over. Her mother's arm seemed about to fall off. While shouting loudly for help, Hun immediately helped stop the bleeding by putting direct pressure on the wound. A neighbor who heard the scream came to help transport her mother to Phnom Penh, where she was admitted to the hospital. Even though Aunt Kien was lucky that she did not lose her arm, the healing was extremely slow and uncertain, so it was anybody's guess what her fate might be.

Grandpa Kaing Hak Yi and Mama told Brother Chen and me to keep looking for our relatives in the crowd. But we never heard anything from Grandma Lo Lian or any of our relatives, except my eldest uncle's wife, Aunt Au Kim. As we were walking, she somehow found us in the middle of the crowd. She was crying and looking for her daughter, Ak, who had just recently married a rich businessman from Singapore. Pulling out a handkerchief from her pocket and placing it on Grandpa Kaing Hak Yi's head to avoid sunburn, Aunt Au Kim showed her deep respect by kissing Grandpa's forehead and whispering for him to take good care of himself.

I watched as they spoke to each other, Grandpa Kaing Hak Yi confiding that she had been a good daughter-in-law. Several years after Eldest Uncle Tek married Aunt Au Kim, he died from a tetanus infection, and she took over the care of her son, Sua, and her daughter Ak. Never remarrying, she dedicated herself to working hard enough to send her son to college in Switzerland.

One of my strongest memories from this period is my recollection of a dream that my Aunt Au Kim told us. The night after her husband passed away, she dreamed about bringing him a bunch of his beloved sugarcane. She was walking on a small road to look for him, but the dark and fog made it difficult to find her way. When she finally saw her husband standing in the middle of the road, two wild dogs kept barking at her, preventing her from getting close to him. Aunt Au Kim said that in the dream, she learned that if she had been able to hand her husband the sugarcane he would not have passed away.

Soon after seeing Aunt Au Kim in the crowd, I became very sick, coughing badly and sometimes bringing up blood. Worse, I lost an alarming amount of weight. Many people were afraid to be near me, fearing I might have tuberculosis. Fortunately, two weeks later my cough went away.

After weeks of wondering the streets, Mama and Papa realized we could never return home again. Resigned to a life in exile, we kept moving, carefully to avoid soldiers, street by street. Eventually, we reached a suburb called Kiensvai. A relative of one of Papa's friends had a huge wooden house there, its base built many feet off the ground. Luckily, they allowed us to rest there a few days. Jammed in with many other families, we slept on the hot ground on a piece of leaf mattress.

Each morning when we woke up, the ground was wet with the print of our bodies. The heat was trying to take away even the moisture of our bodies, as if to drive us away.

We had now eaten all the canned sardines we had brought with us. We had traded our belongings for more food. We ate anything and everything in order to survive, from underripened fruits to unknown plants. After a few days, there was nothing left to consume. Starvation was a scourge.

People suffered from diarrhea. Human feces were scattered everywhere. Countless flies buzzed around and landed everywhere we went. We saw elderly people die on the side of the road and on old mattresses. After many days of wandering on the streets, Papa's friend Mr. Sing somehow found a small boat and decided to leave Kiensvai for Kien Kleang village by rowing across the Mekong River. He invited us to join his family. Papa accepted the offer, without knowing where our journey might end.

❀

21.
Into Exile

Mr. Sing, his wife, and his four young children made the escape first across the Mekong. Around noon the next day, he returned to pick us up. It took about four hours to paddle across the deep, blue river. The dark and cloudy sky worried Mama. She kept saying it would rain and the boat would sink. Papa and Mr. Sing paddled the boat, instructing us to sit still and not move. Obeying was easy because we barely had enough space even to straighten our arms or legs. Meanwhile, water was leaking from the bottom of the boat, as well as threatening to come up over the side. Brother Vuong, Brother Chen, and I worked nonstop scooping out the water with broken coconut shells. Grandpa Kaing Hak Yi and my two younger siblings, Mei Juang and Sok, sat still in the middle.

We all felt as if the boat was going to sink at any time. Mama told us to pray to God and Buddha to protect us. When I looked at my family, at each face, it was hard to believe that our lives had become so completely different in a matter of only two months, each day a test of survival. It defied the imagination. The puzzled expression on Papa's face worried me. We were all paralyzed into silence. No one seemed to know what was happening.

After seemingly endless hours of fearing we would die in the river, we finally saw the shadow of the other shore. High above us was a huge and unusual looking group of eagles spreading their wings and swooping back and forth, making strange noises. We had never seen their ilk before and assumed they were looking for food.

As we approached the shore, Grandpa Kaing Hak Yi looked bitter as he held the edge of the boat very tightly with two shaky hands. Our harrowing journey hardened everyone's lives. Mama had grown frighteningly thin and was very weak from malnutrition. She was a different person from the one who had left Phnom Penh only two months before. As the breeze blew against her face, her long, grey hair floated wildly in the air.

I felt confused as I thought back to when we were in our sweet home. We had celebrated the Lunar New Year not that long ago. Mama had been so beautiful, with her new dress made from a soft, brown material decorated with red roses. She had made the dress from a catalog that a friend from Singapore had brought her. Because she had been a well-known tailor in the neighborhood, she was always neat and impeccably dressed. Returning to the present and immediate future, my mind speculated that if I died at this moment, the birds or the fish in the deep, blue, cold, and lonely water would eat my flesh.

Mr. Sing steered from the bow while Papa paddled with a long oar from the stern. I can still see, in my mind's eye, every stroke and every drop of sweat as he struggled to save us. Strong and industrious before this calamity, Papa would try to do whatever was necessary to make a life for us. Every one of us believed he would save us because he was the family hero.

Just as we reached the shore, a big wave slammed into the boat, almost flipping us over. Papa and Mr. Sing quickly jumped off the boat to reduce the weight. Amidst chaotic screaming, we finally arrived at the juncture of another phase in our lives. Daylight was fading, and we were all exhausted, especially Papa and Mr. Sing, who had rowed and steered the boat the entire day without a break.

A crowd of local people gathered and stood alongside the river, watching us as if we were invaders. The brown dusty road promised an uncertain future.

❀❀❀❀❀

Mr. Sing guided us to the place where we were supposed to stay. Mama and I were still dizzy and nauseous from the sway of the boat. It took about thirty minutes to walk with our belongings from the shore to the huge, dark wooden house where the family of Mr. Sing's stepmother lived. Facing the house across the road was a large empty warehouse surrounded by sheets of white tin. They were so loosely spaced, we could see inside where the sunlight shone through.

We were led behind the house to a small cottage, next to which grew different types of wild grasses. Before we set our belongings in the cottage, Mr. Sing told us we must greet his grandma, the landlord, to thank her and pay our respects. She was sitting on a bamboo bed in front of the house, chewing bitter nuts. She wore black satin pants and a white, short-sleeved shirt with safety pins on her pockets, the typical Cambodian attire of the elderly. Appearing to be in her late seventies, she greeted us with a sullen face and unfriendly voice. But when we greeted her with our palms together, a measure of our appreciation for her hospitality, she nodded her head. Her smile transformed her stern appearance.

"Why did the old grandma suddenly become so pleasant, Mama?" Brother Chen asked.

"That was because we showed our genuine respect toward her," Mama whispered, "so she acknowledged our politeness."

A few days later, Papa went out to fish in the bowl-shaped ponds. He brought back a large haul of huge snake-head fish, sharing them with Mr. Sing's family. According to the villagers, many of these large ponds in the area were cratered by old bomb explosions. Papa went scouting for food every day, not always bringing any home. When he was successful, it usually took him an entire day of foraging. Sometimes he came home covered with mud, arms and legs bleeding from the scratches of thorns, yet with nothing more to show for his troubles than a bunch of wild edible plants.

Out of nowhere one afternoon, a little sparrow flew down and landed on Brother Chen's shoulder while he was standing in front of the cottage, and then flew off. Brother Chen got so excited, shouting loudly as he ran around behind the house, chasing after the bird while the creature hopped around on the ground trying to scramble up into a small tree nearby. I thought it was kind of funny to see his reaction to the tiny little bird. But it was right at the time Papa arrived home from hunting for food, feeling tired, thirsty, and hungry. His face contorted with fury and upset, he lashed out in the anger of the moment. He looked around and grabbed a large carrying pole against the bamboo wall. "There you are," he barked, charging forward towards Brother Chen like an angry elephant. In that instance, I knew he could hurt Brother Chen severely. I rushed up to him from behind and snatched the large stick from his hand and hurled it to the ground.

"You can't hurt him," I said, staring at him.

I did not know how I had the guts to talk back like this to my father. My hands shook, and my voice trembled. He was stunned by my approach as his face suddenly dropped, and he turned and walked away quietly without saying a word. Brother Chen was in shock as he witnessed me acquitting myself so bravely.

Somehow, I feared that we were losing our grip on reality.

❀❀❀❀❀

The next two months in Kien Khleang passed by slowly. I sorely missed all my relatives and friends, and we never gave up hope that someday we would return home. But when, I wondered?

And what could we expect to find there? No one knew. Most likely, our home would have been looted and abandoned, just like all the other homes we had briefly occupied along our journey.

✿

22.
The Weird Woman

During the dry season in Cambodia, it is hot and dusty everywhere. Wells dry up, so you have to walk to the river to get water. One day I noticed a beautiful young banana tree that grew next to the well where I used to draw water. Every day, I watched the purple flowers that grew out from the trunk of the tree growing bigger and bigger. A bunch of young bananas soon followed, making my mouth water as I dreamed of eating them.

One early afternoon while I was planting a papaya tree next to the cottage, Mr. Sing's stepsister appeared in front of me. "Hi, Auntie," I greeted her. I had never spoken with her because she rarely talked to anyone in the house. She looked kind, but I never saw her smile, which I noticed was happening more and more with adults all around me. She always wore black, which must have meant she was in mourning, but to a young kid like me, she was also just weird.

She asked me, "Will you do me a favor, young man?"

I was concerned about her and wondered what Auntie wanted. But I did not want to make her upset. I nodded and said, "Yes."

"Wait a minute for me. I will be back in a moment." She disappeared, but a few minutes later, she returned with a long scythe.

Nobody was at home. Mama and Papa had gone out to look for food. Grandpa Kaing Hak Yi had gone to the river to take his afternoon bath. All my siblings were napping in the cottage.

"Follow me," she said.

I began to wonder what was going through her mind. We meandered along a narrow path where the wild grass and plants nearly blocked our way. The thorns of the wild mimosas on the path scratched my feet. Finally, we arrived at the well. I realized that we had taken an unusual way to get there.

She briefly gazed at what I had come to know as *my* banana tree.

"Please hold it still," she ordered.

She aimed at the tree with the scythe while I obediently held it with my two hands, but also closed my eyes, fearing she might miss the tree and accidentally cut off my head. With my eyes closed, I heard many strokes strike their target. Finally, the tree began to fall. I felt as if a giant, obese monster was bearing down on me. I quickly stepped aside lest I be killed by its weight.

I sat on the ground, trying to catch my breath. My two hands were in pain. She grabbed the bunch of bananas and walked away without looking back.

"Auntie," as I had addressed her earlier, was a strange woman. Occasionally she would stand by the door and watch us. At other times, in the afternoon, she watched us through the window of the attic, her face half covered. None of us understood her. Mama said she had a mental disorder and told us to stay away from her. The rumor was that her husband had left her for another woman and never came back. His absence caused her to be severely depressed, and eventually she went crazy.

Most of the time she would stay in her room the whole day, refusing to eat anything. No one would bother her because she got easily upset. At night, however, she would walk around the house while everyone else slept, often to the kitchen in search of food because Mr. Sing usually left some there for her to find.

One afternoon as we were getting ready to eat our dinner, Papa asked me to warm up some leftover dried fish in the kitchen. When I went to get them, I saw they had disappeared. When I told Papa, he angrily reprimanded me for not watching them carefully. He was getting testier with me, and I didn't know why. At the time, I couldn't figure out where the dried fish could have gone. But looking back, I'm sure it was "Auntie" who took them, and now that I think about it, thefts large and small were happening more and more often, as even ordinary people stole food to survive. There were harbingers everywhere of the desperate and violent times ahead.

❀

23.
The Little Piglet

Life was hard, and it was becoming dangerous as well. Food became so increasingly scarce that Mama and Papa were forced to trade clothing for food. I was struck by sadness and didn't know what to do when I watched Mama exchange her new clothes so we could have a meal. I worried about everything, constantly harboring a premonition of some misfortune about to befall my family. Everything was escaping our grasp. I often overheard Mama and Papa sigh about food, wondering how we were going to live. Many times, I found myself wishing that this was just a bad dream. At night, I would sometimes open my eyes from a deep sleep and wonder where I was, only to find myself lost among the many distant points of light in the dark night sky.

One morning before sunrise, I awoke to raucous sounds coming from a truck being loaded. Curious, I ran closer to discover it carried pigs whose piercing screams cut through the entire area. The driver was a black-outfitted soldier. As he backed up the truck to unload the animals, he accidentally hit the gate of the warehouse. The bumper hooked to the gate, tearing down a part of it and making it unable to close. As the creatures were unloaded, many escaped and ran for their lives in different directions.

That evening, the villagers eagerly hunted for the runaway pigs. As it got dark, we could see bright flames and smoke blaze up in the air as the captured pigs were slaughtered and cooked. One of the neighbors came from the back road with some barbecued meat that he wrapped with banana leaf. He handed it to Papa and told us to enjoy it. Papa carefully held out a small piece to each of us. I will never forget how delicious it tasted. Reluctant to swallow it, I savored chewing it until it dissolved into liquid.

We staved off death from starvation by gulping down everything that even looked like food that we could find. Every day, I felt perpetually hungry, and my body trembled with sweat.

In the afternoon the next day, as I was on my way to the river to wash myself before the sun set, I began to feel weak and tired. Unexpectedly, a small piglet ran by. With my newly awakened desire for meat, I thought it would be good to roast this piglet for a meal. The creature seemed to be running for its life, as if someone was chasing it. I leapt as fast as I could to block the little runt, but rocks tripped my feet and my body fell to the ground. Not bothering to see if I was injured, I quickly extended my arm to grab its leg. All I wanted was to grab this little creature and see Mama and Papa's joy when I brought it home for a meal.

That was easier said than done. It was a challenging fight, with much pulling and screaming from both sides, fearful as I was that this creature would attack and bite me. As it continued to struggle to get free, my arms were getting tired and its sharp kicking hooves peeled back my left index fingernail. My finger began to bleed and hurt so much that I had to let the piglet go. But then, somehow, I managed to spring up and chase after it. I would get close to the runt again and again, almost catching it by its tail, but then missing it each time. After a relentless pursuit, we ended up at the side of the shore while I gasped for air and the piglet trembled miserably with fear.

Finally, the little one bravely jumped into the water and tried to swim away from me. But the current was against it, preventing it from traveling any distance. I stood at the shore, breathlessly watching it float in the water with its nose in the air, so desperate to breathe in order to survive. The sight was so poignant that I suddenly realized I could not let this little creature drown.

After a few moments of hesitation, I went down to the river, grabbed the squirming little fellow, and brought him back to the shore. I held him very tightly. The poor creature cried from fear and frantically wriggled to flee from me. As I looked into his poor, innocent eyes, however, his squeaking voice abruptly stopped. I could feel his fast heartbeat. He was trembling with fear. He seemed to be asking me for mercy. Suddenly, I saw that this little one's life was as important as that of any human being. I felt extremely guilty. I realized that starving for food had deliberately misled me into threatening and possibly slaughtering a living being.

Tears rolled down my cheeks. I talked to the piglet as if it could understand me and my apologies. I said goodbye and good luck to the pathetic soul, and then let it go. The poor little creature ran for its life without looking back. For the first time, I had glimpsed my own potential to be a dangerous, cruel savage. I realized that how I had just experienced myself was not really me. I turned my face to watch the blazing sun sink below the horizon.

That night, my body was sore and painful. I broke out in a rash all over. The next day, a neighbor came to the cottage and told us that the warehouse was giving away dead pigs. Papa and Brother Vuong went to collect some meat to bring home. Although its green color and strange smell suggested it might be spoiled, Papa sliced the meat into pieces and dried it. He said we all had to eat in order to survive. Fortunately, none of us got sick from our suspicious meal. Not everyone was as fortunate.

✿

24.
Kla Krohuem and the Sixteen Buddhist Nuns

After a couple of months of staying at the cottage, we were sad and surprised when Mr. Sing told us that his Grandma wanted us to leave. He wasn't being mean or inhospitable. The dreaded village authority, the Khmer Rouge, was prohibiting strangers from other places taking residence there, and Mr. Sing's family could be no exception. Without knowing where to go next, Papa decided that all of us should walk to his hometown, the village where Grandma Kim Hoa and Brother Vuong's family lived, which my parents informed me was about one hundred sixty kilometers away. We resignedly decided to set out that very day, wondering what the future held in store for us. Sometimes, I felt I was about ready to collapse from all that hunger and walking.

When we left the village in the late afternoon, the weather was miserably hot. To avoid the heat in the day-time, we slept in the shade on the streets, and at night we resumed our journey. The roads were rocky and dusty. Many people were worried and not quite sure what to do, walking and wandering toward an uncertain destination. One evening before the sun set, we arrived at a small rural village called Phoum Kla Krohuem, hidden along a narrow, red, and dusty road.

When Sok, my younger brother, began shaking with fever, his lips even turning pale, Papa decided to settle at a rest stop before nightfall. We wandered throughout the area for some time while Papa looked for a place for us to lie down, but every corner was occupied with hundreds of desperate refugees pouring in from all over the country.

Out of the blue, a big truck drove up close to where we were standing and abruptly stopped in a murky cloud of dust. Those in the back of the truck screamed as the sudden stop threw them on top of one another. The driver quickly jumped out to unlock the back door while impatiently shouting, "Get out! Hurry up, get out!"

Emerging from the dust cloud was a group of at least sixteen elderly Buddhist nuns, dressed in white robes and displaying shaved heads. Some were speaking in Vietnamese. They appeared to be distressed and confused. I was stunned at how they were mistreated. As I was always taught Buddhist practitioners were benevolent people and were to be the utmost respected in all circumstances. I couldn't figure it out; where was the rule of law?

A skinny, middle-aged man helped this group of frail and unsteady women gather their belongings as they struggled to get back on their feet and out of the truck.

Mama told Brother Vuong, Brother Chen, and me to go and help them get down off the truck so they would not fall. Several of them were especially weak. The white robes of some were stained with a yellowish substance that carried a foul odor and attracted swarms of flies. As they thanked us for helping them, all of them were in tears.

❀❀❀❀❀

Later, the skinny, middle-aged man told Papa that he was exhausted from helping the nuns. "I do not know how I ended up here. I am only a cleaner in the temple, but all of

a sudden, we were told to leave. Without any more explanation, we were roughly loaded onto the big truck and drove
away to an unknown destination.

"This is miserable," he said, frowning. "I thought the
driver told us that he was going to move these nuns to another
temple. Now they are left in my care when I can hardly take
care of myself."

After wandering farther in the rest area, Papa finally found
a spot under a wooden house where we could spend the night
with the nuns. One of the most emaciated and smallest nuns,
named Co Tri, loved talking to me as I was watching her touching my younger sister Mei Juang's hair. In spite of the day she
had just endured, she smiled a lot. As Mei Juang and I sat by
her while she ate a boiled green eggplant, we asked her how
she had become a nun. She sadly shared the story of her
childhood.

"I left home and became a nun when I was fifteen," she
began. "My stepfather tried to force me to marry a rich businessman who was a lot older than I was, telling me that this
would be an opportunity for my future. At the time, my
stepfather did not work. Only my mother took care of me, as
well as my stepbrother. Stepfather often came home late with
the smell of alcohol and in a bad mood, scolding both me and
my mother.

She paused and began to sob.

"Unfortunately," she continued, "when I refused my
stepfather's wish for me to marry, he came home one evening
so furious with me that he grabbed me by the hair while I was
asleep, pulled me out of my bed, and chopped off my hair with
a pair of dull scissors. I cried and cried out in pain and screamed
for help, but my mother did nothing. I could not take this
anymore. I loved my mother, but she could no longer protect
me. That same evening, I left home without saying a word to
anyone. I escaped by hiding in a Buddhist temple not far from
home."

She smiled bitterly, and tears streamed down her cheeks. Taking a deep breath, she went on.

"Later, rumor spread that my stepfather was searching everywhere for me in order to kill me. I then decided to give up my life and live in the temple. The abbess had my head shaved, and after a period of initiation, I became a nun. Soon after, the master of the temple transferred me to another one far away from home. Since then, I have never heard from my mother. That has been my fate."

I learned so much from this tiny little woman who had the courage and strength to find her freedom. Early the next morning, we sadly said goodbye to all the nuns and moved on with our journey.

We looked quite different from the villagers in Kla Krohuem, where we were now about to stay. Children ran around naked. Women breastfed their children in public. They stood and watched every step we took toward the core of the village as we dragged our belongings in a cart with three wheels that squeaked constantly. We passed by many villagers' homes, and almost every one of them had a tiny, wooden spirit altar erected near its entrance. The top of the altar was covered with palm leaves and grass. Mama said that the altar was meant to chase the evil spirits. One farmer warned us to be cautious walking around this area because *Mjas Teuk Mjas Dei,* the earth spirit, was everywhere and we might run over it, causing illness or some other punishment from the soul of Mother Nature.

Sok's fever was getting worse, his body doubled over on the torn mattress that we found for him. I disregarded the farmer's warning and told Brother Vuong that I was going to look for some herbs. I met a kind villager who gave me a bunch of lemongrasses that I brought back to Mama to boil for Sok, hoping to reduce his fever. He immediately broke into a sweat and soon felt much better.

When Sok was a little boy, he often got sick with fever. Papa spent a lot of money for his medical treatment. One day,

Mama decided to take Sok to Wat Ampe Phnom and asked the head of the monks to ritually adopt him so he could become *chaw lokta* (the monk's grandson). If so, Sok could recieve more blessings to ward off his illnesses. This was a common ritual in Cambodia.

❀❀❀❀❀

One day while still in Kla Krohuem village, Papa told me and Brother Chen to look around for branches so he could make a cooking fire. But it was hard to find even a twig because there were few trees in the area. As we walked along the road, Brother Chen joked that he might have to break up one of the villagers' spirit altars to make a fire for cooking.

Oddly, after walking about a kilometer, Brother Chen suddenly had a severe stomachache. His face turned blue and he sat on the ground, sweating in pain and holding his belly. We all had to stop. I told Papa and Mama about the earlier joke he had made.

Papa angrily turned to Brother Chen. "You should have learned to respect *Mjas Teuk Mjas Dei,* the earth spirit, in this area. Now we all have to go back and ask for forgiveness." As we hurried back toward the sacred place, Papa continued to lecture him. Once Brother Chen apologized in front of the sacred place for what he had said, his stomach-ache immediately went away. Mama warned him to remember this as a lesson about the courage needed for survival.

❀

25.

At the Shore
of the Mekong

At the end of a long summer day, the evening country air was still red hot. I was always exhausted from the broiling heat of the day and the constant work. My feet were blistered, cut, and covered with thorns from the long day's walk. We finally parked our belongings at the side of the road and prepared for sleep, feeling as if we were dying from hunger. Fortunately, Papa had a piece of yam for each of us. On the road that morning, he had exchanged it with a farmer for his old shirt.

The dawn chorus of birds woke me up the next morning. My body was wet and chilly from the heavy night dew, and my face and arms were covered with bumps from mosquito bites.

After many days and nights of trudging from one village to another, we finally reached the shore of the Mekong River, bordering the Kampong Cham province. Thousands and thousands of people from all over the city of Phnom Penh were anxiously milling around at the shore, waiting for the ship from Kampong Thom to arrive. I watched everyone struggling through their turmoil and hopelessness. The noise and confusion were immense. Some cried out loud that they had already been there for days hoping to be taken to a land where they could start a new life. Yet the ship had still not arrived.

There were even more serious concerns than frustrated hopes. The slope to the river was steep and had become muddy from people repeatedly walking over it to get water. The morning of our arrival, a large group was in the water screaming fearfully. We were told that some children had gotten stuck in the mud as they tried to bathe, and were then unable to escape the strong currents that swept them away. Their bodies were never found. We heard that over the past several days, many people had drowned in this river and many others had committed suicide. For many, death was a reprieve from suffering.

Before the day grew too dark, I left the crowd in search of a place to empty my bowels. I had to walk for a long time to find an isolated spot, which unfortunately was rocky and thick with wild plants. As I was about to place my feet on a big dead trunk, a giant snake about three meters long slid out from the bush and slithered over my feet. I jerked back, screamed in fear, and ran backwards. When people along the shore heard me scream, they came running, not just to help me and not in terror, but in eagerness for a meal.

On the way back to my family, I spied a lonesome, depressed-looking Caucasian man dressed in a light-brown suit and squatting on a rock. An expensive leather suitcase lay on the ground next to him. His blond curly hair was long and messy, and his clothes were caked with mud. He was sitting in the crowd, but he was in a world entirely apart. He was possibly in his early thirties. I assumed he must speak French and approached him with genuine concern, saying, "*Salut, monsieur.*"

After a few seconds, he reluctantly turned his face to me and repeated my greeting, "*Salut.*" His face was dour and angry, and his lips were purple. He looked sick, appearing not to have eaten for many days. I thought he might have gone crazy due to all that had happened. Curious, I asked, "*Ca va, monsieur?*"

Instead of responding, he began to cough violently.

I became frightened and ran off.

Upon returning, I told Brother Vuong, a medical doctor, about my concern for the Frenchman. I hoped he could do something for him. However, Brother Vuong looked at me and replied, "At this moment, I don't even know how to cure myself." Even though I understood that he was upset by our circumstances, I had never heard him so discouraged. His despair baffled me, and I asked him what was wrong. Brother Vuong was a generous and good-hearted person. He said "yes" most of the time when I asked him for a favor. Now I was worried about the Frenchman and worried about how he was going to survive. How would he find his way back home from this place where he didn't belong?

I turned around and stepped towards Mama. She stood alone in the shadow of a tree, facing me with her arms wrapped around herself. Anxiously, I whispered, "Mama, I found a poor Frenchman sitting alone. He looked very sick." She stared at me with a hopeless look of understanding, but her silent, aloof reaction left me speechless and worried. As the night crept in, I became increasingly worried about the Frenchman. I could not help but tell Brother Chen that something could tragically cut the guy's life short.

"I just don't know what to think; we are all in the same situation," said Brother Chen, empathy in his voice.

I began to wonder how everything in the world suddenly became so different and went so drastically wrong.

In the middle of one night at the shore, Brother Chen screamed in pain as he felt something horrible happening to his big toe. His scream raised the hair on the back of my neck. I woke up shaking with goose bumps all over my body and didn't really know what was wrong. I thought the snake was coming after my family. Brother Vuong rushed in to check the bite mark with a flashlight and said it was from a field mouse bite. Although his toe bled badly, Brother Vuong was his usual compassionate self and squeezed out the poison.

We were more fortunate than most of those who had been exiled from the big city.

After only a few days of chaotic life and bewilderment by the Mekong River, Papa saw a ship appear on the horizon. We were all relieved and overjoyed. At last we would be able to move on with our journey, hopefully, to Grandma Kim Hoa's house.

We had no idea how long our journey would be or how much more dangerous our life would turn.

✿

26.
On the Way to
Grandma Kim Hoa's House

Thousands of people were in line trying to jam onto the crowded ship. When it was finally our turn to board, I held Grandpa Kaing Hak Yi's hand as we walked up the plank. Suddenly the crowd pushed us from behind, trying to make its way through and causing Grandpa Kaing Hak Yi and Mama to almost fall overboard.

We tried to bring on board as many of our meager possessions as we could carry. However, a guard forced us to leave things behind in order to prevent the boat from sinking.

By the time we got on board, the ship was already packed, so we were ordered by the ship's authorities to sit on the deck with the last of our belongings next to us. There was no space left to even stretch our arms or legs. After the ship pushed off from the pier, Mama was terrified that it was overloaded. Whenever the waves slammed against it, the water lapped onto the deck and the entire ship rolled violently.

It felt as if we had gone back to primal nature.

The day was getting dark. As the ship moved down the Mekong, I sat next to Grandpa Kaing Hak Yi and watched the scenery of that late-summer afternoon through the mist. Everyone on the ship was confused and worried. I kept asking Mama how our lives were going to change. But she only sat there in anxious silence. Mei Juang and Brother Sok leaned their heads against Mama's shoulders and wrapped their arms tightly around her.

We looked forward to seeing Grandma Kim Hoa. I only vaguely remembered the last time we saw her, which had been several years before. I remembered her as a very caring person who enjoyed cooking my favorite foods for me. When I was a young boy about five years old, I suffered from a severe case of chickenpox. My body was itchy, and I had a high fever. She held me in her arms and fed me porridge with delicious sausages.

❀❀❀❀❀

One day, the situation swiftly changed with no warning or explanation. We simply stopped hearing from her. To this day, I wonder what happened to her, but my heart sinks knowing how most of the records from those years were destroyed. Millions of people like her lived beautiful lives but disappeared without a trace.

The next day, we arrived exhausted in the province of Tbong Khmum. After disembarking, we carried our belongings and pushed ourselves to the limit to walk approximately one hundred kilometers without stopping. After several days, we reached a village called Piem Cheliang. Reaching it was a tremendous accomplishment and a great relief, but Papa wanted to continue, which was difficult for us to understand. While we were debating whether to stay or push on, he saw we were near an old wooden bridge that led to the village where Grandma Kim Hoa lived. At that moment, a black-suited soldier detained us with a pointed rifle and aggressively interrogated Papa.

"You do not belong to this area," he said with menace in his voice. "Go back to where you came from." He emphasized that the other side of the bridge was only for the old villagers, the *neak mool thaan*, and that we did not belong there.

While we remained on the roadside deciding what to do next, two trucks drove by, so big that the ground trembled. Piled high with new, colorful household items, they swiftly sped across the old wooden bridge to the other side of the river.

The sight of someone successfully crossing the bridge depressed me. While I squatted and dispiritedly watched the other side of the bridge, I could see that the entire village was shaded by green foliage of all kinds. The area was deadly quiet, except for the chatting of a few old women who were standing at the riverbank to fetch water with two naked young children. Their clothes were old and torn. I wondered about my future. If Grandma Kim Hoa only knew how close we had come to her village!

To the family's stinging disappointment, Mama and Papa decided to look for a place in Piem Cheliang, where we could settle down temporarily and wait for another occasion to visit Grandma Kim Hoa.

✿

27.
In Piem Cheliang

For the next month, time crept by slowly in the camp. Eventually, the Khmer Rouge authorities allowed us to reside in Piem Cheliang, in a very old wooden house next to a monastery. The first evening of our stay, Papa found a large, old, rotting grey blanket on top of one of the shelves in the back of the monastery. Mama took a long time to shake off the dust and gave it to me and Brother Chen as bed covering at night. When the next morning came around, our bodies were swollen with red itchy bumps. Later, Brother Vuong inspected the material under the sun and found hundreds of bedbugs crawling all over the blanket.

One morning, out of curiosity, Mama and I went into the pagoda, which had been devastated by bombs. It was heartbreaking to see how many statues had been destroyed, the walls cracked, and the roof falling down in many places. There were many leaks through which rays of sunlight streamed in all directions. Many statues of Buddha had been deliberately broken by the rampaging revolutionary soldiers into pieces and were missing arms and legs. The walls grew thick, dark green moss. We saw the building had been abandoned for quite a while because of the vast number of screeching bats and the intense smell of their excrement. It felt like a place full of mystery that Mama and I were the first to discover. As Mama and I kneeled to pray to the broken Buddhist statues for protection, I could sense the vibration of the spirits.

"How could such a sacred place be deliberately damaged like this?" Mama asked.

She shook her head with a sigh in disbelief and wiped the tears from her face with the back of her hand.

A skinny old monk silently appeared from behind and took us by surprise, gesturing with his hand and speaking with fierceness in his voice: "You must leave now before you are caught by the authorities. This is a forbidden zone."

Mama and I were scared by the warning and left quickly.

We were allowed to stay on the second floor of the wooden house behind the temple. Because it was built of wood and bamboo, there were many spaces in the floor where we could see through to the room underneath, which was a warehouse where the monks had stored coffins and gravestones. To me this was an ill omen—we were human beings living over objects for the dead.

The first night I slept in the house, a dream came to me. The Khmer Rouge shot my entire family to death. In the dream, the monks put us in those same coffins and buried my family behind the temple. I woke up with palpitations, crying. Brother Chen had shaken my arm to awaken me from the nightmare.

Several days later, Papa met his childhood friend Ban, who had become a Khmer Rouge soldier. My siblings and I called him Uncle Ban. He was tall, slim, and had two large wide ears. He seemed to know a lot about everything in this village. According to Uncle Ban, all boys and girls at the age of twelve were drafted and trained to become Khmer Rouge soldiers. They became official soldiers when they reached the age of fourteen and knew how to use firearms.

Papa and Uncle Ban whispered to each other whenever they met behind the pagoda so that we could not understand what they were saying. Uncle Ban dressed in black, seemed very nervous each time he came to our place to meet with Papa, and would leave in a hurry.

Later, Uncle Ban helped Papa dispatch a message to Grandma Kim Hoa, letting her know we had arrived in Piem Cheliang. One afternoon I snuck out to the woods to collect sapodilla *lamut* in the cemetery behind the pagoda. It was a type of brown, fleshy fruit with a sweet, floral aroma. The fruit was partially eaten by bats that left remains scattered all over the ground. I brought them home, and Mama helped carve away the bite marks and let us eat the rest.

As I was on my way back, Brother Chen told me excitedly that Grandma had just arrived and wanted to visit us. He pointed inside the room and repeatedly said, "Grandma is here, Grandma is here!" I was so excited that I broke into tears. I ran into the room and saw Papa and two other elderly people sitting there.

Grinning widely at me, Papa introduced me. "Your Grandma is here." I had not seen Papa look so happy for a long time. I came into the room, hugged the younger woman, and called her "Grandma." At that moment, the other woman called me by my birth name as she reached for me with her frail hand and then burst into tears. I felt as if she could fall down and break a bone at any time. She grabbed me tightly, and I could feel that she was only skin and bones. She had become so small. I told myself that my beautiful Grandma now looked completely different than she had many years ago. Naively, I somehow still expected her to look the same, even though she had suffered so much in her life in the jungle.

Traditionally in Khmer culture, it is a high priority to respect and care for the elderly. Kids are taught from a young age to be familiar with the society's norms of politeness and are always to pay respect toward their elders. As I looked at my most revered elder, I tried to figure out how Grandma Kim Hoa had changed so drastically. I could not find the words to express how much I had missed her, but I told her I had missed her a lot. I suddenly started crying. I wasn't sure whether I was crying because I missed her or because life had become excruciating for us.

Soon, the owner of the coach came to tell Grandma Kim Hoa it was time for her departure. Brother Chen and I both held Grandma Kim Hoa as we walked out with her. She told us, "A close friend of mine named Thao lives alone at the corner of the road by the river. Please go and visit her to check and see how she is doing. I have not seen my friend for several years, not since the Khmer Rouge took over governing this area." Grandma Kim Hoa held my hand as we approached the coach. There were tears in her eyes. She was so weak. She kept repeating my name as if she was about to say something, reluctant to leave us. But the visit was over.

As the coach moved away, she waved her bony hand at us through the window as we watched her disappear down the dusty road. It was the first and last time we saw each other for many years. I was very upset and confused. My world was turned upside down. That evening, we talked about Grandma Kim Hoa. The entire family was heart-broken, and worse, terrified about our future as our country tumbled into utter chaos.

✿

28.
The Drowning of the
Khmer Rouge Soldiers

The following day around noon, Brother Chen and I fetched water from the river near the old wooden bridge. While filling our buckets, we happened to see eight raucous young Khmer Rouge soldiers packed into a large truck speeding harshly across the bridge, disturbing the surrounding villagers by loudly singing the Khmer Rouge anthem. Brother Chen and I turned toward the commotion and witnessed the truck suddenly careen out of control, crash into the rail of the bridge, and flip over into the river below.

The singing voices of the soldiers turned to howls and cries for help.

We onlookers were all in shock. But not a single one of us approached the river. As the truck sank deeper into the water, the noise gradually died down. Only the driver of the truck climbed out of the water. Completely soaked, he sat under the bridge for a moment and then slowly walked away. The whole incident seemed surreal. Brother Chen and I were shivering from witnessing such an event, the likes of which we had never seen in our lives.

Several days later, the Khmer Rouge in the village came by where we lived and commanded Papa, Brother Chen, and me to help the local villagers pull the truck out from the river.

While on the riverbank, we spotted several dead bodies that had floated to the surface. They were as puffed up and bloated as balloons ready to pop. Some had their face down in the water while others had their face up. The entire village was filled with the rotten, sickly smell of the dead and the buzz of the flies. It took us several heartbreaking hours to drag the old truck out of the river.

The next day, the Khmer authorities ordered us to return to the crash site and remove the corpses from the water. The order was sickening as well as disrespectful. Fortunately, by the time we made it to the river that morning, the villagers had already removed the carcasses and lined them up by the riverbank, covering them with banana leaves. The foul, rotten smell continued to stink up the entire area. Meanwhile, the surface of the river trembled with thousands of baby fishes, nibbling and scuffling to fight over the flesh of the dead.

Papa, Brother Chen, and I later helped the villagers carry the remains to bury them next to the monastery. I felt a quiver of fear, and my stomach churned with disgust when, on the way to the burial, small fishes, crabs, and crevettes slipped out from the corpses. By the time we were done with the burial, it was close to sunset. One by one, we wandered back to the village feeling degraded and dead inside.

As we were tossed back and forth in our stormy daily life, my thoughts of Grandma Kim Hoa became less frequent. One evening, something very unusual happened. Two young female Khmer Rouge soldiers wearing black came to the pagoda. They both spoke in Mandarin and looked worried and nervous as they talked to us. Meanwhile, a male Khmer Rouge soldier stood by the door with a rifle in his hand, sternly watching the two girls conversing with us. Mama and I were very surprised because it was unusual to see Khmer Rouge who spoke Chinese.

They came to talk to refugees from Phnom Penh, looking for someone they might know. One of them asked us in Mandarin if we knew a woman by the name of Liang Mei Ching, who happened to be my former Chinese teacher. We told her that we knew the person, but we had no idea where she was. She took down the information and politely smiled as she turned her back and walked away. This woman confounded Mama and me, and we wondered how she knew my former Chinese teacher. And how did my Chinese teacher know these Khmer Rouge people? We were deeply suspicious but had no idea what to do about it.

Days later, we heard the wrenching rumors that the two Chinese Khmer Rouge girls were executed by the head of the Khmer Rouge in the village. Mama worried herself to death for many days, fearing people would think we were somehow related to the two young female Khmer Rouge soldiers.

✿

29.
The Blind Old Woman and Her Casket

Unexpectedly and without warning, one morning after we had been on the run for weeks a Khmer Rouge soldier charged into the village where we had been staying and coldly announced that refugee arrivals were to be "allowed," as he put it, to live in a new open land called Cheuteal. Papa quickly had our family registered to go. We all thought it would be the best opportunity to restart our new life. As days went by, more and more people migrated to Piem Cheliang, all of them registering to go to Cheuteal. Our family was assigned to the earliest arrival, and we were allowed to be the first to move in.

That same day at noon, while the village of Piem Cheliang was quiet, I decided to sneak into the area described by Grandma Kim Hoa so I could look for her friend, Thao. I put on my dark clothing and covered my head up with *krama* to disguise myself as someone from the local area. Mama and Grandpa Kaing Hak Yi were very worried I might get into trouble by intruding on the old villager's home.

Following Grandma Kim Hoa's instructions, I found a very old wooden house at the corner by the river. The house was on stilts, which raised it about two meters above the ground. The stairs were old and moldy, and they squeaked as

I put my weight on each step. Some steps had disintegrated from age, so I had to take care not to fall to and hurt myself severely. I had a quick look around to make sure no one would see me. As I was about to knock on the door, I heard a low shaky voice. I called out, "Is this Grandma Thao? Are you Grandma Thao?"

"Yes, I am. Come in, but who are you, young man?" she asked in surprise.

"My Grandma Kim Hao told me that you lived here. She said I should come and check in on you."

She was small, wrinkled, elderly, and nearly bald. But she was very alert and beamed with delight the moment she heard Grandma Kim Hoa's name. She had difficulty standing upright, and after talking to her for a few seconds, I realized that Grandma Thao could not see me clearly because she was nearly blind. She told me she lived alone in this old wood house, could only walk slowly, and relied on her sense of smell, touch, and hearing to help her manage her daily life. The walls in her room were falling apart, making me wonder how she could survive during the stormy season.

Then I noticed a casket next to where I was standing. I was shocked and felt uncomfortable. While we were sitting next to a small, empty bamboo table, I grabbed Grandma Thao's hand and asked her, "What's going on, Grandma Thao?"

Sadly, she replied in a voice choking with emotion, "Years ago, I left Vietnam with my boyfriend and came to this village to start a new life. At that time, this place was so beautiful and full of nature. I loved hearing the flow of the river every day. Unfortunately, one day he fell off a coconut tree and became paralyzed. I took care of him until he passed away.

"Later, I cried every day until my eyes were red and swollen. One day I woke up, and suddenly everything was dark. Many times, I have thought about taking my own life so I would no longer suffer. But as a Buddhist, committing suicide would not be a solution. Killing myself would have resulted in a punishment stretched out over five-hundred lifetimes before I could reincarnate to another human being. I decided that I needed to live to keep my soul alive."

Grandma Thao also told me that she had trouble keeping food down. I later learned that was because she was causing herself to throw up after she had a meal. She confided to me that she slept in her casket every night, just in case she would not wake up the next day. Placing her hand on the casket, she continued, "I want to be sure that I am buried properly when I die. I don't want my body tossed in the woods like the Khmer Rouge did to others."

I was quite disturbed by what she told me. Then she said she had to go to her garden to get something for me. For an old, blind, elderly person, she impressed me with her inner strength and wisdom. She insisted I stay where I was and wait for her return. Then she carefully shut the door behind her and stepped outside. I was worried and peeped through the broken wall to see exactly what Grandma Thao was doing. I was anxious she would fall and kill herself on the broken stairs. My mind kept envisioning a disaster about to happen. However, she managed to reach the ground safely.

I was astonished! She quickly started crawling on all fours toward the bush by the river. Afterwards, she came back with a bag of ripe tomatoes, handing it to me and then rushing me to the door to leave. I was stunned and unable to understand how she could do such a thing in her condition. As I was about to slip out the door, she asked me to come back in several days, when her bananas would be ripe and ready. Unsure what she was talking about, I nevertheless left her house, strangely excited.

❀

30.
The New Open Land
in Cheuteal Village

Mama and Papa asked Brother Vuong and me to go scout out the location where we were being moved. Brother Vuong took me on an old bicycle, and we left Piem Cheliang around afternoon.

The road was rocky and muddy and led us to a narrow path where tall grass grew all over. We could barely see through the grass; it seemed never-ending. When we finally arrived at Cheuteal village, the sun was already setting. Surrounded by thick jungle, it was a newly constructed village with only forty or so houses, partially built of leaves and bamboo.

The cottages on the left and the right were in rows parallel to each other, with a road in between. Behind them were hundreds of termite hills lined up one after another. The base of each cottage was built about a meter off the ground. Each roof was covered with hay and leaves thatched loosely enough that you could see through to the sunlight. For our family, Brother Vuong and I chose a cottage in the middle of the right row.

Night fell soon after we arrived, and we rushed to eat our meal in the darkness. We had salty dried fish and potatoes that Mama had wrapped in banana leaves for us. We had to make sure we would have enough food for the next couple of days.

While I was eating the food, I turned my face toward the dark, clear sky.

I watched the stars twinkling so far away. I felt as if I were falling into a deep well and would never find the way out again. The quiet of the night reminded me that there were only the two of us in the midst of thick foliage, accompanied by only the sounds of night animals and insects. Due to our long and exhausting day, we fell asleep right after the meal.

During the middle of our slumber, Brother Vuong was awakened by the howling of wild animals. He shook me hard in an effort to wake me up. I was drowsy and not sure what was happening. He loudly and repeatedly commanded me, "Move in quickly, the wolves are coming to eat us." I now heard many ferocious sounds very close to the front of our cottage. Brother Vuong and I were not sure, but we thought that what we heard was either wolves or coyotes. Whatever they were, we were certain they were dangerous and about to prey on us.

We then saw the animals, having accustomed ourselves to the dark. The beasts' blinking eyes slowly approached us, followed by the formless shadows of their bodies. Brother Vuong luckily found a long bamboo carrier that he swung ceaselessly in the air as we screamed and made frightening noises to scare away the creatures.

Without warning, they stopped howling, went quiet, and disappeared into the night.

To be safe, we kept screaming and yelling to make sure that they would not return.

That first night in Cheuteal felt as if the universe was using us for bait to fish the wild. Having escaped the night predators, I awoke at the crack of dawn, only to find I had been pricked with what seemed like thousands of needles, my body swollen and full of red spots from mosquito bites. My extremities ached and were painful to move. My throat was sore from screaming. I was terrified that my family and I were going to be struck down by malaria. Many people we knew who were exposed to such jungle life had become very sick, many dying from various diseases. Our priority, basic survival, gave us no time to speculate about dire possibilities.

While in Cheuteal, Brother Vuong and I worked nonstop together, trying to strengthen the cottage so that it would not be destroyed by a strong wind. He sometimes became frustrated from working so hard, splitting so many bamboo trees that his hands bled. Nevertheless, he persisted on the sun-drenched roof, carefully and patiently knitting the bamboo sticks through the thick leaves one after another. I stood at the bottom to pass him bamboo as needed.

For no apparent reason, Brother Vuong started shouting as he hopped off the roof and ran furiously toward the thick foliage behind the cottage. I was paralyzed by his inexplicable and sudden movement. I did not understand what he saw or what had happened. I was scared as I cried after him, "Brother Vuong, what's happening?! What's happening?!"

A few minutes later, he emerged from the woods, disappointedly reporting to me, "I saw a small wild pig wandering around in the bush. I chased it, but it was too fast for me. I thought we could have a good meal."

❀❀❀❀❀

Two days later, we went back to Piem Cheliang to help with the moving. Thrilled to see us, Brother Chen eagerly held out a banana for each of us. He told us that he had more to share when we moved to Cheuteal. That same day, I sneaked into the village to say goodbye to Grandma Thao.

The moment she heard my voice, she became distressed. "I am so upset. Someone stole my bananas off the tree. I was saving them for your family, but someone stole them." I did not know what to say, except to assure her to take care of herself and that someday I would come by to see her again.

The minute I returned, I asked Brother Chen where he got the bananas. He looked at me warily and replied, "Two days ago, I went to fetch water from the river and found a tree with a bunch of bananas. I thought they were wild, so I chopped them down and took them home."

I barked at him, "The bananas belong to Grandma Thao! You stole from her! She was upset. Where are the rest of them?"

He informed me that he had buried the bananas in the ground. I insisted we go see Grandma Thao and apologize to her. When we arrived at her place, Brother Chen confessed he had taken the bananas, which scared me into thinking she would get very angry with us both. Luckily, she was happy that it was her own grandson who took them.

"I kept them for you boys anyway."

Later that night, when we said farewell to Grandma Thao, we left her not knowing if we would ever see her again. On the way back, I felt dubious about Brother Chen. I began to distrust his unpredictable behavior.

Soon after moving into Cheuteal Village, life became even harder and much crueler.

The Khmer Rouge constantly forced us to perform hard and often agonizing labor, day and night, such as working in the rice paddies, cutting down trees in the jungle, and making houses. Everyone in the village, young and old, was ordered by the Khmer Rouge to work on different kinds of duty. Sister Mei Juang and Brother Sok were put with a group of children who were under ten to collect human feces and mix them with dirt to make fertilizers, which is one indication of how some of our tasks were senseless, while most of them were just cruel. I was sent to burn down and clear the surrounding forest for plowing and sowing. During these days of difficult and sometimes harrowing labor, many of the elderly and the very young suffered from heatstroke, and many of the elderly even died from fatigue, disease, or physical abuse.

Soon after, I overheard Papa mutter to Mama in his sad and disappointed tone of voice, "This is the meaning of our Cambodian saying, *Chheam dab poh krabei*—'flood of blood soaked the buffalo's belly.' This is their method of execution. They starve us and exhaust us from overwork."

Across from our cottage lived Mr. Kaing, his wife, and his two daughters, who were seven and six, and a five-year-old son. One late afternoon, Mr. Kaing came over to our cottage and told us that he knew something about *feng shui*, the traditional Buddhist way to design with the spatial flow of energy in any given area. There were hundreds of termite mounds piling up behind our cottage. He said the land looked like it used to be an ancient cemetery where each tomb was filled by a termite mound.

Throughout the rainy season, many of us who had been exiled from our homes in the big city were sent to clear forest, build dams, and dig in the ground with our bare hands across lakes and rivers to form pools which would prevent flooding that could destroy rice fields. On one extremely hot day, we were piling soil to build a flood-prevention ditch to protect the village itself.

Out of the blue, a young woman in her early twenties breathlessly pedaled by us on her mini-bicycle, her long hair flowing behind her. She was nicely dressed, in a bright white shirt and new black pants. Panicked, she sweated profusely as she sped toward nowhere in particular, away from some undefined danger. By that point, I am embarrassed to say, I was too physically and mentally exhausted to even wonder or care about what was going to happen to her.

One day, while a group of us were clearing the forest, and I was near to tears because my small hands were bleeding from working with the machete, I noticed an emaciated old man who I learned was *Pou* Boran (Uncle Boran). He had a long, white mustache. His skin was covered with rashes all over. He approached me and asked if I was willing to accept a *tael* of gold for a can of rice. In tears, he told me that he did not want to die a starving ghost. Speechless, I stared at him sadly. When it was time for us to rest for our usual meager meal of rice and water, I opened my container and offered to share it with him. He turned around, looking at us, and began to mutter with barely repressed fury, "The Khmer soldiers are just a small group of people. Why don't we all grab their weapons and beat them to death so everyone will be free from this life of suffering?"

Everyone gazed at him in terror and said nothing. His words were disturbing. I wondered how the hell this could be. I asked myself, what was wrong with this world? Would violence ever be the only solution? I felt trapped inside my head with fear and anxiety.

Since that day, I never saw *Pou* Boran again. I was wondering what happened to him. Although a rumor spread that he was too sick to go to work, everyone was too exhausted to worry about other people's problems.

Later, I learned that *Pou* Boran had come to this village alone. He shared the cottage with other roommates. He was separated from his family during the forced evacuation in Phnom Penh.

Days went by without change. The monotony was nearly as bad as the work. Very few of us had ever worked outside in fields before, which made life even harder and more absurd.

One dark, misty morning, I was getting ready to go to work in the fields when I heard a man shouting a few cottages down the road from us. I looked outside and saw a man shouting in a harsh voice with wild gestures, "He is dying, he is dying!"

Curious, Brother Vuong and I rushed down to see what was happening. It took me a moment to recognize that the man was *Pou* Boran, lying flat over a torn straw mattress on the bamboo floor. I followed Brother Vuong to kneel next to him, watching him making a strange rattling sound, his white pale face struggling for air as he tried to clear the secretion in the back of his throat. A moment later, the old man drew his last breath and slowly fell into his eternal slumber. That was the first time I ever saw a man die in front of me as his ironically words kept hitting me in my head.

"I don't want to die a starving ghost."

Soon after, Brother Vuong and a couple of roommates quietly helped carry the body to the nearby woods for burial. I felt numb, but at the same time I thought his death finally gave him freedom. When *Pou* Boran's body was lifted off the floor, we were all startled and disgusted to discover hundreds of white, clear, oval bedbugs congregated in clusters on the upper part of his back. It reminded me that we were not too different from any of these insects, who were also starving and craving food. I could think of nothing else, but my mind kept ruminating in different directions with guilt and anger as I wondered what would happen next.

Over the four decades since the horrors that afflicted my country, I thought back about what *Pou* Boran had said. To this day, *Pou* Boran's image has remained imprinted in my memory. Of course, I was too young to know it then, but over the years I have come to appreciate how often my parents and grandparents tried to turn many of our experiences—both good and bad, beautiful and horrible—into life lessons.

❀❀❀❀❀

Every night after moving into our Cheuteal cottage, we heard strange noises that sounded like someone digging into the ground beneath us. We asked our neighbors if they had heard anything like this sound. They had not heard anything, but speculated it could be animals digging for food. Curious, Grandpa Kaing Hak Yi and I decided to search under the cottage to find out where the digging sound was coming from. But as soon as we climbed down from our living quarters to the ground, the sound ceased.

❀

31.
A Kingdom of Terror

Several days after our arrival, heavy rain poured nonstop, flooding the whole jungle and the village. Numerous villagers suffered from poisonous snake and insect bites. Some children died from drowning while their parents were away laboring. Many older people died from illness and starvation.

Hoping to take advantage of the flood by catching fish, Papa sneaked out to exchange gold for a huge fishnet from an old villager. The next evening, he and Brother Vuong left the net spread out in the swift flowing river overnight. The next early morning, the nets were bursting with hundreds of poisonous snakes of many colors, but no fish, which was a great disappointment for us. However, the silver lining of this nightmare was that neighbors helped to remove the snakes, which they took home for a meal. Unfortunately, some neighborhood children stepped on the snake bones after they had eaten them and got bad infections.

A few days later, the Khmer Rouge came to our place and confiscated the fishnet, declaring that it was not supposed to be a personal possession and belonged to the community. Without that resource during the month when the village remained flooded, we ran out of food. The vegetables, bitter melons, beans, sugarcane, and squashes we had been working so hard to grow around our cottage were now all washed away by the flood.

One cold morning just before the sun came up, we were marching in a line toward the forest and passed by the storage shed where the Khmer Rouge kept their food supplies. About four meters away from us, we heard a man shriek and scream while emerging from a cottage. I recognized it was Pu Chhuan (Uncle Chhuan), who wore no clothes above his waist. He was dragged with a rope around his neck by two young Khmer Rouge soldiers. His face and body were covered with raw, bloody cuts.

"Please let me free. I swear I would never do this again." He trembled as he cried, then kneeled, pleading for his life with his hands in the air. A third Khmer Rouge soldier whipped him from behind with a stick and then turned to us with the stick pointing in our direction. He barked, "Look at this! I want to show you all that this is the consequence of stealing."

I half shut my eyes, too afraid to witness the hostile scene. Following other villagers in line, I quietly strode across the woods. His piercing scream weakened and gradually disappeared in the distance. I felt lost as I just couldn't figure out what feeling underlied my anger. Everyone seemed to act as if nothing had happened.

I recalled that a few days before, I had spoken to *Pou* Chhuan. He was a nice man who always displayed a friendly smile, even if his life was about to break into pieces.

The following evening, after a long day of harsh labor, a neighbor quietly came to our cottage and whispered to Mama that she had discovered a bloated dead corpse hung on a tree in the woods nearby. She was attracted by the cluster of flies, but immediately took off.

I had no doubt that it was *Pou* Chhuan, tortured to death by the Khmer Rouge. Even today, his mournful cries leave a piercing pain in my heart.

To address the food crisis, the Khmer Rouge picked five women to hike to Prasith Mountain for five days to dig wild potatoes for the whole village. Unfortunately, Mama was one of the women selected. This concerned us greatly because Prasith Mountain was well-known as a source of malaria so severe that people rarely survived. They would travel through the flooded forest in a small boat, a trip that took from dawn to midnight. If they would not contract malaria, they would develop food poisoning or be eaten by wild animals. The chances that someone sent there would fail to return were perilously high. Acutely aware of those facts, when Mama left for Prasith Mountain, she entreated me and my siblings to faithfully pray to the spirit of the jungle to shield us from any harm.

Two days after Mama's departure for Prasith Mountain, the Khmer Rouge selected Papa and three other men to sail a small boat to Krouch Chmar. The Khmer Rouge commander gave them only seven days to cut down eight hundred bamboo trees and bring them back to others who needed to build houses.

Mama and Papa were so afraid the Khmer Rouge was plotting against our family that we did not dare to complain about anything we were ordered to do. However, Papa had mixed feelings about his assignment, thinking that he would take the opportunity to visit Grandma Kim Hoa and Brother Vuong's family instead of obeying the Khmer Rouge commander.

After Mama and Papa left, I felt obligated to take care of Grandpa Kaing Hak Yi and my younger brother and sister. Two days later, Mei Juang's eyes turned bloody red with an ugly yellow discharge. Brother Vuong collected rainwater, boiled it, and used it to clean Mei Juang's eyes. However, the redness did not go away, and her eyes became dangerously swollen. Then Mei Juang began telling us that she couldn't see clearly. She became so debilitated that Sok and I had to carry her to the bathroom whenever she had to relieve herself.

Brother Vuong predicted that if the inflammation did not subside, Mei Juang could become blind. I was upset because I did not want to see Mei Juang suffering.

Suddenly I remembered Aunt Sai Fong, a resourceful neighbor who lived several houses away from us. Mama often mentioned that I should ask her for advice whenever she and Papa were not home. An hour after being told what happened to Mei Juang's eyes, Aunt Sai Fong came to me with a strange ball of smashed, slimy, dark-green leaves. When I asked her what it was, she said, "It is a secret herb given to me by my ancestors. You do not need to know its name. If I tell you, the spell will be broken, and it will no longer work." I wondered if what she said was true.

She continued, "You must place the poultice on your sister's eyes and return for the next day to pick up a new supply, and then repeat the treatment until she is better."

When on the second day I came by Aunt Sai Fong's place to pick up the mashed herb for Mei Juang's eyes, I noticed a bunch of hibiscus leaves on her bamboo floor. I guessed that this was her secret herb. At first, I was worried that the smashed green leaves might poison Mei Juang's eyes. But, miraculously, after three days the redness in her eyes went away.

✿✿✿✿✿

One stormy evening, after a long hard day of labor, Brother Chen came home with blood dripping all over his body. He had accidentally cut his ear with a scythe while he was clearing the jungle. In order to stop the bleeding, Brother Vuong quickly helped him wrap up the wound with tobacco leaves. That night I felt like there were many dead monsters coming to life. The rain was heavy, and the wind was so turbulent and strong that it blew off the roof of our cottage, completely soaking us all.

During the storm, Mei Juang was nauseous and vomiting from food poisoning she had contracted from eating some unknown leaves in the woods. My younger brother, Sok, fearfully hiding himself from the storm under a wet blanket, shook with a high fever from malaria. Our cottage was trembling and threatened with being torn apart by the violent weather. Grandpa Kaing Hak Yi grabbed hold of the pole with his two hands to prevent it from being blown away by the strong wind.

Brother Vuong pushed me up to the top of the roof to fasten the leaves and hay so they wouldn't fly away. Each flash of lightning and subsequent crash of thunder was a gruesome event for me, sending a shiver down my spine. All of Mother Nature was in terrifying fury.

The following morning, two very young Khmer Rouge girls appeared in our village to distribute medication for each household to help prevent illness. The pills were round and dark, reminding me of rabbit poop. They were meant to cure headache, diarrhea, fever, and many other diseases. One of the girls grabbed a handful of the pills and told me to have Sok take four pills three times a day to help cure his fever. Distrusting them, I feared they might try to poison Sok.

As soon as they left the cottage, I hurled the pills as far away as I could throw them.

Late one afternoon, just before the sun went down, Grandpa Kaing Hak Yi went out alone to wash himself in a puddle near the rice fields, about half a kilometer away. As the evening grew darker and he had not returned, I began to worry that something had befallen him. Just as I was about to run out to search for him, his dark shadow slowly rose up in front of me. As soon as he stepped into the cottage, I was alarmed by the sight of three huge, blood-sucking leeches dangling from his calves. Brother Chen and I frantically struggled to get rid of them, eventually succeeding. Surprisingly, they did not seem to bother Grandpa Kaing Hak Yi Perhaps by now he had seen too much in his life for these bloodsuckers to be much of a bother.

❀❀❀❀❀

I counted the days waiting for Mama and Papa to return home. Naively, I was hoping that Mama would bring us lots of food from Prasith Mountain, as we had nothing left to eat. One late afternoon, right after coming home from our labors, I decided to go alone into the thick foliage to search for wild potatoes. Unexpectedly, dark clouds suddenly rolled in, blocking out the sun I would need to rely on to find my way back. Holding the wild potatoes in my hands, I blindly ran and ran. With every step, I became more afraid. I was scared of becoming lost. My heart raced as I ran ever deeper into the jungle, trying to find my way out. My head was filled with frantic visions of a large black snake winding around a tree as I speculated about what could happen if I became lost.

Suddenly, the sun broke out between the trees. In the sunlight, the forest was beautiful! I was reminded of the paradise I had grown up in and felt at once that I was safe, as Grandpa Kaing Hak Yi had often instructed me on how to use the sun for direction. By the time I arrived home, it was dark. Grandpa Kaing Hak Yi had been very worried, but now everyone was greatly relieved and happy to have the wild potatoes for dinner that night.

❀❀❀❀❀

I continued to miss Mama and Papa sorely but knew how important it was to stay strong for Grandpa Kaing Hak Yi and my younger brother and sister. Late one drizzling and freezing afternoon, I heard the neighbor's children cry loudly, "Mama is back, Mama is back!" I rushed out to look for my mama, but I couldn't find her. In fact, she was standing right in front of me, but had lost so much weight and become so tiny that I didn't recognize her.

I will never forget how her thin, light, yellow-flower shirt now hung loosely on her. She had become so weak that she walked slowly in that cold misty rain, with two arms covering her chest. I almost cried out in happiness to see her back, but I became even more worried because she looked so different from the last time I saw her.

In spite of my misadventures, I was one of the lucky ones. Rumors were rampant that thousands or more had died in the so-called revolution. As I welcomed Mama's return, a couple of neighborhood children were wandering in the road, waiting for mothers they would never see again. I began to notice that the Cambodian world I had grown up in was shrinking. People were slowly disappearing or vanishing all around us.

Mama told us that because of constant flooding and violent rainstorms, the place where her group of women had gone to dig wild potatoes was wet and rocky, with no food to be found. One woman died of a poisonous snake bite the night of their arrival. On the way back, due to the bad weather, another woman accidentally fell off the boat and drowned, no attempt to rescue her being successful. The boat leaked and then broke into pieces. Luckily, though Mama did not know how to swim, she was able to hold tight to some flotsam and float along with it to shore. Relieved that she was safe, we also feared that she might be persecuted for not bringing anything back for the villagers as she was assigned to do.

A few days later, Papa came back in the early evening with hundreds of bamboo trees fastened together as a thick platform bamboo raft, under which there was a small storage space where he hid poultry, corn, rice, and beans. Papa and two other men had floated the raft along the river to the village. That same night, Brother Chen and I sneaked out and transported the food supply to the cottage.

The next day, the Khmer Rouge commander learned about Papa's work skills when Papa had gone to see Grandma Kim Hoa. While he was there, Brother Vuong's parents helped him cut the bamboo trees, a valuable skill to our captors.

Life was bitter and dangerous as the rule of the Khmer Rouge became increasingly hostile. The soldiers forced us to work day after day, from dawn to dusk. There was no food to eat, yet still they criticized us after work. And we were not allowed to talk in a group.

In the midst of the madness, Papa was happy to bring back food for us from Grandma Kim Hoa. We hid the poultry and corn under our blankets and ate them in the middle of the night.

Looking back on those days during my childhood, I've been lucky enough to have learned a lot of great life lessons and survival skills from one of the world's most hostile and violent places.

✿

32.

Khmer Rouge Brainwashing

Over the next twelve months, every night, after the long day of wicked labor we were forced to endure, the Khmer Rouge commander added to the cruelty by calling a village meeting. During the meeting, he would try to find fault with anyone and said that we should trust no one. Repeatedly, he warned that praying to any god or spirit or following any religion was strictly prohibited.

"There is no such thing as God or spirit. There is only one Leader, Angkar, the ruler of the Khmer Rouge."

I had no idea what he was talking about, but the anger in the commander's voice told me that Angkar was someone or something terrible.

Eventually, I pieced together the truth from many conversations with different people. The Angkar, I learned, was the name of the ruthless Communist Party of Kampuchea. The Khmer Rouge's top leadership called themselves *Angkar Padevat*. The Khmer Rouge commanded all Cambodians to obey Angkar Padevat as our supreme authority.

I hated the way he talked to all of us as if we were idiots. Yet no one dared to say a word. We all kept quiet, worried for our safety, our very lives. Stories of executions were common, and every time I heard one, I couldn't help but think that their hostility toward us was rooted in their twisted understanding of Buddhism, which they considered to be primitive super-stition with no place in their cruel vision of a utopian future.

Constantly pounding his fist, the commander not only railed against God but even contemporary comforts. "In the past, you always relied on every modern convenience in the city, like an electric iron or an electric rice cooker. You got used to just turning the switch, and everything was there to serve you. You should know that these things no longer exist. Now each morning when you turn on the switch, you will see a shovel. Then you turn on another switch and you will see an ax. Then you will realize the whole jungle is waiting for you to clear it. I am sure you will enjoy the way it is now. Those who worked for the capitalists are the ones who betrayed our country. We must eliminate them. You have to work very hard to enjoy the crops you grow. Only those who work hard will be allowed to eat. Whoever disagrees or has any problem can come and talk to me."

The meeting went on and on until very late at night so that I almost fell asleep from exhaustion. The brainwashing became torture, and I fought to keep my eyes open. When he finally concluded, we all clapped our hands as we all shouted after him, "Long live Angkar," feeling relief and pretending to appreciate what we had heard.

On the way home from work one evening, walking along with me was Ming Chanda (Aunt Chanda), in her late sixties, her skull covered by short, thin hair. Her skin was mottled and peeling from exposure to the sun. A large, heavy goiter bulged out in her neck. I noticed drool dripping from her lips when she talked. She lived with her daughter across the road from us. She coughed as she cut in impatiently with her trembling anger in my ear.

"Young man, you listen to this," she said. "A Khmer Rouge teenage girl called me a young girl. She asked if I enjoyed my life in the muddy rice fields." Ming Chanda looked perturbed as she continued. "I can't believe how disrespectful she was. I am old enough to be her great grandma. I wish I could just choke her to death." She shook her head and sighed breathlessly. "This is what we call *chha'oeng srek sbek haw* [the bones scream, the flesh calls]. This is it. Our world is ending."

Her words slammed against me like an angry thunderstorm.

One early morning, right after the night of a violent rainstorm, the sky was still filled with thick dark clouds. Three male Khmer Rouge soldiers in their twenties moved back and forth in front of our cottages. One of them held a wide-blade machete on his shoulder and shouted authoritatively, "Hey! All of you, get out now! There's lots of work waiting for you."

The order left us with little time to prepare. We lined up on the path, marched through the muddy bushes behind the cottages, and did as we were ordered to do, moving toward the woods, shredding leaves, and smashing branches strewn along the way. Light rain began to fall when we began to work, and turned into a drenching downpour that soaked us for the rest of the day. I was starved and shaking until my mind could no longer think clearly. While we toiled, the bullying voices of Khmer Rouge soldiers behind us yelled, "Keep working! We don't have much time to seed the crop before nightfall."

After the long day of labor, I plodded alone through the drizzle on the trail back to the village, searching for edible wild plants on my way. Passing by a giant termite hill, I heard a strange twitching noise. Turning around, I saw Ming Ni (Aunt Ni), a sweet, tiny Cambodian woman who was well known in the area. She lived alone a few houses away from us and was about the same age as Mama. She had long dark hair and dark skin, wore a thin grey long-sleeve shirt with an old colorful sarong, and was sheltering under a tree by the termite hill. Her whole body was completely soaked. She wrapped her arms around herself, shivering violently, her teeth chattering uncontrollably, her lips turned blue.

"Ming Ni," I called out hesitantly.

She shrunk back apprehensively, staring at me as she reacted in a low shaky voice, "Young man, I feel so weak. My whole body aches and turns hot and cold every minute. I don't know what's wrong with me."

"But Ming Ni," I replied, "you can't be here alone by yourself. You must hurry up. Go back to the village before it gets dark. You could get attacked by wolves." I spun around, and without giving her a chance to say a word, I grabbed her frail arm and tugged her along to force her to inch slowly forward.

As we struggled on our way, Ming Ni politely repeated how grateful she was to me for helping her. She exclaimed sadly, "I feel like my time has come. I am ready to go. I have lost all my relatives and wonder where they are." She paused for a moment and then added, "I have an old hen and a little white chicken at home that I want to give to you."

I was greatly moved and humbled by her touching generosity. The rain began to pour hard again. It slashed at us the whole way back to the village. As soon as I got home, I made Brother Vuong aware of my encounter with Ming Ni because I knew he could do something to help her. Brother Vuong immediately dug out two white tablets from his big, brown gunny sack, warning me to make sure that no one saw me deliver them to her. She was astonished when she saw me climb into her cottage, repeatedly expressing her appreciation.

Right before sunrise the following morning, I went out behind the cottage. While standing there peeing, I noticed a mysterious shadow moving toward me. It was Ming Ni. She held a small, brown, featherless hen and a little white chicken in her hand. Looking at me with her fragile smile, she said, "These are for you. You decide whatever you want to do with them." She handed them to me, quickly turning around and sliding away into the early morning shadows. Speechless, I hesitated to turn back home with these prizes. It seemed shameful to accept such valuable gifts from this frail woman. Her generosity totally overwhelmed me.

❀❀❀❀❀

Life went on. The Khmer Rouge continued to force us to cut down everything from small branches to large trees in the jungle around us, and then dig up their stumps and roots until we had completely eradicated everything. We then smashed into the huge termite hills that remained in order to level the land. Out of this deforestation arose dark clouds of millions of insect swarms, as well as crawling hordes of tiny white insects.

Many people were so maddened by hunger that they fell upon the white larvae. Groping into the earth with their fingers, they stuffed the larvae into their mouths, ensuring that any juice that dribbled out of their mouths was pushed back in. Savoring the taste, they declared the larvae a delicacy. I overheard several older adults mutter to themselves, "These are alright to eat. They are a good source of protein." Some gathered handfuls and carefully drowned them in containers partially full of water to prevent them from escaping. I feared that in spite of my disgust I might soon end up just like them, voraciously eating the larvae.

While we were cleaning up the forest, Brother Chen found a thick green snake about a meter long, curled around a tree limb. He bravely unwound it, bit it to death, peeled off its skin, and roasted it on a fire. Later, he enthusiastically shared it with me. But I was disgusted. Hungry as I was, I just could not bring myself to eat it.

"You are stupid; just try it. It tastes delicious," he taunted me, gorging himself on the rest of it.

Soon the forest land behind our backyard was chopped and cleared, except for a gnarled mass of thick, wild, giant bamboo trees and an old krasang tree that was full of sour, hard-shell fruit we used for cooking. The old villagers told us that the remaining vegetation served as an ancient boundary.

Way up toward the top of the old krasang tree, a hundred pouch-like nests of various sizes and shapes hung at many levels along flexible thin branches. Sometimes, dark and shiny blue-feathered birds with long scissor tails flew back and forth among the trees. When resting, they hung upside down on the limbs. Old villagers reported that snakes often crawled into the tree to steal the birds' eggs, often fighting with the birds and spitting venom on them. Often enough the venom would hit the fruit, which in turn could make anyone eating it very sick, sometimes even enough to die. Despite the reports, whenever the Khmer Rouge were not around, people sneaked out and ate any fallen fruit that fell to the ground.

On parching hot days, the soldiers ordered us to drag piles of dry, withered vines, branches, and roots and throw them into the holes where we had recently dug out the trees' roots. We then burned them to fill the holes in order to smooth out the soil. As the heavy flames and bright cinders swirled up, crackling angrily in the hot afternoon air, the wind swept them away. We ourselves felt about to be roasted in the sweltering heat of flaming fire under scorching sun.

Suddenly, a massive flock of green parrots appeared out of nowhere, flashing their wings and squawking angrily while circulating above us in the sky. Some older adults informed us that these birds gave us warnings of impending disaster. Mama ordered me and Brother Chen to leave the creatures alone and stay away from their nests, telling us that they just wanted to live peacefully like any of us.

The same evening, as we were strolling in line on the way back to the village from a long day of exhausting work, a distant noise of angry birds alarmed us. Their piercing shrieks sounded as if they were ready to attack. The turmoil lasted for a while, and then subsided without further incident. That night before we went to bed, Mama spoke to us with her oracular tone. "The forest spirit may have been disturbed. These creatures are grieving. Their sounds are warning off those who try to invade their territory."

The next morning before daybreak, Mama and Grandpa Kaing Hak Yi were terrified when the Khmer Rouge commander stopped by our cottage and called me and Brother Chen to join some twenty young teenagers to clear portions of the forest and start planting. We who were the "chosen ones" took a long time to reach our destination. We trudged along in a single line, snaking through murky waters and almost impenetrable foliage. Slashing vines and branches with a long scythe, the person in front cleared the path for the rest of us. As soon as we arrived at the designated space, the Khmer Rouge com-mander immediately ordered us to clear the area for growing corn and potatoes. He divided us into small groups to uproot the trees, some of which towered thirty feet above us. We each had our own spade, ax, or scythe with which to do the work. As we began to work, I wondered, *why are they forcing us to do this? How did we get here? Will we survive?*

By the time I arrived, I was already exhausted from the forced march. My whole body was shuddering. Although I tried hard to focus on doing my job, I was dizzy from both the intense jungle heat and lack of food. I feared that the Khmer Rouge commander would think I was lazy and remove me from the group. But I knew he would tolerate no complaints or excuses. He stood watchfully while we dug up the trees, warning us against relying on the strength of others and slacking off. He repeatedly admonished us that we must do our fair share.

As we were chopping at one of the giant trees, a wild black boar appeared out of the jungle and sped past us. Instantly, everyone shouted excitedly, and we chased after the creature with axes and spades. The entire forest became a war zone with an army of teenagers chasing the boar. I feared we would accidentally hurt one another, but we finally captured the beast, with everyone left unhurt. We could hear the piercing, grunting sound of the creature running across the woods.

Gradually, the noise of its slow dying faded away.

All of us exultantly carried the dead boar out from the woods and placed it on the ground under a big shady tree. The

Khmer Rouge commander designated some of us to stay in the shade to help slice the flesh of the dead boar and wrap it with wild leaves. Many of us eagerly anticipated the big meal it would make for us. But when I saw its bloody, maimed body up close, I felt nauseous and lost my appetite. I was not the only one disillusioned.

The Khmer Rouge commander ordered us to bring it back to the village to be kept for future consumption, keeping only the creature's organs for our own meal. Obediently, we immediately found a big, old rusty gasoline tank and boiled the boar's organs into a watery organ soup with wild squash leaves and potatoes. We each hollowed out our own coconut shell or bamboo tube into a soup bowl, then stood in line as ordered to receive our portion. Most of the famished male teenagers howled with joy as they received their generous portion. But even though I was starved, I had little appetite for the soup after having witnessed the boar's mauled, dead body.

A crowd of women were also there. Among them were two ethnic Cham girls, who did not want their portion. The Khmer Rouge commander raised his voice threateningly to the two girls. "Come here, you two, you must try it. It tastes good. This is your portion; take it!" When they gently declined, he furiously commanded other teenagers to force two pieces of organ down the girls' throats.

The boys laughed while they cheerfully followed orders, shouting to the girls, "You're stupid; you should try it. It tastes good. This is your portion. Now take it!" The Khmer Rouge commander stood in front of us, screaming at the girls. "It was not that bad, just as I told you. We must share our food equally." The two girls were in tears as they were forced to swallow the boar's organ. Watching their turmoil, I forced myself to eat my portion, my legs trembling. Soon the meal was over, and we were ordered immediately to return to our labor.

On the way back to the village, some teenage girls sang the Khmer Rouge's songs as we marched along the trail.

"We are the group of young girls who help transport food supplies and ammunition to the front line, as American imperialism melts away and is completely destroyed…"

"Yeung Khnhom Chea Krom Neary Doek Sbeang, Doek Krob Min Teang Tov Samorphoum Muk, Chakraport Amerik Rorleay Antoray……"

✿✿✿✿✿

The soothing melody of the song tranquilized us from the tensions of our day, enticing me into gradually losing myself, my will, my being, to the collective world of Khmer Rouge delusion. I thought I might be the only one aware of being thus seductively brainwashed. As far as I could tell, the others succumbed completely and without resistance.

The country had first entered a political conflict, then internal war and external involvement, and eventually the brutal regime of Pol Pot left the civilians suffering, resulting in the deaths of nearly two million people for reasons I am still trying to fathom more than forty years later.

✿

33.
When Being Educated is a Detriment

Early one afternoon, a Khmer Rouge guard summoned all the kids to an urgent meeting. We gathered on a platform without walls under a large, steeply pitched roof and squatted in front of the man. As he spoke, his lips stretched into a cold, suspicious smile. My tummy growled.

"Angkar [the Khmer Rouge Party] needs people who have special talents. If you know anyone in your family who was a teacher, doctor, or someone who can speak English and French, it is very important to let us know. Angkar will have a better job for them."

He pointed his finger toward a big storage shed with its wooden door half open. Through the fading sunlight, we saw sacks of dried corn and grain stacked on top of each other.

"These are kept for emergency backup food supplies," he said, "but Angkar is willing to share it with those who are smart and have higher education. They deserve to be treated better than others."

The man walked quietly back and forth with his arms folded across his chest. He wasn't so much looking at us but gazing *into us*. I was too afraid to look him in the eye.

As soon as the meeting ended, I anxiously ran to find Brother Vuong. He was behind our cottage, splitting logs for our cooking fire and to keep mosquitoes away. I breathlessly called out, "Brother Vuong! Angkar said they are looking for someone who can speak French and English and…"

Before I could finish, he angrily flung his ax aside and hissed, "You know nothing!" He stared at me furiously. "You know nothing. Shut your mouth and don't ever tell anyone about me." He turned his back and stepped into the cottage. I had never seen him so upset and was confused.

Later in the late afternoon, I became worried when I could not find Brother Vuong. I ran toward the muddy field behind our cottage, about half a kilometer away from the village. There I found Brother Vuong standing alone under a tree in a bush, quietly watching the sunset. He didn't notice my presence. Between us was a big pond, so clear I could see the dead branches and green algae lying on the bottom. I shouted excitedly, "Brother Vuong! What are you doing here alone? I was so worried about you."

Turning, he looked at me with a wry smile.

Without thinking, I quickly stepped into the pond and began wading toward where he was standing. When I reached the middle, where the water was up to my waist, I noticed something on the surface crawling towards me. Instantly, I recognized it was five or six huge leeches. I frantically pushed my way toward the shore, shouting and furiously swatting away at the leeches. Brother Vuong burst out laughing when he saw my reaction. He quickly extended his arm to help me out of the water. We hugged each other and we laughed until we cried at my scare and fortunate escape. That was the hardest we had laughed since we had left the city.

❀❀❀❀❀

One early morning, on my way to collect some water in the muddy field very close to where we lived, I saw a group of people standing in line under a tamarind tree. Their faces were covered with pieces of black cloth. I hid myself by the dam and watched the Khmer Rouge talking to them and then marching them toward the forest. That evening, one of the neighbors was crying because her brother was taken away in that group.

She was in tears as she said the Khmer Rouge had taken him away after he told them that he could speak French.

On the way to the rice fields, I overheard my neighbor talked quietly with a worried tone of voice to his brother, urging him to bury his eyeglasses under the ground because the Khmer Rouge commander had begun to search for people who wore eyeglasses. My heart dropped as I suddenly felt a sense of impending doom was befalling all of us.

The Khmer Rouge believed that if you spoke foreign languages, your mind was polluted by Western culture. Or if your skin was light, that meant you were lazy and took advantage of the poor who worked hard out in the rice fields under the scorching sun. Therefore, you were not pure or trustworthy. You either needed to be reeducated or eradicated.

The reason why the Khmer Rouge wanted to recruit the educated professionals was so they could murder them.

❁❁❁❁❁

One late afternoon, right after Brother Vuong had returned from labor, he unexpectedly received an order from the Khmer Rouge commander to prepare to leave the village and join his family. He was informed that his sister was coming to pick him up. She had grown up in an old village under the Khmer Rouge regime and had lived there for a long time. We were alarmed at the news.

It was not much later that day when his sister arrived, dressed in black and looking worried. She did not talk to us, but her eyes were soaked with tears. Brother Vuong did not appear to be happy to meet his sister. They were both busy tying his belongings to the bicycle, including the huge pack of medications that he had kept since leaving Phnom Penh. Telling us bravely that he had to leave, he put his hand on my right shoulder. "Take care, you, and love yourself, too." We were all gathered together in front of the cottage. Sadly, but without tears, we wished him luck. We hated to let him go, as he had become part of our family.

I recall that when we were back home in Phnom Penh, he drove up to our house on his motorbike and parked it in front. Leaving the engine running, he rushed into the house, digging out some money from his safe locker.

"What are you doing, Brother Vuong?" I asked.

"I want to give some money to a skinny homeless old man to buy food. He sits at the corner of the street a few blocks away. He's starving, I'll be right back." Brother Vuong smiled indulgently at me and hopped back on his motorbike, revving the engine. I wondered how any bad thing could happen to Brother Vuong, such a kindhearted person.

I watched him bike away with his sister, fading into the distance until he was out of sight. I felt numb with fear that Brother Vuong had to go away from us. I wished him peace. We could only try to believe that his life would be better.

I was reminded of not so long ago, when we had so much fun together. He taught me to speak English while I taught him to speak Chinese, because he wanted to have a Chinese wife. Whenever he had a school day off, he would come over and stay at our house. At night before bedtime, as he helped my siblings and me with our homework, we talked a lot about our future plans. When he started to earn money from his own practice as a medical doctor, he said he would take me to travel around the world. Our first choice was to go to Hong Kong so that we could see movie stars in person. He promised me that he would never forget me when he became rich, and I believed him.

After Brother Vuong was gone, the Khmer Rouge interrogated all of us in the village in order to learn about our past histories. We all became even more afraid and distrustful of one another. Gradually the village population declined as people were led into the woods by the Khmer Rouge and disappeared forever. Yet the villagers were so terrified that none of us would talk about it. ✿

34.
Karim, a Native

One extremely dry and hot morning, we stood in line to receive our orders for the labor of the day. The Khmer Rouge commander pointed at me and told me to lead a buffalo to a muddy swamp in the middle of the forest. "Make sure you bring it back before the sun sets," he told me. I was happy about the assignment because I would not have to labor in the field. However, it turned out to be a huge, ugly, hairy old buffalo, and I was scared that he might go mad and run over me or attack me with his two long, sharp horns. Leading him, I took it easy and walked slowly toward the swamp where I had been ordered to take him for the day. Naturally, I didn't want to stress him out because we had to learn to get to know each other.

It took me a long time to reach the swamp. As soon as I arrived, I strapped the buffalo under a small tree. There was a boy there who looked about my age watching a buffalo of his own. I learned his name was Karim. He spoke Cham, the minority language, and he told me he was from the nearby village of Neak Mool Thaan. He was skinny, small, and had very dry, dark-brown skin. As we talked, I learned that Karim was smart, quick, and very friendly. I admired and thoroughly enjoyed the way he had so much fun with his buffalo. Showing me the way to ride on a buffalo, he had the creature slide back and forth across the swamp.

"Come, hop on, we can ride together. Don't worry, you will be fine," he reassured me. I hesitated for a while, but then when it came close, I hopped on its back and managed to sit behind Karim, holding tightly onto him while the creature began to move faster. It was not as fun as I thought it would be.

Suddenly, I noticed my lower leg was touching something slimy on the lower left side of the buffalo's belly. Looking down to find out what it was, I screamed with disgust and fear.

"Ugggh!" I yelled. "A leech! A huge leech is on my foot!"

Karim was laughing, unconcerned with my plight. "That's a buffalo leech. Don't worry about it. Once it sucks enough blood from the buffalo, it will let go."

I was not reassured by Karim's explanation and feeling extremely uncomfortable. My calf kept rubbing against the slimy leech as the buffalo continued moving around. Finally, after Karim and I got off, I discovered that there were more leeches, at least half a dozen, stuck to the buffalo's belly. Even though the sight disgusted me, I wanted to impress Karim, making him think I was fine with it. For me, at that moment, to get to know a person from this native area was a privilege. I didn't want him to think that I was afraid.

That afternoon, Karim taught me to speak a few words of his native language.

"*Ngoac Sai O?*" he asked slowly. "That means, did you eat your meal yet?" Karim also taught me how to count to five by repeating, "*Sa, Toa, Klao, Bag, Lmeu.*"

I thought Karim was lucky to be a native villager because he probably didn't have to worry about having enough food to eat. He told me that his buffalo loved to hear sound, so he taught me to pick certain types of leaves to fold into certain shapes and then whistle through them to make the sound of a wild bird. I competed with Karim in making bird sounds until my jaw got tired.

Unexpectedly, a Khmer Rouge soldier appeared on the other side of the swamp, holding a long scythe on his shoulder. He was about the same age as Brother Vuong. Shouting sternly, he demanded that Karim leave immediately. Obviously frightened, Karim immediately turned to me and said, "I've got to go." I didn't even have a chance to thank him for such a good time.

Soon after he left, as the sun was going down, I dragged the buffalo back to the village. I was so hungry, it seemed to take forever to get back. As soon as I arrived, I strapped the buffalo under a tree next to the Khmer Rouge commander's hut, as I was told to do. When he saw me, the commander came out, looked at me, and said, "You are not allowed to spend time with Naek Mool Thann. He is a native." He added, "You are *pror-cheer-chun thmey*, new population—different from us."

I did not say a word, but only bowed at him to show him respect. I did not know what he was thinking, but I was petrified that he was going to confine me. The whole time he spoke to me he smiled inscrutably, so that I couldn't tell what he was really thinking. To my great relief, he finally told me to leave. I forgot how hungry I was, both from relief at escaping the commander and from fear of coming across wolves or coyotes on the road. I ran the rest of the way home. Never knowing what might happen to someone being ordered about by the Khmer Rouge, Mama and Grandpa Kaing Hak Yi were greatly relieved to see me return safely.

I never knew what happened to Karim. To this day, I often think of him as an innocent boy with a kind heart who was considered to be "different" from the rest of us, and who undoubtedly paid the ultimate price for that difference.

❧

35.
Cassava Scraps

In the heart of the monsoon season, my new close friend, Tang Su-Weng, mentioned he had discovered a cassava field not too far from the village. (Cassavas are the starchy, tuberous roots of trees eaten in tropical countries.) He pulled me aside and excitedly whispered that some *neak mool thaan* (original local villagers) had just completed their harvest. He wanted us to sneak in and forage for abandoned scrap cassavas. As we stealthily ran through the forest, I was excited at the thought of finding food to bring back to the family.

At the edge of the vast clearing, a wrinkled, grey-haired man squatted under a huge tamarind tree. He was dressed in black and smoked tobacco wrapped in a leaf.

I bowed my head and asked him politely, "*Pou* [uncle], may we collect leftover cassavas?" The man looked at us with suspicion and slowly nodded his head. He flicked the cigarette to the ground and briskly walked away. Su-Weng and I entered the field.

Except for the cries of wild birds, it was quiet and deserted. We hurriedly scoured the plowed furrows for discarded cassavas. I took a broken branch and started digging into the hard, sunbaked soil as fast as I could. Eager to share my excitement with Su-Weng, I panicked when I looked around and couldn't find him. I frantically screamed his name over and over, wondering where he could be. Clutching my shirt full of cassavas tightly against my belly, I kept scanning the field for Su-Weng.

"Thief! Stop! Don't move or I'll shoot!"

A Khmer soldier clad in black, with a *krama* wrapped around his head, charged at me from the other side of the field. I ran for my life. The sound of gunfire and bullets zipped past my head. Paralyzed with fear, I stumbled over exposed tree roots and pitched forward, spilling cassavas to the ground. I struggled to regain my balance and raced toward the thick forest.

Fearing that I was bleeding, I kept feeling around my body as I ran. Too exhausted to keep up the pace, I paused in the middle of thick foliage, gasping and trying to catch my breath. I shielded myself behind one of the giant trees. I heard the sound of snapping branches growing close. Suddenly it was dead silent. At that moment, I realized I could be shot and killed.

Bang! Bang! Gunshots broke the silence. *Bang! Bang!* The shots kept coming.

A few moments later I heard the soldier's footsteps receding. Having no more strength, I slumped back against the tree trunk, my calves sore and cramping.

I noticed a strange tickling sensation behind my ear. I had disturbed a nest of red fire ants. They trickled down the back of my shirt, but they didn't bite. I quickly removed my shirt and shook them off.

I needed to find a way out before darkness fell. After wandering in fear for a while, I found a familiar path and ran toward home. Nearing the village, I was stunned to spot a Khmer Rouge soldier emerge from the forest and aim a rifle at me. I started zigzagging in case he opened fire. I darted through the back doorway of my cottage and found Grandpa Kaing Hak Yi napping. I stepped past him and peeked through the woven bamboo wall. My body trembled at the sight of the soldier approaching, his rifle still at the ready.

I tore off my black striped shirt and grabbed a dark green one, hoping he wouldn't recognize me. Then I jumped out the front door and kept running until I reached an area flooded from recent torrential rains. I was too scared to look back, afraid he might be catching up to me. The rains had engulfed the road and swallowed the forest floor. I sloshed into the water, looking for trees to climb. The only ones I saw were in deeper water, but I didn't know how to swim.

Desperate, I grabbed some thick reeds to resist the pull of the strong river. I pulled myself down into the murky water and slowly let my face rise up until my nose broke the surface to breathe. A horde of hairy field rats splashed chaotically back and forth as I struggled to keep my head above the surface. Cold water filled my nostrils and rushed down my throat. I lost my grip and panicked while the current swept me away.

I awoke to a familiar voice yelling in my ear. I violently coughed up water. Tang Su-Weng's older brother, Tang Su-Kwong, kept pushing on my chest to force water out of my lungs. He lectured impatiently, "You're so lucky—you would have drowned if I hadn't jumped into the water to rescue you. You shouldn't get into the water if you don't know how to swim!"

By the time I arrived home, trembling and shivering, it was completely dark. Mei Juang and Sok sat and huddled against the bamboo wall, staring at me with puzzled looks. Grandpa Kaing Hak Yi quietly told me, "You have a bad odor and should wash yourself thoroughly." I asked where my parents were. In a shaky voice, he said, "Khmer Rouge soldiers ordered everyone in the whole village to report for an urgent meeting." He cautioned me not to go, but I wanted to see for myself.

When I arrived, I saw people gathered around the fierce flames of the blazing campfire. They were seven or eight rows deep. I crouched low, hoping I wouldn't be noticed, and waited until I could join the outer edge of the crowd. I saw that Papa and Brother Chen were standing at the center, so close to the fire that their faces were red. I knew something bad was about to happen. A soldier stood with his rifle pointed at them. I recognized the soldier as the one who chased me.

Brother Chen was tied with vines. Papa dropped to his knees in front of the Khmer Rouge commander and pleaded for mercy. "Please give my son a chance. I promise he will never steal food again."

The commander barked, "Stop making noise!" His solitary voice echoed through the forest. No one dared to say a word. I noticed Brother Chen was wearing his black-and-white-striped shirt, identical to the one I wore earlier. The soldier must have mistaken him for me.

Mama rushed out from the crowd and fell to her knees at the commander's feet, crying, "Please forgive my son! Please forgive him! He's only a child."

There was a long moment of deafening silence. Then the commander ordered Mama and Papa to stand up before the entire village and loudly swear, "If you steal, you will be shot to death."

I crept quietly away from the crowd and hid in the yard, weeping with guilt. Much later, the rest of the family returned. As soon as Papa saw me, he exploded, "Where have you been? You must be the one who stole the cassavas! Chen said he didn't do it. You make my blood boil! I'm going to beat you to death if you don't stop stealing!"

"But, Papa ..." I tried to explain.

"I don't want to hear another word out of your mouth," Papa interrupted.

Grandpa Kaing Hak Yi broke the silence. "Try not to be too hard on the boy. Don't forget, he's the one who finds and brings home most of the food we eat."

A moment later, Papa burst into tears, covering his face with both hands, and said, "I just don't know what to do."

That was the first time my father cried in front of me.

When enough time passed for emotions to settle, we sat quietly in the darkness, devouring a late-night dinner of field crab soup with banana trunk.

The next day at the crack of dawn, Mama told us about a dream that came to her in the night. A man dressed in black had snuck under our cottage and listened to our conversation. Mama believed the dream was ominous. She became paranoid, repeatedly warning us to watch what we said to one another. As we prepared to leave for the day's labor, no one spoke.

By then we had learned that talking could get you killed.

✿

36.

A Neighbor Boy's Lost Soul

Tha was the next-door neighbor on our left. He was a kind boy who was tall and skinny, with very light skin and long hair. He was the same age as me. One late afternoon, when the sky was about to turn dark, we heard his mother crying loudly and calling his name. "Where is Tha? Where did Tha go? Why is he not home yet? He told me he went out to catch field crabs. He should be home by now."

I peeked through the bamboo stick wall and saw his parents and younger brother standing in front of their cottage, waiting impatiently for Tha to return home. Papa and Mama were also worried and tried to console them, without knowing quite what to say. We all hoped the boy would return home soon.

When daylight first appeared the next day, I heard my other neighbor's voice nervously announce, "I found your son's body. He was found drowned near the ditch. I'm sure that is your son. Come with me."

Papa quickly jumped out of our cottage and followed the group as they ran toward the ditch. Among them was Tang Su-Kwong, the same man who had once saved me from drowning. Soon, I heard the weeping sound of Tha's parents. They had found Tha's body. With several other neighbors, they were carrying the body back home. His mother was weeping hysterically. As soon as they placed his body on the ground in front of their cottage, his mother threw herself to the ground, beating her chest and weeping uncontrollably.

Afterwards, the Khmer Rouge came by and ordered some of the neighbors to take the body away for burial. Shortly after, while the eyes of Tha's parents were red and swollen from crying and their clothes still muddy and wet, the Khmer Rouge unceremoniously ordered the rest of the village to line up and march toward the forest for another day of labor.

A couple of nights later, I was awakened by a strange noise coming from Tha's family cottage next door. "*Heuuu, heuu, heuuu.*" Unable to sleep, I woke up Mama and told her I heard something. She murmured drowsily, "Try to sleep. We have to work hard tomorrow." The next morning, she told me, "What you heard was the spirit belonging to the next-door boy. He drowned, and he was cold. His spirit tried to return home, but he could not get into the house because no one performed a ritual ceremony for him, no Buddhist chanting." Mama continued dourly, "The boy may not be able to reincarnate for that reason. His soul will wander around in the jungle until he can find another person to replace him. We have to pray for him."

The shivering noise lasted for several days. One evening on the way home from labor, Tang Su-Kwong approached me and said, "You were so lucky. The boy drowned at exactly the same place where I pulled you out of the water."

I walked back home thinking about how lucky I was. But the moment I entered the front door, I noticed Grandpa Kaing Hak Yi had a strange look on his face. He opened the palm of his hand. There, lying in the middle of his palm, were his two front teeth. Then he pointed through the hole between the bamboo sticks at the bottom of the cottage and spoke very strangely.

"Do you see anything down there?" he asked, lisping through the gap where his two front teeth used to be.

"See what, Grandpa?" I responded.

"Why are there so many human skulls on the ground?" he asked with foreboding tone.

"No, Grandpa, there are no human skulls on the ground. Your eyes must be blurry."

I didn't understand what was in Grandpa Kaing Hak Yi's mind, or why he said something like this. He had become so different, and it made me sad to see him that way. I wondered if he was slowly going crazy. This was indeed a very sad day for everyone.

✿

37.
Into the Woods

For six months, my family and I had been struggling to live in the jungle under the domination of the Khmer Rouge. Under their severe orders, we worked day and night trying to cultivate land for growing crops and vegetables, but in a cruel irony, we still didn't have enough food to survive. After a busy harvest from the very difficult cultivation, we had to gather corn and rice and preserve them for future use. No matter how much energy we spent on working, we were always starving because we were not allowed to keep any food at home. We never got to eat anything produced by our labor.

One hot afternoon while returning home from our labor, my neighbor friend Tan Liang and I found wild grapes hanging from a tree in the middle of the jungle. Although the adults in the village always warned us that the wild grapes were poisonous, we couldn't walk away without trying them because they looked so delicious. However, the tree was too tall for us to reach them, so Tan Liang had me sit on his shoulders, and I used a stick to make the fruit drop from the branch. The grapes tasted both sweet and bitter.

A few minutes later, our throats became very itchy and sore. We were afraid and started crying. We ran home for help, thinking we were going to die. My heart was beating irregularly, and my breathing was fast. Mama and everyone in the family were deeply concerned. But other than losing my voice for a couple of days, I turned out alright.

Not long after that embarrassing incident, we all came back from our labor in the fields and had nothing to eat. Mama brought home some wild leaves she had picked in the woods. She thought they were Sluk Cabah, some Cambodian herbs, so she boiled them in a pot of water. We ate them all. However, the next morning she was worried that the leaves she cooked for us might have been inedible and poisonous. As luck would have it, we all felt fine.

The following morning at daybreak, as I was leaving the cottage on the way to labor in the woods, a short, grey-haired woman in her late seventies who lived across from us broke down and sobbed loudly like a child, throwing herself onto the ground in front of me. I didn't recognize her at first because her face was covered with grey powder. She barked mournfully at me with her sharp voice: "Young man, young man, help me! Look at my face! My son-in-law, Liek Meng, did this to me. He threw wood ashes in my face. He insulted me, calling me 'Old Thrush.'"

She tried to catch her breath but choked and coughed loudly, continuing to sob while crawling on hands and knees toward me. "Young man, I have not eaten in over two days. I cannot live with him anymore! He does not give me anything to eat. He is so cruel. I do not know what to do. Please help me."

I was suddenly overcome with sympathy for the old woman. All at once, her whole body shook as she labored to breathe. I backed away, turned around, and rushed back to the cottage, calling out for help. Mama and our neighbor, Tang Su-Weng's sister-in-law, came out to help "scrape the wind" out of the woman's body. Afterwards, they carried her to rest in the space beneath her cottage.

Right after that, I met Liek Meng in the rice paddy. I approached him cautiously and said, "Liek Meng, brother, you appear to be a good person, but we all feel very sad for what happened to your mother-in-law this morning."

Liek Meng did not say a word, but his eyes became misty as he looked at me with a friendly smile. While leaving, I added, "Every action you and I take has consequences."

Several days later, after returning from labor, Tang Su-Weng's sister-in-law told Mama that she saw the Khmer Rouge commander taking the old woman to the woods. After that we never saw her again. No one dared to ask about her disappearance. Her disturbed emotional state has remained in my memory. She disappeared, led by the Khmer Rouge commander, just like all the others, into the woods, which became one of many of the horrible "Killing Fields" around Cambodia, where nearly two million of my people were murdered.

✿

38.
Ren and the Charcoal Kiln

Pu (Uncle) Sai Tong was a refugee just like us. He was tall and thin with long grey hair. His deeply lined cheeks loomed over the sparse, long, wiry grey beard that clung from his chin. This seems a description of a very old man, but he was probably in his thirties. He was a friendly person who spoke openly and affectionately toward my family, yet Papa kept reminding us to be cautious around him because the Khmer Rouge commander had recently appointed him to supervise everyone's work.

Every morning, just as daylight broke, he ran around in his tattered white sleeveless T-shirt and loose dark pants, shouting for people to stand in line and hear their work assignments.

One evening before sunset, Pu Sai Tong unexpectedly appeared at the front of our cottage, calling my name. He was accompanied by Ren, a boy around my age with dark circles under his eyes and sunken, sickly pale cheeks. Ren had previously worked together with me a few times in the fields. As soon as I stepped out of the cottage, he stole a glance at me, smiling bravely but sadly. "It's your turn to guard the charcoal kiln overnight," Pu Sai Tong commanded, motioning for me and Ren to follow him. I was always fascinated by our charcoal kilns, which are mounds of earth used to burn wood into coal. Someone needs to monitor the process to ensure that the flame doesn't get so hot it burns the wood into ash instead of transforming it to charcoal.

As we started to go, Mama quickly grabbed a black long-sleeve shirt and handed it to me, anxiously reminding me to look out for wild animals. Pu Sai Tong led us through the village as the sultry sun dropped below the horizon, casting an oppressively bright orange-red over the whole region. When we reached the other end, he pointed across a large plough field to a small path and emphasized, "Keep walking until you see the charcoal kiln. Be sure to stay awake. Don't get lazy. Keep close watch over the strong flame so it doesn't overly burn the wood." With this brief instruction, he departed.

Ren was unusually brave. The first time we met, he and I had been sent together with a group of other villagers to tend to the seedlings in the muddy rice fields. After slogging over the ground for only a few minutes, I noticed blood dripping down my left foot. I was repulsed to see a two-inch, dark, slimy slug clinging to the lower part of my calf. "Help me get it off!" I cried out, jumping to my feet and brushing it away with my hand. Everyone was too disgusted to come near. Everyone but Ren, who rushed over, fiercely pulled the bloodsucker from my leg, flung it to the ground, quickly broke off a stick from a nearby tree, and battered the creature into pieces. When finished, he dismissively lectured the rest of us, "It was only a leech. Why do you have to be so scared?"

Another time, Ren and I were ordered to guard yellow swayback cows grazing in the fields. We were each assigned one huge cow to watch. While we were leading them down into the woods, Ren pulled out a small ax from around his waist, angrily staring at me and ordering, "I'm going to kill the cow and you have to help me. We'll share the meat."

Astounded by his words and shaking with fear, I whispered to him, "Ren, you're scaring me. I'm not going to get involved in this."

He turned and looked at me. Sounding intensely frustrated, he encouraged me, "Don't be afraid. This is my responsibility. We're starving."

"No, Ren, I'm scared what would happen if we were caught, so I don't want to."

Enraged, he yelled at me, "I said you don't need to worry! This is my responsibility!" The escalating desperation in his eyes suggested an imminent lack of control that terrified me. I was too frightened to speak.

We headed toward the open fields, where many wild, flimsy *daem sleng* (a strychnine tree) scattered throughout the woods bloomed with bright orange fruit. Although they looked delicious, adults in the village often warned that the fruit was bitter and deadly poisonous. Abruptly, Ren tied his cow under one of the tree branches and exclaimed angrily to himself, "The fever recurs again."

He looked around for a second, ran toward one of the trees, and climbed up it. I watched him struggle up to a fork between branches. With shivering hands, he tightly grasped a branch, plucked a fruit, and heedlessly peeled it with his teeth. "No, you can't eat this, it's poisonous!" I yelled up from the base of the tree. But he didn't care what I said. No sooner did he take the first bite than his face contorted with a frown. Despite the pain, he voraciously chewed on in an effort to devour it, then swallowed hard to force the last piece down his throat.

After climbing down the tree, he anxiously looked me in the eye, let out a heavy sigh, and explained, "Sieu, the seed can help reduce my fever. If I die, please help carry my body to my mother. I don't want it to be devoured by the woods."

Suddenly, my friend collapsed onto the ground. Curling up, he wrapped his hands around his head and began trembling, teeth chattering violently. I was terrified he was dying. His eyes rolled up as his breathing slowed and deepened. Rubbing his arm, I shouted in panic, not knowing what to do: "Ren, what's happening? You must have poisoned yourself."

But Ren surprised me after his collapse; he came to, regaining consciousness. Very slowly, he sat up, wiped away large drops of sweat running down his face, and looked around, trying to remember what happened. In a tired, faint voice, he moaned, "My joints are sore and achy."

Since then, I've often recalled him as a unique piece of work. As Ren and I continued along a small path through the woods, I spied a column of thick white smoke drifting upward and raging across the forest. Daylight gradually began to fade by the time we reached the charcoal kiln, which casted a shadow that looked like a giant grave. Ren raised his voice with excitement when he discovered a wild papaya tree behind the kiln. It was about two meters tall, with two fist-sized green papayas dangling from the tip of the tree. Ren peeked at them curiously for quite some time, until the night suddenly turned impenetrably dark and dead quiet, except for the startling crackling of burning wood from the stoke hole of the kiln.

On its right side was a heap of wood we used to keep the smoke going. We both chose a spot to stay warm and sat facing each other near the entrance of the kiln. As the night progressed, hundreds of translucent insects swooped back and forth around the stoke hole of the kiln. Ren's eyes reflected the flames and grew wide with excitement when green-and-black lizards suddenly darted out of nowhere after the bugs. Grabbing a long thin branch on the ground, he wildly smashed the lizards as quickly as he could so that not one of them managed to slither away. He fastened them to the branches by their necks and later baked them over the flame. I sat passively by and watched him enjoying his meal, guzzling the lizards as fast as he could.

Still, I was afraid of being caught and punished, so I struggled to stay half awake until daybreak. With the coming light, I could see that some of the papaya leaves had fallen to the ground and the fruit were gone from the tree. But I couldn't see Ren. In vain, I looked around for him. Could he have left without even telling me?

I scurried back home through the cold, dead silence of the morning forest. I kept looking around to make sure I wasn't noticed. As soon as I reached the village, I saw a Khmer Rouge standing in front of one of the huts, his machete in hand. I heard a woman crying loudly from inside the hut, "I beg you, please don't take him away." I wondered who the crying woman was and what had happened to Ren. But I have never seen or heard word of him since.

I fear the worst.

❁

39.
Do Moral Rules Change When
You're Starving?

Right after returning from the field after a heavy workday, Mama and I heard some muttering coming from the next-door cottage of our neighbor, Tang Su-Weng. Curious, I peeked through the bamboo wall to see what was happening. Suddenly, a huge black dog dashed out from under Su-Weng's cottage, yelping and running in the direction of the old village.

"Oh no! Motherfucker, we missed it! We didn't do it right," said Tang Su-Weng's brother, Tek, disappointedly. His outburst shocked me, but he continued, "No way could we have missed it. We must get him. Eventually this creature will soon forget the pain, and he'll return again," he said, as if he was trying to reassure *us*.

Later that night, I came across Tang Su-Weng in the backyard. Curious to know about the dog, I asked him, "What happened earlier? I saw a big black dog yelp and run out of your place."

He softly whispered in my ear, "That dog came from the older village to our cottage scavenging for food. My brother tried to kill him. Please, promise me you won't tell anyone."

What he told me was unnerving.

Trembling, I insisted, "This has nothing to do with me!"

That same evening, someone next door started vigorously sharpening a machete, the sound of which sent shivers of terror through me. For centuries, a machete was a simple tool to be used in the fields. But lately they had been used by berserk Khmer Rouge soldiers and villagers who were losing their minds

Several days later before the sun set, as I was about to step into the cottage, I heard a noise coming from Su-Weng's cottage again, this time from under it. Again, I saw the same huge black dog snatching bait that had been laid out on the ground. Abruptly, the creature's shriek pierced the woods. My heart pounded as I witnessed his head fall to the ground. Blood gushed from his decapitated body, seeping into the ground. Tek immediately darted from the cottage and ran to drag the dog's head and body into a large brown bag. At the same time, Su-Weng and his sister-in-law helped pour soil on top of the spreading pool of blood.

I realized I had just witnessed an inhumane act and that if the Khmer Rouge owned this dog, I could be in trouble. They might force me to bear witness against my neighbor or else I would stand accused as an accomplice. I quickly stepped into my cottage, but not before Tek noticed I had seen what had taken place. That same evening, while I was still anguishing over witnessing the brutal execution, Tek unexpectedly showed up at our cottage. He handed me a bamboo container. "This is some soup for you to enjoy." I was angry the moment I saw him come into our cottage with this obvious bribe. But I said nothing as he set the soup down. After he left, I picked up the bowl of soup, saw a piece of dog meat floating in it, and threw it out the door as far as I could.

For the next few days, I had trouble eating anything.

❋❋❋❋❋

Early the next day, while we were lining up to leave for labor, there appeared two young men dressed in black, each bearing a machete on his shoulder. They were known to live in the village from where the dog had come. They wandered from one cottage to another, their faces blotched with angry red burns. I guessed that they were looking for the black dog, but I was too frightened to look them in the eye. I wondered what tormented me more, the death of a starving pet dog searching for food or the fact that Tek had murdered the dog to prevent himself from starving. It was a moral dilemma I never thought I would have to face. We were all starving and doing hard labor, as if we were in prison. Do moral rules change in such a world?

After Tek decapitated the dog, Papa ordered us not to have any more contact with Su-Weng's family, warning us, "I do not want you to be involved any longer with those people. Stay away from them. Otherwise, our family will end up in big trouble."

I will never in my life forget the horror of that dog being butchered. I could not see myself condone such acts of inhumanity and barbarism, no matter what the cost.

✿

40.
The Floating Chickens

We were awakened by the Khmer Rouge commander's loud voice in front of our cottage, shouting, "Hey, you, stop!" Wearing black clothes with a red *krama* wrapped around his waist, he demanded, "I need a young boy to guard the rice fields now."

There was no choice. I had to step out of the cottage. I trembled as he looked at me and said, "Our village needs you to guard the rice fields. You must be there every day before the sunrise to keep the birds from eating the grains." Handing me two long bamboo sticks, he commanded, "Hold onto them. Let me show you the way to get there."

I stood anxiously as he stared coldly at me, holding a long-handled hatchet on his shoulder. My two arms pressed tightly to my breast, I politely bowed to greet him.

"Let's go," he said, roughly.

Again, I had no choice. I had to tag along after him. I looked back and saw Mama looking at me from the cottage. Rightly, Mama was always worried whenever Brother Chen and I were pulled out to do something for the Khmer Rouge. Now I became frightened as I realized I had never before walked alone with a Khmer Rouge. Studying his face, I clearly remembered him to be the one who had declared at the meeting, "Keeping one is no gain, losing one is no loss."

For a long time, we walked, meandering through wild, bushy foliage until we arrived at the destination: rice fields in the middle of nowhere, about two kilometers from our village. My stomach ached with hunger. I was unable to determine how large these paddies were because the thick rice plants prevented me from seeing where the fields stopped. This quiet was broken only by the sounds of wild birds singing to one another in their different languages. I kept wondering how I had come to be here to work as a scarecrow.

My arms were tired and sore from clapping the bamboo sticks together—*whack, whack*—to scare the birds away. Over the next several days, I learned how to be invisible and quietly do my work. In Cambodia, rice grain ripening before the harvest, before they develop into rice itself, are called "pregnant crops" because they are full of rice juice. It was my job to chase birds away from eating the pregnant crops. One day at the rice field, I was so hungry and suddenly felt so dizzy that I could no longer stand up. I impulsively grabbed a handful of rice grain and gorged myself with one juicy and delicious mouthful after another and buried the empty husks in the fields. But the shell of the rice cut my tongue and burned my throat when I swallowed them. My whole mouth was sore and swollen.

As soon as my mouth and throat recovered, I chewed the grains, this time carefully sucking out only the juice.

❀❀❀❀❀

Every day before heading back to the village, I sneaked into the middle of the rice field to reap the grains and hide them in my pocket to bring them home for Grandpa Kaing Hak Yi and the family. Taking rice grains in this way made me fear for my life. Yet it was worth the risk. I was always exhausted, always hungry. I couldn't resist the temptation with each delicious drop of the pregnant rice grain's milky juice that ran down my throat.

One afternoon, an elderly native man from the old village quietly appeared, sitting under a large tree at a corner of the rice field, across from where I worked. Even from that distance, I could see his dark, brown, wrinkled skin and short, thin, grey hair. Every bone in his body seemed to show through his skin. Shirtless, he had only an old *krama* wrapped around his waist. I was greatly excited. I had not seen a single human being in this area since I started to guard the rice field. Quietly squatting under the tree, rolling his tobacco with wild leaf, the old man ignored my existence. He stared in the other direction and looked unspeakably sad.

Slowly but respectfully, I stepped forward and greeted him, "Grandpa, how are you?" (In Cambodian culture, young people always refer to the elderly as Grandpa or Grandma even when they are unrelated.)

The sad old man blew the smoke out of his mouth and reluctantly responded, "Well, I am doing fine."

I continued, "What are you thinking, Grandpa?" He was quiet and ignored my question. I kept asking him, "Why do you have to smoke, Grandpa?"

He smiled as he turned his face to me. "This tobacco helps my day go by faster."

I asked, "Do the leaves taste good that you roll the tobacco in?"

"No, but I have no choice," he answered.

I volunteered, "Well, I came from the city. I just want to tell you that people in the city smoke cigarettes with paper."

He replied, "Sadly, you know, I have lived in this jungle since I was born. I never had a chance to visit the city of Phnom Penh. I heard it is beautiful."

After a moment of respectful silence, I asked, "Sorry, Grandpa, I don't mean to make you feel sad."

The old man exclaimed, "I wish someday I could have a chance to smoke a cigarette that is rolled by paper, at least before I die, so my life would be fulfilled. I heard it tastes so good. Is that true? I would be willing to exchange anything for a piece of paper." He looked very sad and pale with his bony wrinkled face.

I told him, "I don't know the difference, Grandpa, because I don't smoke."

Suddenly I thought of the book I found in the mansion when we were leaving the city. Excitedly, I looked around to make sure no one else would hear our conversation.

Approaching closer, I whispered, "Listen, Grandpa, I have a book. If I bring you some paper for rolling your tobacco, what can you give me in return?"

The old man suddenly broke into a big smile, becoming cheerful and animated when he heard me mention the paper. "You must tell me the truth. You're not going to lie to me, right? Listen, I have young chickens to exchange with you. I've never done this before, but I can offer you some chickens."

After further conversation, we both agreed to meet each other the next morning at the same place. I would bring him twenty sheets of paper from the book, and he would bring me four young chickens.

I was so excited that I could hardly sleep the whole night, thinking about being given the four chickens. The next day before I left for the rice field, I dug out the book from a bag. Noting again the title, *How to Breathe Fresh Air,* I tore twenty pages from it. I carefully folded and inserted them in my pants so that no one would know.

At the rice field, I kept waiting and looking around for the old man, but he was nowhere to be found. Finally, by the end of the day, as the sun was about to set, he appeared under the tree. I hurried to him and asked, "Where are the chickens, Grandpa? Why are you so late? I have some papers for you." The old man replied, "I didn't wake up early enough to catch the chickens—they had already left their nest to find food. But I promise you, I will make sure to catch them tomorrow before daybreak. If you already have the papers with you, may I have them first?"

Disappointed, I hesitated. "But Grandpa, I thought we promised each other yesterday?" As soon as I handed him the stack of papers, he tore off a small piece, rolled it with tobacco, and quickly began smoking. His very first breath of smoke made him ecstatic. He smiled at me, "Young man, you have finally fulfilled my dream."

I couldn't help but wonder if he would still keep his promise. Looking at his face full of happy wrinkles, I shared in his delight. That evening after I left the rice field, I decided to quit thinking about the chickens. I didn't want to set myself up for disappointment if he broke his promise.

The following day, right before sunset, as the rice paddies gradually faded into twilight, the old man appeared with four beautiful young chickens with their legs tied up. He carefully laid them under the big tree. He anxiously waved his hand to me and whispered in his soft voice, "Young man, you can only take two chickens at a time, so you'll have to make two trips. You don't need to worry; I'll sit here and wait until you come back to pick up the other two." What he was telling me made anxious, but I listened carefully to his instructions as he untied the legs of two chickens and placed each of them with its breast lying on my palm, one on my left hand and the other on my right hand, their heads facing my body. "Listen carefully. I want you to remember. This is the technique you use to hold chickens in the dark; they don't like it when you tie them up. Just let them float in your palm and they'll be fine. They won't cause you any problems."

Then the old man warned me, "Remember, if one of us gets caught by the Khmer Rouge soldiers, you don't ever mention anything about me, and I will never tell anyone about you. It will be our mutually agreed responsibility, do you understand?"

"Yes, Grandpa," I responded nervously.

"Good." Then he added, "Everything is now a matter of life and death."

Seeing that I did understand, he changed his tone and added, "Be safe and come back fast to pick up the other two."

I left the rice field with two chickens on my palms and dashed as fast as I could, not worrying about anything except to bring them home so everyone could be fed. For my safety and the old man's, I knew I was in a race against time until I returned for the other two chickens and brought them safely home. I managed to move quickly along the meandering trail until I reached the village.

The road was still. The moment I stepped into the cottage, everyone in the family, especially Grandpa Kaing Hak Yi, was happy to see me come back safely. They were all even more delighted, and shocked, to see the chickens. Papa instantly took them from me and noiselessly choked them. However, Papa and Mama both were opposed to my returning for the other two, fearing it was too risky. Mama said, "It's too dangerous on the road, and you might encounter wild animals or the Khmer Rouge." Yet I insisted on going back because I had promised the old man, who would be worried about me if I did not return. I promised Papa and Mama that I would be careful.

As I darted along the road on the way back to the rice fields, the evening began to grow darker. I could see each of the villager's homes as they started fires under their cottages to chase away mosquitoes. I could smell the distant fires burning. By the time I reached the rice field, the whole area was wrapped in almost complete darkness. The old man was glad to see me back but there was no time to celebrate my success. As soon as I arrived, and while I was still breathing heavily, he quickly placed the other two chickens on my palms, simultaneously warning me, "You have to leave now. Be careful on your way back."

I did not say a word. I nodded my head and immediately took off, maybe faster than necessary. I ran so hard that my calves soon became achy, and I was feeling extremely fatigued. The muscles of my legs started spasming. I realized I could no longer clearly see my way in the darkness. I could only sense the bottom of my bare feet pressing on sharp objects with each step I took. The pain took its toll, and I started sweating, trembling, and feeling dizzy. Hundreds of flies and insects kept landing on my face, crawling on my lips, and blocking my eyes. Giant bats flitted back and forth in front of my head, hunting night bugs and making all kinds of harsh, squeaking noises. Animals howled and whooped and stared at me, their eyes glowing eerily from the dark bushes on the sides of the trail. I surprised myself by suddenly becoming more fearless with every step that I took.

My mouth and throat were dry and thirsty, and my whole body sweated profusely, but I kept running until I only saw trees and branches in front of me. Then I realized I had taken the wrong trail and was heading into a dead-end. Taking deep breaths to avoid panicking, I turned around and tried to backtrack down the trail until I could find a familiar way back. In the darkness, I stumbled over sharp branches and landed heavily on my elbows and knees. Despite my clumsy falls, the two chickens did not seem to be bothered.

When I stood up again, they were both lying peacefully in my palms.

At first, I feared I would be unable to get up and continue on my way. Fortunately, I was not seriously injured. As I struggled to stand up, I felt the soreness in my arms from holding the chickens. But I did smell the burning wood of the villagers' fires as I headed toward the cottage. I was so utterly exhausted that my vision became blurred, and I was terribly hungry and thirsty.

My race against the Khmer Rouge and the jungle beasts was over. I have never forgotten that late-night feast. Food never tasted better. We ate four chickens in the dark, and even chewed all the bones into pieces. But it was also the lengths we had gone to find our meal that made the food taste better.

I'd come a long way. I remembered how I used to get really angry at Grandpa Kaing Hak Yi when the chickens he bought me at the market ended up on the dinner table. It made me terribly upset to eat them. Now that I was starving, I ate chickens without a second thought.

✿

41.
Escape from the Khmer Rouge

It was the mid-spring of 1976. One cold evening, our whole family was again called out to sit in the middle of the crowd. It seemed that we had done something wrong. During the meeting, the Khmer Rouge commander ordered every family there to wrap up their belongings and get ready to move to the Phnom Han Chey (Mount Han Chey) early the next morning. The area was known for malaria. The commander said there was another dense forest that needed to be cleared. Every family, that is, except ours. We were terrified, not knowing why we were singled out to stay behind.

Without any explanation, the Khmer Rouge commander ordered our family to stay where we were and wait for him to return from Phnom Han Chey in fourteen days.

Early the next day, it was still dark and cold when the other villagers began to form a line to leave for Phnom Han Chey. Tang Su-Weng and my other friends and neighbors came over to say goodbye.

Mama turned to me. "Go find something for them in our backyard."

I cut a few pieces of young sugarcane I had planted two months earlier. Although it wasn't really ready to be served, I cut some anyway and gave them to Liang, a good friend of mine, and his four siblings, Nam, Kheng, Yong, and Soy.

Mama told them, "Sugar will help keep your energy up for your trip."

While I was cleaning off leaves from the canes, a scorpion stung me. My whole right arm went numb. I neither felt pain nor had time to think about it because I was so worried about what was going to happen to us. Mama's tears ran down her cheeks. We waved goodbye to our friends and neighbors slowly walking toward Phnom Han Chey, accompanied by the Khmer Rouge commander and a few other soldiers carrying rifles.

I recalled the first evening meeting in Cheuteal, when the Khmer Rouge commander gathered only the young teenage boys and girls for the meeting. He announced, "At some time in the future, I will help arrange for all of you boys and girls to come together as husbands and wives."

When I came home and shared with Mama what the Khmer Rouge commander had said, she gave me a silent worried look. She then murmured that she would rather see me marry one of Liang's sisters, Kheng or Yong, as they seemed to be good girls and were around my age. I thought Mama's mind was out of touch, as she seemed to carry too much in her head. At the same time, I kept wondering what my future would be.

❋❋❋❋❋

Now the whole village was dead quiet, with no humans except our family and no sound other than wildlife. We all feared for our lives, wondering what would happen next. Unexpectedly that early evening, a vaguely familiar man dressed in black appeared with his bicycle at our cottage. It was Uncle Ban, Papa's childhood friend whom we had first met in Piem Cheliang. He leaned his bicycle against a termite hill in front of our house and ran into the space beneath our cottage. I knew right away that something was not right.

I overheard Uncle Ban excitedly tell Papa and Mama, "Ever since Brother Vuong arrived back at the family home, things have not been the same. The whole family has been shunned by everyone else and is being watched by the Khmer Rouge."

Turning to Papa, Uncle Ban continued, "Your mother asked me to come here and warn you that the Khmer Rouge has a plan to terminate everyone in your family. You have to leave right away, in time to join a group of Vietnamese, farmers and fishermen who are on their way to Vietnam. You must arrive at Rocky Diamond Village at precisely the right time so you can merge into the group as they leave the village. This is your only chance for survival!"

He anxiously looked around for a second and exclaimed, "The premier of China, Zhou Enlai, passed away recently, and Chairman Mao's health is in accelerated decline. This is seriously worrisome. No one can possibly know how far this is going to go."

Uncle Ban gave Papa the directions to Rocky Diamond Village. Once assured that Papa understood what he had to do, Uncle Ban hopped on his bicycle and left the village.

Immediately, Papa and Mama helped us pack, getting us ready to leave the village as soon as possible. We threw away anything we could not fit into a small bag. Sok had to let go of a baby bird he found during the flood. Many such personally treasured things were abandoned. Gathering what necessities we could, we left the village in the middle of the night. Characteristically, in the midst of this panic and chaos, Mama reminded us with her shaky voice to wear long-sleeved clothing to avoid mosquito bites.

As we fled through the night, whenever a bright light appeared in the distance, Mama and Papa silently signaled for us to hide and not move. Sometimes we laid on the ground for what seemed an eternity until we were certain no Khmer Rouge were anywhere near. We did not dare to rely on any light other than the moon to find our way.

From a lifetime of moving through the jungle, Papa had a very reliable sense of direction as he led us through the jungle. Our path was bushy and muddy, but we had no time to complain. Brother Chen and I had to guide Grandpa Kaing Hak Yi by the hand because of his poor vision and partially hold him up by his arms because of his weakened condition. Sok was crying because he stepped on a bamboo thorn. Our bodies were covered with mud and scarred by scratches from the thick vegetation. Many long hours of alternately running and walking and pushing hard through the thick foliage had exhausted all of us, yet we could not allow ourselves to fall asleep. All along the route, we heard strange animal noises, which Grandpa Kaing Hak Yi said were coyotes howling. Whatever they were, we were lucky that none actually confronted us.

Time crept by.

Finally, the first appearance of light in the sky began to approach. We passed a pineapple grove that looked as if it had been recently deserted. Most of the pineapples were dried and dead, but we spied a few remaining ripe ones. Both thirsty and hungry, Brother Chen and I begged Papa to let us sneak into the field to pick some. He reluctantly gave us permission, and we ran into the field, desperately grabbed hold of the pineapples and twisting them out of the plants. We managed to get five or six. But as Brother Chen attempted to snatch more, I urged him to leave the field before anyone grabbed us for stealing.

When we emerged from the pineapple fields, our entire bodies were burning and itching like crazy from being scratched by the spiky pineapple leaves. Using fingers in place of knives, we broke the pineapples open. Grandpa Kaing Hak Yi kept cautioning us to eat the pineapples carefully so that we would not be poked, but we gorged an entire one down in just a few seconds. As soon as we finished eating, Brother Chen's and Sok's noses began to bleed, and all of our throats and tongues became itchy and numb. A few hours later, however, everyone was fine, and we continued on our journey.

The following night, we could not sleep very long or very well. We were terrorized with fear that the Khmer Rouge would find us far from where we were supposed to be.

Long after nightfall, we reached the edge of a remote abandoned village. All the cottages were isolated from one another, intensifying the sense of emptiness. We were worn out and immediately fell asleep in bushy shrubs along the side of a ditch.

I was jolted awake by the unexpected sound of footsteps on crisp leaves. I shook Mama to wake her up. A tiny, wrinkled woman dressed in black with long, thin grey hair limped as she approached us. The old woman held a bunch of small branches. When she saw us, she fell back on her heels in surprise. She looked around to make sure no one was watching, and then tossed the branches to the ground and waved her hands excitedly at us. She whispered in a low tone, "Hurry, don't be afraid! Come with me. You'll be safe in my hut!"

Papa hesitated a moment before exhaling and nodding in agreement. We followed her down a narrow trail to the other side of the ditch. A shirtless skinny man in wraparound black pants stood in front of a weathered old hut surrounded by a thick growth of bean and corn plants. He had an ancient face and watched us with concern. A lit cigarette dangled from his lips. He signaled us to follow him into the hut. We noticed a Buddhist Pali (scripture) tattoo across his chest. Papa whispered that the characters were talismans meant to give the old man supernatural armor against any type of harm.

The man said in a tone of great relief, "You are indeed fortunate to arrive here when you did or else you would be in great danger." He sighed deeply as he pointed to the empty cottages in the area. "We have lived here for almost our entire lives but rumors spread that Vietnamese troops were going to attack our village, so Angkar evacuated everyone to a new labor camp. My wife was paralyzed by a high fever and couldn't walk, so they ordered us to stay behind until they could come back with an oxcart." He paused, then turned to look at his wife. He continued, "It has been months since they left, and we still haven't seen even a shadow of another human being." The old man offered to let Grandpa Kaing Hak Yi rest on a bamboo bed. Then he shared some baked cassavas and urged us to stay the night.

After we ate, he showed Papa how to follow the stars high in the sky for direction. "A comet appeared several days ago with a tail like a brush," he said. "I believe it is an omen."

He paused for a moment and turned to look at us with a serious expression. "Nature is letting us know that war will soon happen again." Pointing to a large star, he noted it had recently become blurry and less bright, foretelling that a supreme authority was about to fall.

The old man's wife excitedly interrupted, "Not long ago, the lunar eclipse occurred. It lasted several hours. It was *Rahu Chab Chann* (the celestial demon) attempting to gorge on the moon. Since then, we've had famine throughout the whole region. It was really a sign that disaster is upon us."

Early the next morning, his wife nervously warned us to be very cautious on the dangerous road ahead. Then they surprised us by sharing a small container of dried peanuts. Food and water were scarce, and either one was precious to find. I chewed the peanuts slowly for a long time, afraid that I would be hungry again if I swallowed them too quickly. While the morning was still dark and cold, we left the elderly couple and continued our journey.

When we arrived in a devastated village, we passed by the ruins of house after house that had been destroyed by bombs with no one in sight. Each step we took was filled with fear of stepping on unexploded shells or landmines. A nauseating, rotten odor prompted us to walk as fast as possible to get past the village.

We kept our eyes open, looking for water and plants or animals to eat, but found none. Mama pulled long grass stems from the ground and told us to suck the roots for water. After long hours of walking, we reached the edge of the jungle just as daylight was fading. Papa decided we should stop for the night. We hid in one of the few remaining houses. The roof was destroyed and the walls blackened by fire. We were surrounded by silence, except for the squeaking rusty hinges on the broken front door swinging back and forth in the cold wind.

Papa warned us to stay quiet while he took Mei Juang to fetch water from a nearby lake. A short moment later, they returned without water. Papa looked pale and worried. Mei Juang's eyes were wide with terror. She said, "We found dead bodies scattered on the lake shore, covered with flies. More bodies were floating in the water." All of us were terribly thirsty and hungry. Mama tried to assure us that everything was going to be alright, but her face betrayed her.

As the darkness descended upon us, I moved carefully across the broken tiled floor through the building, looking for a place to release my bowels behind the house. Wild grass pushed up through every crack. Dim moonlight illuminated a tree and streamed through the shattered window. Outside, I noticed something dark moving in the branches above me. I rushed back to Papa and excitedly whispered, "Papa! I spotted a giant rooster resting in a tree behind the house. I can catch it easily!"

Papa looked at me for a second and said quietly, "This place is empty. What you saw must be a wild rooster." He clasped his right hand and said in a low tone, "Grip its neck tightly and hold onto it for a few minutes until it stops moving. You must be careful. Don't make any noise! We don't want to attract any trouble."

I nodded, and before Papa could finish his words I turned and ran to the backyard. My head was filled with visions of a feast. I took a deep breath and stretched my hand to grab one of the tree branches, slowly pulling it out of my way. The giant sleeping rooster did not notice or react with suspicion. I snatched the bird's neck with my left hand and pulled the creature out of the tree. A brief shrill scream escaped its throat as it gasped for air and began to fight back. Its sharp claws scratched my arm and neck while it spread and flapped its powerful wings, struggling to free itself from my grasp. I held fast to its neck. After long minutes of fighting, the giant bird weakened and swung loosely, unconscious. I yanked the bird to the ground, believing I had strangled it to death.

My heart pounded and my body trembled, having just wrestled with this poor feisty bird that did not expect such a sudden attack. Just as I was checking on the burning pain from the sharp claw scratches, I was shocked to see the creature hold up its neck and slowly get up off the ground, half alive, stretching out its wings. It began staggering in the shadows across the yard, in search of a way out in the dark. A sudden chill went down my spine. I quickly dashed back to Papa. He was digging a hole in the ground behind a broken wall.

"Papa, Papa! I killed the bird, but somehow it returned to life!" I explained.

Mama had been listening to our conversation, and whatever we said gave her stress and anxiety.

"Go back, and wring it hard and fast until you hear a snap," Papa instructed hastily, "so the creature will die instantly without suffering."

I found the creature by the bush, still slowly lurching with uncontrolled movements. I took Papa's advice, quickly hunching over and pressing the bird to the ground, gripping its neck, and twisting it with force until I heard a popping sound. It took only a second. The creature was executed quietly, dropping flat to the ground.

Papa made a fire in the pit, wrapped the giant bird carefully, and cooked it in the ground. I was happy that everyone had a delicious meal. But as I thought about what I did, I was disgusted with the brutality of my conduct, even though I was desperately hungry. I felt sad and guilty and wondered how I could have committed something so utterly gruesome.

Soon the darkness deepened as the night grew. Papa instructed, "Sleep separately, just in case. If something happens, one of us might still survive."

Grandpa Kaing Hak Yi and Brother Chen and I slept next door in another broken house. In the middle of the night, Brother Chen screamed and woke everyone up.

"I saw a man with no arms and blood all over him," Brother Chen said, obviously shaken. "The man told me to get out of his way because I was sleeping in the doorway. 'You're blocking my entrance!' he said to me."

What Brother Chen told us gave Sok, Mei Juang, and me the shivers. So, we all moved and slept next to Papa and Mama.

The next day, Mama said this whole area was full of dead spirits. "They didn't pass away properly. Death was sudden and unexpected. The spirits remain on the site of their death —they're confused and might not accept that they have died." Mama cautioned us, "Respect the surroundings; other-wise we might be cursed by them."

I was immensely relieved once we left the house and continued on our way.

During our days and nights in the jungle, we were famished, so we ate all kinds of wild leaves, fruits, and insects. The weather was extremely hot and so dry that we had to drink rainwater from puddles that were sometimes full of larvae and mosquito eggs. One blessed day, while we were resting in the woods on a steep hill, Brother Chen and I discovered a clear puddle that was large enough to make a small pool. Without hesitating, we both scrambled down and quietly slipped into the pool, soaking ourselves for what seemed like hours. Later, Grandpa Kaing Hak Yi came along and joined us in the water. Strangely, the immediate area surrounding the pool was clear and clean, not a tree or even a blade of grass growing. Suddenly, Grandpa Kaing Hak Yi noticed small, sharp objects scattered throughout the area. He instantly cried out to us, "Get out of the water! Be careful, and don't step on the sharp objects or you might get a serious infection. This place has been bombed. That's what created this pond." Pointing at the sharp objects, he explained, "Those are the fragments from the bomb."

Later that day as we continued on our journey, we came upon a deserted village that looked as if it had long been abandoned. We were all exhausted, and everyone's feet were blistered, wounded, and swollen from walking so many miles under a sky so red and hot that it seemed as though the heavens were angry and about to burn us up. Fortunately, Grandpa Kaing Hak Yi had no complaint so far, which was a great relief because we were all concerned for him. As we walked by the cottages, we observed that most of their walls were collapsed or had been blown away by the wind. The soil in this area was hard, red, and rocky.

"It would be hard for anyone to survive here," Grandpa Kaing Hak Yi said. "Because of the lack of nutrients in the soil, no one could grow vegetables." From the distance, we saw a few people walking slowly and oddly, as if ill. Strangely, no one took notice of anyone else, as if afraid of talking to anyone. Everywhere we went, we were annoyed by the buzz of mosquitoes and flies landing on our eyes and lips. Vultures flew back and forth in the sky, making weird noises. Occasionally, we heard the sound of distant explosions. Eventually, we realized we had come to another dead zone.

We learned later that we had arrived at our destination, Rocky Diamond Village. Each of its cottages had a well in the front. Papa chose to stay in a cottage with a well full of cloudy water; all the others had wells that were almost completely dried up. Papa and Mama nervously told us to stay inside the cottage and watch for the group of Vietnamese we were supposed to meet here. Then I heard Mama ask Papa in a worried tone what would happen if we could not find the group.

✿

42.

With the Cheungs

Rocky Diamond Village seemed to be deserted. I sneaked out to fetch some water, found a rusty bucket on the ground, and as I was casting it into the well to draw water, a woman suddenly surprised me from behind. She was in her late twenties, with pale skin and very short, thin hair.

In a frail Chinese (Mandarin) tone of voice, she warned me, "Oh, be careful, don't use that well. A lady who just used it died a couple of days ago of severe infection. Wounds opened all over her body, and flies ate at them. She always used this well to wash her body. Sometimes the water she washed with dripped back inside the well."

In broken Cambodian, she then introduced herself to me as Mrs. Cheung. She pointed to a nearby cottage. "We live there in that cottage, with the big tree in the front." She asked, "Are you trying to escape to Vietnam?"

I dared not say a word.

I knew Papa would be angry with me if I told anyone that we were escaping.

Mrs. Cheung's tears ran down her cheeks as she opened her heart and said, "I miss Vietnam so much, the country we are from. How am I going to go back? I dare not imagine. My family and I are waiting for an opportunity." She continued,

"So many people die in this village every day, one after another. Look at my hair." She touched her hairless head as she said, "Look, I was so sick I lost all my hair. My husband, too. We're all going to die if we stay here."

We were interrupted by Sok, who ran up to me and yelled, "What makes you take so long? Mama is getting upset. She doesn't want you to get bitten by mosquitoes."

Mrs. Cheung asked, "This must be your younger brother?"

"Yes, he is," I responded. I fetched the water in the bucket and walked after Sok, telling Mrs. Cheung I hoped to see her again. The moment I got back to the cottage, I cautiously explained to Mama that I had met Mrs. Cheung at the well, that she was from Vietnam, and that she wanted to leave this place just like us. Papa was so angry and paranoid about Khmer Rouge soldiers by then that he could have killed me for talking to a stranger.

The same evening, Mrs. Cheung and her husband unexpectedly dropped by and whispered to Papa and Mama that their family was planning to escape across the border. They both begged Papa for advice. I vividly recall our small group sitting stock-still and listening to Mrs. Cheung's words as she warned us through her tears, "The mosquitoes in this area are as strong as the Khmer Rouge and as dangerous. They could take your life at any moment. We have to leave this area as soon as possible. At the same time, we are terrified of stepping on landmines."

Papa did not say a word, making me very uncomfortable. He finally responded, "Stay calm. I will try to talk to the leader of the Vietnamese group once they arrive."

Mr. and Mrs. Cheung excitedly went on and on about how they ended up here. But we were all so tired that Papa finally had to tell them to return to their shelter and that we would let them know when the opportunity came to leave. After they left, my racing mind kept speculating about Mrs. Cheung and her family. I wondered if they had been able to survive in this place without speaking any Cambodian.

As we were about to fall asleep, we heard the sound of approaching clanging cowbells and the squeaking of ox-drawn carts. At first, the moonlight was not bright enough to tell who was approaching, but then Papa excitedly called out to all of us, "They are here! Finally, they are here!" His excitement swept up all the rest of us, and then he marched out to speak with them. His bravery took me by surprise. After they introduced themselves, their leader came up to greet Grandpa Kaing Hak Yi and the rest of us. He spoke only Vietnamese, none of us understanding a word.

There were about twenty families in the group, all farmers and fishermen. They all greeted Papa as if they knew him well. According to my father, the Khmer Rouge and the Vietnamese government had an agreement to allow this group to return safely to Vietnam. Papa also told the group leader about the Cheung family, asking that they be allowed to come along with us. Happily, the leader agreed. The Cheung family consisted of five people: Mr. and Mrs. Cheung, their six-year-old daughter, Mr. Cheung's younger sister, and Mrs. Cheung's younger brother. The group leader arranged for them to hide separately in different oxcarts.

One of the families had a baby monkey, which had a metal chain lock around its neck and was tied to a wooden post in the back of their oxcart. The monkey was making screeching sounds and jumping up and down, looking frustrated and angry.

❀❀❀❀❀

Early the next morning we left the village, trying to avoid the blazing heat. Grandpa Kaing Hak Yi, Mei Juang, and Sok were arranged to sit in one oxcart, while Papa, Mama, Brother Chen, and I walked along the country road with the group. The group leader warned everyone in our family except Papa not to say anything because we could not speak Vietnamese.

As we traveled toward the Vietnam border, we soon reached another small village, where people were celebrating the Cambodian New Year. They all wore black, and the females had *krama* wrapped around their heads while males had them folded around their waists. A group of ethnic Cham danced with bamboo sticks as they sang the Khmer Rouge songs, "*EE Yong Salong Tuy Tuy Pati Yue, Yong Salon Tuy Tuy Pati Yue Yong Salong Tuy Tuy Pati Yue.*"

My father whispered to me that they were songs of revolution, which I didn't understand. They seemed annoying to me.

The faces of the young soldiers looked very sad and nervous.

Marching along the road, we passed by a creek and were frightened when we saw several Khmer Rouge soldiers, whom we feared would inspect us. Fortunately, they did not. Some of the Vietnamese in the group left to find food. Terribly thirsty, Mama and I decided to climb down to fetch some water. Reaching the creek, we were immediately repulsed by an unpleasant smell and the buzz of flies everywhere. Mama snatched my arm from behind, exhorting me to leave right away as she pointed to the creek, "Look, there are several dead bodies in the water!"

Stunned, we scrambled back and rejoined the group.

On the way, we walked by a group of young adults sitting gloomily by the side of the road. Curious why they were not with the others, singing and dancing, I turned back and peeked at them again. Shocked, I suddenly recognized a familiar face. "Mama, I can see Brother Vuong!" I whispered to her. "There, that's him, Brother Vuong. He's alive!"

Both moved and excited, I choked up and tried to calm myself down. For a moment, Mama and I forgot what we were there for. Accompanied by the sound of the bamboo dance and the New Year songs, Mama and I approached Brother Vuong and greeted him with great excitement. But when he turned toward us, he looked as if we were not there. Emaciated and pale, he failed to respond to the hoard of flies that landed all over his body.

Moving closer to him, Mama confided in a low tone, "Escape, or you are going to die. Go now, you can hide in the oxcart."

Brother Vuong glanced at her with his bitter smile, and then at me, as if trying to recognize who we were. Finally, he responded, "Leave me alone, I am not going anywhere. I am suffering from parasites and diarrhea. I'm going to die soon anyway."

Anguished, Mama turned to me and nodded in resignation.

"You have to leave now," she said matter-of-factly.

Turning away from Brother Vuong, we trudged back to the group, agitated and anxious. My legs shook from hunger, and I was confused and sad over seeing Brother Vuong in such a desperate condition. I also worried that he might go crazy and start talking about us to the Khmer Rouge. I kept turning over in my mind what he must have been going through these past months since he left the village with his sister.

After that day, I often thought about Brother Vuong's troubled eyes, how they were lost in another world. Mama and I never imagined that we would see him alive again. I felt guilty and wished I had not seen him because of the pain it caused Mama and me. His appearance and reaction to us threw me into total confusion. However, when we saw him there was no time to dwell on his condition because we had a dangerous trip to face in a few hours.

The Cheungs' appearance suggested they had gone through many unpleasant experiences. Mr. Cheung wore loose, bright blue shorts over a flaccid body. His floppy belly protruded as if there were a heavy balloon hanging inside. He was in his middle thirties and was tall and awkward. His eyes looked worried, as if some harm was about to befall him. His wife was thin with sunken cheeks. Her skin was yellow and seemed stretched to cover her bones. When she spoke to me, her voice shook, and she had to catch her breath every few words.

Mr. Cheung told me that he and his family had come to Cambodia as tourists in April 1975. Their plan was to visit Phnom Penh for a couple of weeks. But when the war broke out, the Khmer Rouge took over so suddenly that the entire family was stuck there, unable to leave the country. His family tried to escape right after the Khmer Rouge took over, but his sister suddenly fell sick, and they were obligated to stay behind to take care of her. Due to the language barrier and a desire to avoid any further trouble, Mr. Cheung's sister pretended to be mentally ill and his wife, Mrs. Cheung, pretended to be deaf. I felt privileged that they confided their secret to me. They made me promise not to tell anyone. Whenever Mr. Cheung's sister spoke to our family, she first looked around to see if any strangers were within listening distance. Sometimes she laughed or screamed loudly without any observable reason.

Mrs. Cheung and her sister-in-law both suffered from malaria, and in the time we spent with them, came down with chills, fever, and vomiting. My family felt deep sorrow and sympathy for them, but we could do nothing.

While we were taking a break on the road, my eyes were blurry and my head drowsy from the heat and lack of food. Mama approached, informing me that she had discovered an old temple nearby. She insisted we go to beg the spirit of the temple to give us a safe trip to Vietnam. She also asked Mrs. Cheung and her young daughter to accompany us. We sneaked away while the group was taking a break. The walk took us about ten minutes along a bumpy road with soil that was strangely red, as if someone had spilled red paint all over the road.

I worried, "Mama, what if the Khmer Rouge discovers us here? We don't have the protection of the group. I think we should go back."

"Don't worry. *Mjas Teuk Mjas Dei*, the earth spirit, will help seal us off from them."

I was skeptical.

To occupy my mind as we walked, I asked Mrs. Cheung, "Please teach me a few words in Vietnamese."

Reluctantly, Mr. Cheung replied, "Me and my husband only speak very poor Vietnamese even though we were born in Vietnam. My parents owned a big 7up soft drink corp-oration in Cholon and we helped them with the company. My husband had a business there as well, but at home we only spoke Fujianese. We never had a chance to go to school to learn Vietnamese properly."

By the time Mrs. Cheung finished her story, I was becoming conscious again of the road to the temple. I did not like walking on the road, which seemed never-ending.

When we finally reached the temple, I saw that it was a small, old, dilapidated structure that was hidden in the brush and surrounded by many big trees. Only one or two walls and a statue of one of our local divinities were left standing. Mama said that a bomb might have exploded in the area, which was stone silent aside from the sound of little birds.

The silence made me suspicious.

"Mama, this isn't safe," I pleaded. "Please, let's go back!"

"This will only take a few minutes," she insisted.

At first it was hard to find the way into the temple because all of the rocky walls had chaotically fallen.

Mama looked around in awe. "This place must be over a hundred years old."

In the center of the temple, on the left side of the deity, stood a wooden pole into which were carved phrases with many Chinese characters laid out in numbered rows. Next to the deity was a tiny bamboo-tube container, full of small bamboo sticks. Mama pointed to the sticks. "See there? For-tune sticks. You can use them to tell your future."

Mama, Mrs. Cheung, and I immediately kneeled down in front of the deity and begged the holy spirit of the temple for blessings. Mrs. Cheung's little girl, however, was upset for some reason and stood behind us in silence. Following the short prayer, Mama grabbed the fortune stick container from the altar and started shaking it as she made a wish. Once a stick slipped out, I helped her match it to its corresponding number on the wooden wall, which explained her future. The fortune said that her journey would be smooth and successful, bringing a relieved smile to her face.

Mrs. Cheung grabbed the fortune stick container and, likewise, knelt down to make a wish. She then quickly shook out a stick and hurried to the wall to match the corresponding number. Shockingly, she burst into tears. Deeply concerned, Mama asked her what happened. Through her wailing, Mrs. Cheung replied, "I picked a bad stick. It said that I won a battle, but no one recognized me as a warrior. That means that my future is bad."

Upon hearing this, Mrs. Cheung's daughter let out a piercing scream. Mrs. Cheung covered her daughter's mouth with her hand, asking her what was wrong. Rubbing the little girl's belly, she inquired if she had a stomachache. The little girl shook her head and kept crying. Mama and I didn't know what to do. We felt anxious for the little girl, and, worse, out of fear that her screaming might bring the wrath of the Khmer Rouge down upon us.

Mrs. Cheung kept nervously asking her daughter what was wrong. The little girl finally replied through her crying. She spoke in Fujianese, so Mama and I could not understand. I asked Mrs. Cheung, "What did your daughter say?"

Interpreting for us, Mrs. Cheung said, "My daughter had a bad dream last night in which she lost all her teeth and her mouth was full of blood."

Mrs. Cheung hugged her daughter, both of them distraught. Mama and I were not sure what to think. We were concerned, but hardly knew what to believe about the little girl's story. Mama went back to the altar and prayed for Mrs. Cheung and her daughter. I was deeply disturbed. I feared that bad spirits possessed Mrs. Cheung's daughter. Suddenly, Mrs.

Cheung angrily screamed at her daughter, "Why do you tell me all this? Don't you dare say that again, or I am going to slap you!" The little girl bit her lips and tried hard to keep herself from crying.

Now desperate to leave the temple, we rushed back to the group, Mrs. Cheung holding her daughter's hand the whole way. No one said a word, not knowing what to say. We were all quiet and afraid that we might say something that would only make matters worse. My head felt full of heavy rocks when I heard Mrs. Cheung anxiously mumble how desperate she was to return to Vietnam. Peeking at her, I saw that she was teary-eyed, pale, and lost in her thoughts as she walked with her daughter over the bumpy and rutty road. As we trudged under the flaming, red-hot sky that bore down on us as the day drew to a close, I yearned to make them feel better.

But there was nothing I could do to stop the nightmare.

When we finally returned to the group, everyone told us they were wondering what had happened to us. But there wasn't anything that we could think of to tell them that would make any difference in the coming days.

✿

43.

To the Vietnam Border

The next morning, we headed toward the ominous Snoul forest. The road was dry and dusty. The heat of the sun continued to strike us mercilessly. The temperature was over one hundred degrees Fahrenheit. The leader of the group, fearful of any delay, kept firmly pushing everyone to keep moving forward. I remember him continually emphasizing, "The circumstances along our journey are unpredictable, so for safety's sake we need to make it to the border of Vietnam as soon as possible."

One day we were delayed when we encountered an unexpected, furious thunderstorm. We huddled under the branches for hours, trying to stay dry. Yet the weather left trails of destruction on our way, greeting us with puddles and endless rows of muddy potholes.

My feet were dead tired and my calves ached with every step I took. Although Mama's lips were dried and cracked from lack of water, she never complained. Occasionally, she gave me an encouraging smile that revealed her missing front teeth but also her indomitable hope. Over and over again, she kept up our spirits by promising me and Brother Chen, "When we get to Vietnam, I am going to buy you a lot of ice cream. I am going to cook your favorite foods and buy you a lot of nice clothes."

Mama's words gave me the strength to push forward. She always tried to inspire me with hope and confidence. My mother never gave up hope. Maybe that is where I learned to never resign myself to failure.

Late on the first day of our march, we caught the stench of a jungle in the distance. When we asked, we were informed that we had arrived at the rubber plantations. The group leader loudly announced, "We have no choice. This is the only route we can take. Move faster to avoid mosquitoes and insect bites."

We plunged into the dark forest, the dense and misty area cloaked in the black shadow of thousands of ancient, giant rubber trees. It had rained during the night, and the road was sticky and muddy.

In the middle of the forest, the pet monkey somehow managed to break the lock, escape from the oxcart, and run away. As its owner shouted frantically, the creature quickly climbed up a tree. We were obliged to stop on the road, as the sickening stench of rotten rubber smacked us in the face. Everyone grumbled over the situation, watching the owner throw food at the monkey, trying to entice it to come down. But the poor monkey appeared afraid and kept going higher, without looking back. It soon reached the very top of the tree. After a while, the owner disappointedly gave up, and we continued to hit the road at full speed.

Deeper and deeper we moved into the forest, and soon we could no longer see the sunlight. We could only smell the rotten stench of rubber and hear the sounds of softly tweeting little birds hopping from tree to tree. As we penetrated more deeply still, the stench smelled more and more like the horrible smell that comes from sewers. Not only that, we were persistently attacked by mosquitoes, which exhausted us because of the constant effort it took to swat them away. With each step, we were further assaulted by the muggy and heavy air, the annoying clanging of cowbells, and the babies wailing in distress. Finally, to our great relief, after long hours of marching through this torture, we emerged out the other side of the rubber forest.

It was now late afternoon. As soon as we left the area, many of us became nauseated from exhaustion and began vomiting. It would take some time before we escaped the foul odor entirely. Ultimately, we were still walking along a seemingly endless wooded trail. Encouragingly, the group leader informed us, "We're about forty kilometers from the Vietnam border. I suggest we rest here tonight. Tomorrow we'll have more energy to speed over the road to the border."

That night, everyone was told to get down from the oxcarts and sleep on the ground. In the distance we could hear the sound of mines exploding, one after another. We also heard the sound of machine guns firing very close to us. Terrified, Mama kept reminding my siblings and me to chant our prayers.

When we awoke the next morning, the stench from the rubber field was still on our breath, in our eyes, and in our lungs. Several of us still suffered from nausea and vomiting. The leader urged all of us to pluck up our courage and speed forward. So we did.

✿✿✿✿✿

As we approached the border, two men dressed in black suddenly came out of nowhere. They pointed rifles at us and shouted, "Do you have any gold? Hand it to us now, or else we are going to kill you!"

While we were frozen in shock by this new threat, a bomb exploded behind us, erupting in a dark cloud of smoke. Taking advantage of this distraction, the group spontaneously broke up and scattered in all directions. As we continued speeding forward toward the border, Papa shouted at us to stay close to the leader. I thought I was stepping on fallen trees, but I looked down and found myself treading on corpses, foul-smelling and covered with flies. We ran as fast as we could, hearing Papa's shaky voice spur us on: "Hurry up, this way!"

Everyone tried to run as fast as possible through the forest while avoiding stepping on landmines. Papa was pulling Sok's hand, and Mama was pulling my sister Mei Juang's. Grandpa, Chen, and I dragged behind, frightened and sweaty. When we got within sight of the border, we were accosted from behind by shrill and piercing voices.

"The bandits are robbing the people behind us! Run! Run!" screamed a Vietnamese family. Everything now in chaos, I heard screaming and crying. I turned back and saw Mr. Cheung holding his daughter against his chest. The family raced away from the trail to our right. Landmines continued to explode all around us.

Exhausted and bewildered, we glimpsed the Vietnamese flag in the distance and suddenly became excited and cheerful. Quickly covering the ground, our family and many others from the group were overjoyed on reaching our destination, the territory of Vietnam.

Our elation dissipated when a group of Vietnamese soldiers approached us. Their hands were outstretched in a very friendly welcome, which gave us a little murmur of relief. But one of them ordered all the families to line up together. We grew sober upon hearing they would detain and question us, intending to confirm we were Vietnamese. Waiting for our names to be called for interrogation, we all sweated profusely from anxiety as well as the heat of the sun. A woman in her late forties fainted the moment her name was called. People in the crowd tried to help her by splashing water on her face, cooling her down. We were all worried about what was going to happen to her, but she quickly recovered. Her face was blue and covered with sweat. Mama guessed she had a heart condition.

Papa was extremely nervous and warned us not to speak, as he was the only one among us who could speak a word of

Vietnamese. He told us that we would be sent back to Cambodia if we were found out.

Meanwhile, we heard many gunshots and explosions echoing through the forest. Her face contorted by worry, Mama instructed us to keep praying while Papa was being interrogated by the authorities. To our great relief, he soon came back. With a bitter smile, he told us he passed the language test. Mama's face beamed with happiness. As our family began to march into the land of Vietnam, Mama suddenly burst into tears. She turned around, waving her hand and saying goodbye to Cambodia.

About half a kilometer from the border, we found open ground and rested there. We then began looking for the Cheung family. Mama did not want to give up on finding them. She took me with her, and until the sun went down, we walked around the border area, asking for the Cheung family. But no one knew what happened to them.

We spent our first night in Vietnam under a giant tree. Mama and Papa were upset, and we mourned the disappearance of the Cheungs. During the several days we spent recovering from our exhausting journey, Mama could not eat. My leg muscles felt detached from my body, as if they needed time to grow back.

❀❀❀❀❀

Our arrival in Vietnam in May 1976 was met with much relief, but not without many painful memories. Hundreds of thousands of people were left behind and were still being tortured by the Khmer Rouge. I often thought of one of our neighbors who had told villagers he had worked as a security guard in the city. The Khmer Rouge soldiers in the village concluded he had done something against their regime and took him away. His wife cried for days, eventually going insane over the loss of her husband.

This was why Papa always warned us not to make friends with anyone. He had come to understand, to his horror, that people we thought were our friends could betray us and report us to the Khmer Rouge, who murdered anyone they considered a threat.

Like our family, many new arrivals found shelter underneath the big tree after making it to the southern border of Vietnam. We saw people break down and loudly sob like children, despairing of ever finding their loved ones.

✿

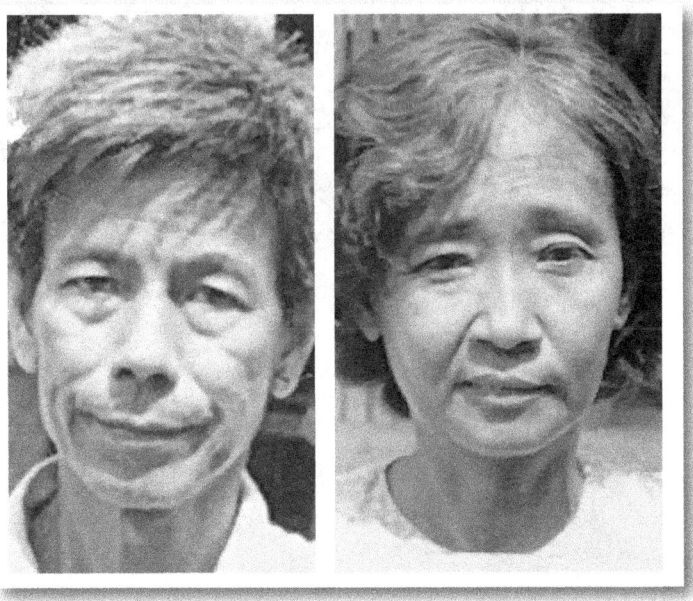

My beloved Uncle Phan and Aunt Kien, taken in 1981 after surviving the Khmer Rouge Genocide

At the border of Vietnam

44.
Life on the Border

Papa soon found a space for us in Mr. and Mrs. Nguyen's backyard, where we could live temporarily. Mr. and Mrs. Nguyen had built everything of bamboo. They grew sweet potatoes all around the house, and they pleased Mama by allowing her to pick the potato leaves for cooking. Because we ate them almost every day, the potato leaves could not grow fast enough for us. When they were all gone, their stems were left fallen on the soil, like executed bodies.

Mr. and Mrs. Nguyen also raised hens and roosters. The roosters often fought over the hens. Each hen seemed to have her own group of chicks to care for. Sometimes the hens fought over food. When this happened, the chicks scattered everywhere, making the area feel like a chaotic battlefield. This reminded me of the human behavior I had witnessed so many times in recent months.

Each day at dawn, the roosters took turns crowing from the trees, the rooftops, and their cages. Their crows were alarm clocks, awakening us to another day of required labor. Although we were in Vietnam and no longer forced to work by the Khmer Rouge, hard labor was still necessary just to survive.

Fortunately, Mr. and Mrs. Nguyen were very friendly and kind to us. They had two children, one four and the other three.

They were a happy couple in their mid-twenties. Besides chickens, they also raised frogs for a living. They owned a large pond across the road, not very far from where we lived. It teemed with frogs of every size. Mrs. Nguyen told Mama that when an exploding landmine had created a huge crater that filled with water, Mr. Nguyen got the idea to hire people from the neighborhood to expand it and then surround it with a huge net to keep the frogs from escaping. Then they turned on kerosene lights at night to attract insects for the frogs to feed on. The frogs croaked day and night, like a choir filling the surrounding area with the sound of its raucous hymns. I visited the pond only once, because neighborhood people said there were still landmines in the area. However, Brother Chen loved to go there and told me everything about it. Mr. Nguyen told him that frog bites during the dry season could be very poisonous and perhaps even fatal.

Despite the danger, Brother Chen went anyway.

Occasionally, Mr. Nguyen brought us live frogs and gave them to us to cook for dinner. Mama did not like the way these animals were treated. She did not want us to be involved in killing living animals and always reminded us how brutal the Khmer Rouge was in torturing people. She often insisted that killing animals was no different. One night at our dinner table, she lectured us on the circle of life and told us Buddhist stories of reincarnation. She explained how animals and humans are related to each other and how they just want to have good, peaceful lives like any of us. I felt guilty hearing Mama's stories because I loved eating frog meat.

Before each meal, Mama wanted us to pray for all the people who were suffering from starvation. She often warned us not to waste any food, explaining, "A grain of rice is the lifespan of a worm." We then prayed for Brother Vuong, Grandma, and all of our relatives, neighbors, friends and all the people left in Cambodia. In great sadness, I ate my meal.

✿✿✿✿✿

While at the border of Vietnam, we continued to hear the constant sound of gunfire, and landmine explosions frequently shook the area. We were not allowed to go out after dark, both to be safe and because of the curfew. So we went to bed immediately after dinner, which was just as well because we were still recovering from our exhausting escape. When night fell, my mind turned to the people who had traveled with us back in Cambodia, wondering whether they had been trapped or killed.

Each evening before bedtime, Mama gathered all of us to sit in front of the cottage and talk about our experience in the jungle. We listened to Grandpa tell us stories from his life, especially about how he used to be a farmer in China. While we had been in the jungle, he taught me and Brother Chen how to catch field crabs and grow vegetables. He also taught us to stay in tune with our environment, and to be cautious and watch out for animals that could kill us when we were foraging for food in the wild.

That summer, the weather in the jungle became scorchingly hot. The unbearable heat lasted for weeks. The puddles in the woods and rice fields dried up and the soil cracked into pieces, destroying many paddy sprouts. One day before sunset, I ran out with a bamboo tube to search for field crabs, only to find dry holes where there once were muddy puddles. Curiously, all the holes were about the same size, about five inches deep. Digging in one of them with my fingers, I caught a medium-size frog that hid at the bottom. Realizing that frogs inhabited all of these holes, I furiously dug one hole after another and caught several of them. As I continued to dig, I also found field crabs hiding at the bottom of other holes. My hands and arms started hurting after several hours of digging in the hard soil. Although some of my fingertips were worn down from my efforts, I continued to collect as many frogs and crabs as possible. As I did, I remembered Grandpa warning me to never put my hand in a dry hole.

Consumed by my need to forage for food, I ignored this warning and vigorously looked around to break up any hole I could find. At one point, I saw one next to a termite hill near the corner of the rice field and broke up the soil at the bottom. When I felt a strange tickling sensation on my fingertips, I impetuously grasped whatever was hidden there. To my horror, hundreds of scorpions came crawling out of their nest! As I ran back home, a sickening disgust shivered down my spine whenever I thought of those tickling sensations.

Over the course of those first few days of our new life in Vietnam, my family and I often spoke of our recent fearful experiences and how our lives had moved from what had felt like hell to a rebirth on earth. My mind kept returning to our friends, the Cheung family, and the kind people we had met in the village of Rocky Diamond, and how we had fled together. I recalled Mr. and Mrs. Cheung once told me that they were from Cho Lon, Vietnam. Indeed, the couple did not look as if they belonged to Rocky Diamond, and they also spoke very poor Cambodian, forcing me to communicate with them in Mandarin. Mrs. Cheung told me that in Vietnam, her family owned a 7up soft drink company and a chicken farm. She promised that if some day by chance I met her again in Vietnam, she would introduce me to a beautiful Vietnamese girl and would give me as much 7up as I could drink.

Whenever we remembered the Cheung family, Mama and I would become very sad. While at the border, Mama, Brother Chen, and I never gave up trying to find the Cheungs. Even though we could not speak or understand a word of Vietnamese, we tried to talk to anyone we came across on the street. But there was never any news of them.

Before crossing over into the Vietnam, we had been living through a surreal, horrible nightmare. Then I realized I was actually in the act of reflecting on the recent past, when for so long I didn't have the time for such a luxury.

As I sat in the Nguyens' front yard, the evening breeze gently caressing my face, I watched the stars brightly blinking in the dark, cool sky. I began to recognize how angry I was at what had happened. But I also felt deeply grateful for where my family and I were now. Our flesh could be fertilizing the now distant soil of Cambodia, and no one would know what happened to us.

No doubt, people were wondering about us, just as we wondered about the Cheungs.

Mr. and Mrs. Nguyen did not ask for more in life than their two young boys. The family was grateful for what they had and, as they said, they only lived for the moment. Mr. Nguyen reflected, "Look, my parents lost everything in Cambodia in 1970 when the government forced us to leave the country. My parents sweated blood to escape. My mother was shot and killed during a robbery. My father died at this border from an overdose of medication. Now, I do not want to worry too much about tomorrow. We have to enjoy every moment that we have because there is no promise of tomorrow."

Mr. Nguyen was a hardworking person who labored from dawn till dusk. He did everything he could for his family. I never saw him complain or get upset about anything. He was active and strong. In his brown shorts, covered with mud and sweat, he moved nonstop but always smiled and had a positive attitude.

One of the most tragic aspects of the war was the presence of thousands of landmines that were planted by the Khmer soldiers. Frequently, they exploded around the forest and along the roads near where we lived. The explosions filled the air with dust and shook the house almost to the point of collapse. People who had lived there longer seemed to have adapted to the commotion, whereas our worried faces distinguished us as new arrivals. At night, my mind was usually only half-asleep. We all kept our belongings next to us, in case we had to resume running for our lives. One night, a bomb exploded loudly very close to us, waking everyone up. Mama, my siblings, and I woke up shaking in fear and confusion, not really sure what was happening. I feared the Khmer Rouge were still after us, and I kept wondering why and how these things could occur.

At the border, everyone had to work very hard to make a living. Mama and Papa were very anxious to look for jobs in order to raise the seven of us. Papa often got upset for seemingly no reason. When he came home exhausted, no one would venture to get near him because he so quickly lashed out. However, we came to understand that his explosive temper was the result of his profound disappointment in the way his life had turned out. We did not have the good life in Vietnam that all of us had expected. He somehow thought we could duplicate the comfortable life we once enjoyed in Cambodia prior to the Khmer Rouge. Eventually, he found a job working as a well digger for very little money. This only increased Mama's anxiety, as she was terrified that Papa would be blown to pieces from hitting a landmine while digging. On top of everything, our natural dependence on him as head of the family was increased by his being the only one of us who could speak Vietnamese.

Most of the people who lived at the border had fled in 1975, soon after the Khmer Rouge took over Cambodia. Many children and teenagers were sent out into the fields to pick fruit, only to be killed when they mistakenly picked up a landmine. Maybe they were the lucky ones, compared to the many physically and mentally disabled people who wandered about the streets and countryside. Many cried and screamed with fear, but no one paid them any attention. Others crawled or rolled on the ground without legs or arms, protecting their remaining limbs from being scratched and bruised by wrapping broken tires around them with cloth bands. When I looked at these handicapped survivors, I realized how truly fortunate my family and I had been. Living at the border were also many Cambodian farmers who hoped to return one day to their homeland when the country was again at peace.

Life was unpredictable on the border, so security was often tight. Frequently, when Vietnamese and Khmer Rouge soldiers came within sight of each other, their inevitable conflict quickly escalated into serious armed fighting. The rest of us then had to run for our lives. Occasionally, however, when the Khmer Rouge advanced near the border, the Vietnam government would temporarily evacuate us to a safer locale further inland. After the shooting was over, we were allowed to return. But this brought us little peace because this chaos that surrounded us never seemed to end.

Not a day passed that we didn't hear gunfire, which was often the result of the Khmer Rouge shooting Cambodians trying to cross the border into Vietnam. We heard that many people lost their lives during these attempted escapes. Others were wounded from gunshots or mine explosions. Because there was little medical care available at the Vietnamese border, families were forced to treat the sick and wounded with their own resources.

Nor was danger restricted to the Cambodian side of the border. People planting vegetables on the Vietnamese side would occasionally hit explosive mines while plowing the topsoil, resulting in permanent injuries, disabilities, or even death. Although the Vietnamese authorities tried to detect and clear the mines in the area, the explosions continued. It was not unusual to find human skeletons. The danger for the children was especially acute because their thirst for exploration made it impossible to know their whereabouts at all times. During their adventures, it was not uncommon for them to find cartridges, grenades, or even guns that had been abandoned by soldiers. Not understanding the danger, the children played with the weapons as if they were toys.

One afternoon, a crowd formed across the road not very far from where we stayed. Several adults were shouting in panic, "Help my child! Help my child!" From a distance, we could hear the piercing sound of two boys crying in pain. Curious, I stepped forward and overheard one of the adults in the crowd state that the two boys found an unfired bullet in their backyard. Not knowing what it was, they tried to break it open with a rock, exploding the bullet. A local nurse rushed in to help treat the wounds on the boys' faces and bodies, which were spotted with many tiny bits of explosive debris. With eyes shut tight and streaming with tears, their screams were heart-rending. Because of scenes like this, Papa and Mama constantly warned all of us children not to go around digging for anything.

In spite of our parents' warnings, we sometimes found canned food, flashlights, radios, or a soldier's nametag buried under the ground. One time, Papa brought home a rusty radio that he found in the ground where he worked. Mama was terrified of all of these discoveries, fearing that any of them might turn out to be an explosive device.

Even caring for refugees had its dangers. Whenever the Vietnamese authorities had forested areas burned down to clear space for refugees to stay, mines exploded and sent out clouds of toxic smoke that undermined the health of those who breathed it in. With danger arising from all aspects of our lives at the border, all of us lived in constant fear and anxiety. But we did not give up our faith and believed all through the crisis that tomorrow would be a better day.

✿✿✿✿✿

Several weeks after settling at the border, Papa returned from work exhausted but also excited. He announced he had saved up enough money to take a trip to Saigon, where he could find a better life for all of us. Carpooling with someone he had met at the border, he left, after anxiously instructing each one of us to take care of Grandpa and ourselves and promising he would return soon. Because none of us except Papa spoke Vietnamese, we were especially worried by the prospect of his being away. Fortunately, the Nguyens were very kind to us. They gave us food, and in return we babysat their two children.

A week later, Papa came back in a small car and a Viet-namese driver, explaining that he had rented a taxi to take all of us to Saigon. He was eager to tell us that we must move out of our present location by the next day. I have never forgotten how excited we were. I could hardly sleep, and I kept reminding Mama that we were going to have a better life in Saigon. With mixed feelings, we said farewell to our new friends at the border. Reluctant to let us go, Mr. and Mrs. Nguyen were in tears the moment Papa gave them the news of our moving out. That same night, they cooked chicken porridge to hold a farewell party for us, and everyone, even the children, went to bed very late. We promised the Nguyens that someday we would see each other again.

We left the border in the early morning. On the road to Saigon, we were all very excited, laughing with joy as the car drove past many small towns. We kept looking through the window, reminding one another that we no longer had to endure the rule of the Khmer Rouge. But from time to time, I noticed that Mama was worried about our future.

✿

Family Picture in Saigon. From right: Papa, Mama, Brother
Chen, me, Brother Sok, Grandpa Kaing Hak Yi
and Mei Juang

45.
A New Life in Saigon

Soon after he arrived in Saigon, Papa found us a one-bedroom apartment. It was on the third floor, number 309, in Pham The Hien near Cho Lon market. To our big surprise, we came across Mr. Sing's family from Cambodia, who once led us when we were fleeing across the Mekong River to his grandma's house in Kien Khleang. They now lived on the second floor in the same building. We also met many other Cambodian families who had escaped the Khmer Rouge. Even though our new home was small, we were happy to be away from the sound of gunfire on the border.

Still, the economy was poor in Saigon, and the people were desperate. We would frequently see people walking around asking to buy anything—bottles, metals, anything that was made of plastic, or old rubber shoes that they could resell for recycling.

The first day after our arrival in Saigon (now called Ho Chi Minh City), a new neighbor took me to a bazaar next to where we lived. In shorts and rubber sandals, we were sitting at an empty food stand, chatting and laughing, relaxed and enjoying ourselves. As we were about to leave, I discovered that one of my sandals was missing. My friend and I looked around for a long time but couldn't find it. I could not understand how

I could have lost it. I was very upset because I had only the one pair and knew that Mama could not afford to buy me another.

In spite of such misfortunes, life was full of excitement during the first few weeks of our new circumstances. However, we were soon confronted with more serious challenges: enormous cultural barriers involving both language and finances. Although Mama and Papa were very frugal with our most basic food expenses, Papa still had to work hard in order to earn money to support a family of seven.

Tall and twenty, Kim Hoan was an older friend and a new neighbor of mine. Separated from his family during the Khmer Rouge oppression, he immigrated to Vietnam all by himself. A few days after Brother Chen and I had arrived in the Pham The Hien district, we ran into a group of kids in the neighborhood who were several years older than we were. Ganging up on us for no reason, they shouted at and chased us down the street, coming close to catching us. As we ran away from them, we bumped into Kim Hoan. Reaching his arms out to stop us, he asked us what was going on. To our great relief, as soon as the bullies saw Kim Hoan defending us, they ran away, never to threaten us again. Although I never understood why bullies feared him, Kim Hoan became not only my personal body-guard, but he would often provide the same protection to other young kids as well.

Our Vietnamese landlord was a tall slim man with short black hair and a thick moustache that almost covered his top lip. Kind and friendly, whenever he came by to collect rent, he enthusiastically took me around and showed me new places in the city. Although neither of us understood the other's native tongue, we made up our own useful sign language. When we first moved into our apartment, Papa explained to the rest of the family that most people in this area were destitute, barely making enough of a living to pay their utility bills. Many would have to steal electricity by inserting a metal hook inside the electric meter so that it registered only a small part of the electricity that they used. Mama was upset that Papa seemed to be excusing their behavior, so she clarified that we were not to indulge in any such conduct. She confirmed the justice of her view by noting that such people were often electrocuted and severely burned.

Our next-door neighbor in Apartment A-310 was Ba Hai. She was a sweet, heavyset woman in her mid-fifties who lived alone and was famous for her delicious desserts. Late every night, she prepared her sticky rice mung bean dessert with coconut shreds to sell the next day. The savory aroma of her freshly baked desserts spread through the building.

One late night while everyone was asleep, I was jolted awake by a thumping sound from Ba Hai's apartment, like something heavy slamming to the floor. However, I was so tired that I quickly fell back into a carefree sleep. The following morning, when Ba Hai's retailers missed her dessert deliveries, they notified her daughter Chin, who rushed to Ba Hai's apartment and forced open the door. She was shocked to find Ba Hai lying dead inside her kitchen, apparently killed by an electric shock. Hearing the tragic news, I was pierced with guilt for going back to sleep that night, thinking that if I had checked on her the moment I heard the loud noise, Ba Hai might have been saved.

Strangely, a similar accident occurred around noon one day. As I walked through the hallway toward the other side of the apartment building, I spotted a woman from apartment A-316 standing by the electric meter. The next thing I knew, her body shook violently, and she screamed sharply. It took me a few seconds to realize she was being electrocuted. In a split second, she collapsed and fell to the floor, unconscious, her face turned blue. I was terrified because I did not know how to summon help in Vietnamese. My heart pounded as I turned in every direction, screaming at the top of my lungs and pointing toward her apartment. Within minutes, a crowd gathered inside the woman's living room as everyone frantically tried to revive her. The disturbing event completely traumatized me, even to this day.

❀❀❀❀❀

In the beginning of our life in Saigon, whenever we went to the bazaar to shop for groceries, Mama relied on our neighbors to interpret for us. But one day in the early morning, Mama and I decided to go shopping on our own. Papa had taught us how to say a few words in Vietnamese and how to bargain for a better price. As Mama and I were on our way to the bazaar, we came across a nice woman who stood on the street selling her produce from a loaded wheelbarrow. In the beginning, she was very nice and friendly while we conversed in our broken Vietnamese and struggled with bargaining. However, when Mama and I began to walk away because we could not agree on a price, the woman immediately set fire to a piece of paper and swept it back and forth across her produce. All the while, she complained furiously in Vietnamese. We continued to walk away, not understanding a word.

Later, we learned from a neighbor that we should never shop in the morning, especially if we were the first customer and not ready to engage in our own negotiation with a vendor. This would make the vendor upset, as it was believed to be a bad omen not to make a sale first thing in the morning. Unknowingly, we had caused the sales of her business to drop for the rest of the day! She had burned the fire and swept it over her produce as a ritual practice, to chase away the negative "chi."

Eventually, we were told by the authorities that we needed to register at the police station in a nearby residential district to live in the city. In the apartment building where we lived, we were assigned a group leader named Co Cam. She was in her early thirties and friendly, always wearing a big smile. She was very kind to us and always made us feel welcome but was also bound by her strict rules. She would keep track of everything everyone did. Every evening, right after dinner, we had mandatory meetings at Co Cam's apartment and listened to her reading the newspaper in Vietnamese. We did not fully understand what was being said—according to Papa, they were stories of the heroes who sacrificed their lives for Vietnam. The meeting would take at least two to three hours, until everyone would feel tired and fall asleep.

Rumor gradually spread that former South Vietnamese soldiers and officials were taken to reeducation camps in the countryside, where they would spend at least a couple of years before being allowed to return home. We also occasionally heard that people tried to escape Vietnam by boat to begin a new life abroad. Some fled successfully, whereas others were arrested and sent to jail.

One late afternoon, Ms. Tu and her four-year-old boy, whom we had met at the border of Vietnam, unexpectedly dropped by our apartment. She was distressed and trembling. Her white shirt and long black satin pants were torn and stained with mud. She reported that two days earlier, before daybreak, the Khmer Rouge invaded the border area where we used to live and turned the whole place into a war zone. They attacked the refugees there, taking many lives, including some of her family members. They wiped out everything, burning down houses—including the Nguyen's house, a conflagration that Ms. Tu had witnessed herself. She broke down in tears and said in a fearful tone, "You all are fortunate you were able to leave the border before anything happened." We were sad and did not know what to say. We wished her good luck and said goodbye. She held tight to her son's hand and wept as she left our apartment.

Every afternoon, Papa and our Cambodian neighbors gathered together and listen to the BBC broadcasting news on the radio. We were all hoping to hear something about the condition of Cambodia. But the news rarely mentioned our deteriorating situation. For many years to come, the atrocities being committed by the genocidal Khmer Rouge remained hidden to the outside world. To this day, I can't make up my mind about whether the silence was politically motivated, racist, or ignorance. Maybe it was a combination of all three.

During that time, the International Committee of the Red Cross, based in Geneva, Switzerland, provided voluntary services to help reunite families who were separated during the war. Mama remembered Sua, the son of Aunt Au Kim, who left Cambodia in 1973 to study in Switzerland as an international student. Papa immediately contacted a friend, who helped write a letter in French to the Swiss Red Cross in Geneva, requesting help in finding Sua.

It took two-and-a-half months to receive a response, which stated that Sua was still residing in Switzerland. Papa promptly wrote to Sua via the Red Cross to let him know that our family fled Cambodia and now lived in Vietnam. To this day, I can still feel how excited we all were, especially Grandpa Kaing Hak Yi, who thought he would soon be in contact with his long-lost grandson.

While we were anxiously waiting to hear from Sua, we heard news on the BBC about hundreds of international students who chose to return to Cambodia, believing the war had ended. Sadly, no one ever heard from them again. Soon after, we received a letter from the Swiss Red Cross confirming that Sua had left Switzerland for Cambodia sometime at the end of 1976. We were all suddenly in shock, confused and traumatized by the news, realizing that our previous correspondence to Sua was too late to keep him from returning home.

Life went on, at least for some of us.

One day, Brother Chen came home shouting excitedly that he came across Ban Somath, our former French teacher in Cambodia, who was now living in the city. Eventually, Mama invited her to come and resume tutoring us in the French language. Meanwhile, she also hired another teacher to tutor us in the English language. Although even our money for food was limited, Mama saved every penny and continued to grant my wish of learning those languages.

Life was up and down for us. My heart broke when I saw tears in my Mama's eyes over our lack of money. I yearned to help my parents bring money home. But how?

Sometime later, I met a neighbor, Nga, who used to live in Cambodia and knew how to speak some Cambodian. After she became someone who I considered my only good friend, she asked if I wanted to go into business with her, selling fruit at the nearby market. Excited by the prospect of finding a way to earn money to help my family, I raced home to tell Mama I wanted to partner with this woman. Although Mama appreciated that I wanted to help, she initially had reservations about my request. However, I persisted until she reluctantly consented, giving me money for the business venture.

I worked very hard and the business went well. However, I was surprised to find that I was not bringing home all the money I calculated I had earned. I reluctantly had to conclude that Nga was not honest with me. I was very upset and depressed for some time. Still, I knew the economy in Vietnam during that time was extremely poor and that many people desperately struggled to survive in any way they could.

❀❀❀❀❀

Life went on. After a while, my French and English skills improved, and I began to eke out some income by working as a private language tutor. Besides easing my financial burden, I was happy to be preparing those who planned to seek asylum in strange lands for a smoother transition.

One day, as I was looking out the apartment window, Grandpa Kaing Hak Yi approached me from behind and said, "I saw a shadow—what was that?"

I replied, "That was me you saw, Grandpa. It was not a shadow." I sadly realized that Grandpa Kaing Hak Yi was no longer able to see because of his cataracts. Due to his impaired vision, we all took turns to make sure Grandpa Kaing Hak Yi was safe when he walked around.

❀❀❀❀❀

Slowly but surely, our family started to get used to life in Vietnam. To our relief, we came across more and more Cambodian survivors who had fled just like us. Many of them were also lucky in that they were able to flee Cambodia just when the Khmer Rouge had begun taking over.

One day, Brother Chen and I found a Cambodian temple in Saigon named Watt Chang Riang Sey. When we went in to visit the temple and listen to the Cambodian monks chanting, we met many Cambodian refugees and shared our survival experiences with one another. Many of their faces were contorted with worry, afraid of what might have happened to their loved ones left behind. Happily, some Cambodian families were able to leave Vietnam to reunite with their families after obtaining sponsorship by their relatives to resettle in France.

❀

Grandpa Kaing Hak Yi

46.
Divining the Future

In 1978, the Vietnamese government started con-fiscating the property of the wealthy, so many of the well-off fled the country as boat refugees. Others left their homes and moved into rural areas, trying to find new open land to restart their lives. The whole city of Saigon, which held a few million people, turned into chaos as increasing numbers fled the country.

While everybody was worrying about the future, people turned to esoteric practices in order to discover what fate held for them. Some attempted to look for help from fortune tellers. Others believed in communicating with the spirit of death to foresee their future circumstances. Some of my friends and I snuck out around midnight and gathered at the balcony by the stairway. In hushed quiet, we would play a game called *Die-Xian*, which people say is like a Chinese Ouija board.

To play, we used a piece of paper written in Chinese or Vietnamese characters and a small sauce tray marked with an arrow. We burned incense and lit a candle. Then three members of the group gently placed their index fingers on the sauce tray, which is called the *planchette* (French) on a Ouija board, and called on a wandering spirit to possess the *die-xian*, the tray. Once the tray seemed to be possessed by a spirit, we asked it questions about our future, and in response, the sauce tray started moving left or right or in a circular motion.

Adults in the neighborhood strictly warned us that it was a dangerous game. If we did not know how to properly send the spirits away at the end of the ritual, it might cause serious consequences. They often told us, "To invite a dead spirit to come is easy, but to send it away is difficult." There was a rumor that once a woman in our neighborhood asked a male *die-xian* to help determine the identity of her future romantic partner. In return, she promised she would be willing to offer anything the *die-xian* wanted as payment. So right after the ritual event, the *die-xian* spirit told the woman that he wanted her for himself. The woman was terrified and did not know what to do. She suddenly became seriously ill and went mad.

Despite all the rumors and warnings, we still thought it was a fun game. One time, we called on a spirit who appeared to be a female ghost. The spirit told us that she was looking for food in the nearby garbage dump when she heard a distant, beckoning voice calling her, which is why she came to us. We all became scared and decided to stop tempting the spirit. Yet it refused to leave and continued to move the dish in circles and zigzags. We all freaked out and took off straightaway. Soon after, we became worried that this female ghost would come after us.

Fortunately, nothing happened.

Still, it was a colorful example of how my culture was in constant and intimate contact with the spirit realm. Trying to determine our future through different forms of divination turned out to be a path fraught with the unpredictable. In an uncanny way, it mirrored our reality at the time, which was in upheaval, and left us in the dark about our future. No one knew how long the chaos or the holocaust would last, or if we would survive.

❀

47.
The Fall of the Khmer Rouge

Unexpectedly, in late December 1978, news spread throughout the city that Vietnam had launched a full-scale strike on Cambodia. They wanted to drive out the Khmer Rouge so that it could no longer threaten the country. The many survivors who escaped from Cambodia and found shelter in Vietnam or Thailand, including my own family, had been traumatized and feared being massacred by the Khmer Rouge. So, they were ecstatic and hopeful when they heard it was under attack.

In January 1979, the news came that the Khmer Rouge had been overthrown by forces from Vietnam. Immediately after, many Cambodian refugees returned home from Vietnam and Thailand, searching for remaining loved ones who might have survived.

As soon as the Khmer Rouge was crushed by Vietnam, Papa sent a messenger to Cambodia to help search for our relatives. While we waited, we desperately hoped that the messenger would return with some positive news. My siblings and I would often sit next to Grandpa Kaing Hak Yi, continually talking about each of our relatives and wondering who might have survived the Killing Fields.

One morning, Papa took our whole family to a local restaurant called Phnom Penh Noodle. This was the first time we could afford to go out for breakfast together. Coincidently,

Papa came across an acquaintance, Uncle Lak, who was now in his late thirties. Tall, skinny, with light skin and a shiny bald head, he was from the same town where Grandma Kim Hoa lived. Uncle Lak and Papa both jumped up and spoke loudly as they hugged each other and started chatting in Cambodian.

Suddenly, Papa's posture changed. He did not say a word as Uncle Lak told him, "I am so happy to see you and your children are all alive." He glanced at us and then continued, "But your mother and everyone are gone. One day, after coming home from labor, I noticed the whole neighborhood was empty. I did not really know what happened, but the villagers told me the Khmer Rouge lined up everyone in front of a pit. They took off their clothing and knocked them down. They executed everyone who was of Vietnamese decent."

Papa remained silent and just looked down.

"How is Vuong?" I asked, trying to change the subject. "Have you heard anything about him?"

"I knew Vuong," Uncle Lak replied with bitterness. "A friendly tall guy, a doctor. It is pitiful. I met him several times in the village. I heard he suffered from diarrhea and passed away."

Mama screamed, "What have we done wrong in our past life to deserve such punishment?"

We were stunned by all the devastating news. I was angry and numb, in denial about Uncle Lak's report. I just could not believe it. We all sat at the breakfast table in shock, grieving the loss of our loved ones. Meanwhile, a waitress repeatedly returned to our table, trying to take our order—we had forgotten we were there to eat breakfast.

Uncle Lak and Papa continued to talk for a long time. I overheard him whisper to Papa that he was going to leave Vietnam soon and head to the West to seek a better future. We left the restaurant feeling a kind of survivor's guilt and hollowed out by grief and emptiness.

We were still mourning and feeling hopeless from the news of Grandma Kim Hoa and Brother Vuong when that same afternoon a messenger came to our apartment to deliver a note from Grandpa Kaing Hak Yi's oldest daughter. It informed us that everyone in her family was still alive, as well as everyone in second uncle Bun Hua's family except his third son, Asy, who sadly disappeared when the Vietnamese troops expelled the Khmer Rouge regime. He was herded by the Khmer Rouge back to the jungle. We had not heard from him since then.

I was thrilled the moment I finished reading the note out loud. Mama burst into tears, and we shouted with joy and jumped about. I cannot describe how it felt to experience such extreme feelings in one day. I saw Grandpa Kaing Hak Yi smile again with his sweet, skinny, wrinkled face, filled with hope as tears ran down his cheeks. He delighted in asking me to read the note for him over and over again.

❀❀❀❀❀

Two years later, around the end of 1980, Aunt Lan managed to find us through acquaintances. She was Papa's sister, so we were all especially happy to find her alive. But we also learned that out of her entire family, only she and her son had survived.

The Khmer Rouge had taken her husband away for interrogation, right after they found out that he served as an official in security for the government in Phnom Penh. She never saw him again. Her daughter died from malaria. She also informed us that Uncle Thai Khieng's wife and daughter survived, though Uncle Tai Khieng himself died while fighting in the front lines against the Khmer Rouge.

Although few in our extended family survived, we were extraordinarily fortunate that our immediate family appeared to be one of the very few left fully intact. It occurred to me that our odds had been practically zero.

As time went by, more and more Cambodians continued to migrate to Ho Chi Minh City, even though it was during a time of economic crisis. Rumors circulated that the Vietnamese government was going to establish three refugee camps. They would first take all Cambodian refugees who arrived in Vietnam after 1979 and move them there, and then next would be the rest of the Cambodians who migrated to Vietnam after 1975. My family and many other Cambodians were disturbed by this rumor, as well as another about the drafting of our young men into the Vietnamese Army. On the heels of these rumors, we witnessed an increase in Cambodians fleeing Vietnam by land and sea to find freedom elsewhere.

❀❀❀❀❀

In September 1979, to our great surprise and excitement, Chea Heng, a son of Papa's cousin, showed up at our apartment. He had survived the Khmer Rouge regime and fled to Vietnam all by himself. Although there were already seven of us crammed into about twenty-three square meters, an excruciatingly tiny living space, we gladly welcomed him as part of our family. He was grateful and excited, hoping to find a better life here.

Chea Heng hoped to reconnect with a brother, Chea Meng, who left Cambodia before the Khmer Rouge took over the country and now lived in France. While Chea Heng was still in Vietnam, he wrote to his brother almost every day. Unfortunately, outgoing mail could take weeks or months to reach its destination, and responses were delayed so long that Chea Heng constantly worried whether his letters had ever been delivered. To address this worry, they sometimes corresponded by telegram, which was extremely expensive.

One midnight toward the end of December 1979, the whole family was sharply awakened by loud banging on our apartment door, accompanied by loud demands that we open it. To our great fright, three security guards barged in, shining flashlights in our faces and asking for anyone who had recently arrived from Cambodia. The most imperious looking of the guards held up a written order and shouted it out, calling Chea Heng by name. The two other guards escorted him to a large truck parked in front of the apartment building.

I overheard the guard in charge inform Papa that Chea Heng was being transferred to a refugee camp in the country-side. My heart pounded at the sight of Papa's and especially Mama's distress over what might happen to Chea Heng, who was all alone and had no idea where he was to be taken. Mama quickly scurried about the kitchen, grabbing some bread, a small cooking pot, and some dried food. She then commanded me to run down and give it to him. I ran as fast as I could and found Chea Heng, who was in the back of a truck that was about to leave. Quickly, I handed him the food through the canvas-covered truck opening and noticed he was surrounded by at least fifty others jammed into the truck bed. The truck jolted forward and Chea Heng disappeared into the night, leaving everyone in the family stunned, then frightened, and finally, depressed.

The following three days were filled with anxiety for Chea Heng. Relief came when a mysterious messenger delivered a letter informing us that he was safe in a refugee camp called Song Be. Mama and Papa immediately began looking for someone willing to check up on him and bring him some food.

Not long after, in February 1980, we were all shocked one evening when Chea Heng rushed into the apartment, as if someone were chasing after him. He appeared tired and dis-traught. Speaking barely above a whisper, he said, "The refugee camp where I now live does not have enough food to eat. Everything is so expensive. I sneaked out of the camp with a middle-aged woman on a bus to Saigon in search of food."

Papa carefully shut the door behind him. He sternly warned, "You are not to go out of the house. I don't want you to get in any trouble with the security guards. And you can't go back to Song Be." While speaking, Papa stared intently at him to ensure that he fully accepted the warning. Papa continued, "You must go back to Cambodia so you can reunite with your parents. I can no longer be responsible for your safety here."

We lived under constant fear that at any time Chea Heng could be caught in the apartment, his last residence before being abducted to be transported to Song Be. To avoid that, Papa took him in the evening to his friend's house near Cau Chu Y Bridge, about a mile away, to let him spend the night there. Four days later, Papa finally found a guide and paid him to lead Chea Heng back to Cambodia.

Our continual worry about Chea Heng's safety found no relief until March 1980. We were delighted to receive a letter from him informing us that he had safely arrived in Thailand, at the Khao I Dang Cambodian refugee camp. The thought of reliving the experience I had under the Khmer Rouge and in a Vietnam refugee camp made me despair for my family and my own future. Meanwhile, rumors also spread that those who were sent to the Vietnamese refugee camps in the countryside would eventually be allowed to settle abroad, if they were sponsored by family members, but I had mixed feelings about leaving. I recalled running across the border of Vietnam, where Mama often told us that our life was going to improve, that she was going to cook our favorite foods, and that we would once again be happy as we had been before that fateful day our lives changed.

After more than forty years since the fall of the brutal Khmer Rouge regime, we survivors of the genocide continue to be haunted by our memories. Our dream of happiness had been damaged, but not destroyed. Our elders taught us well that we need to survive not just alone but together.

✿

My beloved Aunt Lan, taken in 1981
after surviving the Khmer Rouge Genocide

48.
Searching for
My Unknown Future

One afternoon, right after Mama finished her Buddhist chanting ritual, I approached her with a wry smile and kneeled in front of her. "Mama, I cannot stop thinking about my future. I am really worried about it...and I want to talk about it."

Instantly, she frowned and looked me straight in the eye.

I persisted, "Mama, I am eighteen, old enough to plan my own future. I am ready to make a break for it and face any challenges."

With eyes wide open, she anxiously shouted, "A break for it? What are you talking about?"

"But Mama, leaving is a risk worth taking. Who knows? If I can make it to the West, I may wind up with a bright future."

"Stop talking about this!" Mama shouted. "You're not going anywhere."

Seeing that I had upset her, I quickly changed the subject.

I never again tried to discuss my idea of escaping. But my concern for my future in Vietnam persisted, and I continued to dream of leaving. When the right time came, I would be ready.

One evening in December 1981, Papa came home from work unusually early. I overheard him anxiously whisper to Mama that a close friend of his, Mr. Dang, a native-born Vietnamese, had a small fishing boat. He said we could use it to flee Vietnam together with his family. He would not charge any fee up front, but we would have to pay him a certain amount of money if we successfully crossed the ocean and resettled in another country.

Although Papa seemed excited, the rest of us were in shock at the thought of this drastic and dangerous adventure. I instantly thought about Grandpa's Kaing Hak Yi well-being and whether any of us could survive in the open sea. Mama was distraught and refused to give Papa an immediate decision. Naturally, she was fearful about losing any of us. Papa then turned around and addressed Brother Chen and me. "How about the two of you? This would be a great chance to leave Vietnam and start a new life, don't you think?"

Mama intervened. "It's not as easy as you say. Didn't you listen to the BBC news broadcast that many of the refugees who have tried to escape by boat were lost at sea in storms?"

I was conflicted. I was not ready to put everyone in a life-threatening situation, but I also did not want to miss this opportunity. I wondered if any of us, myself included, would be ready to risk their life crossing the ocean. I stared at Mama's eyebrows, knitted together as she spoke to Papa.

"This is too much! It seems like I just get over one crisis and another one occurs. I need to piece my soul together." Her face looked pale and tired.

That evening, Mama suggested we all stop talking about escaping in a fishing boat, which was deeply distressing to her. As much as I wanted to give her relief, I knew I would not be able to let the matter rest. Would I need to go it alone? What would the world out there be like? What country would be my ultimate destination? What opportunities would open up for me? What if I got arrested and imprisoned for trying to escape?

It was late, almost midnight, and I couldn't sleep because my mind was churning with a strange mix of hopes and fears. I sat back against the wall with my knees tucked up close to my chest. With profound curiosity and anxious excitement, I stared vacantly into my unknowable future. I didn't know where my life would end up, but I knew I needed to escape as soon as possible and find my way to the West.

Forty-four years after the mass executions, the survivors who are out there, including myself, continue to be haunted by the memories. According to our scholars, nearly two million of my fellow Cambodians perished under the genocidal rule of the Khmer Rouge, about one-third of the population.

Slowly, we are rebuilding our country and our culture. Life must go on, which was one of the many beautiful lessons that my parents taught me and my siblings.

I believe they would be proud of how it has gone for me.

I vividly recall one evening when we were desperately wondering if we could survive another night in the jungle. Papa entered our pathetic cottage and waved at me strenuously to join him outside. My mother and my siblings looked away, and although I was frightened and shaking, I stood up from where I was sitting on the bamboo floor and walked uncertainly to the door and stepped outside. I remember the sound of crickets and the stars whirling in the sky and the shadows of dim moonlight flickering through the trees. Despite the beauty of Cambodia's natural world I felt sick and hoped it wasn't dysentery or one of the other diseases that were ravaging our camp. When I reached my father, he put his hand on my shoulder, and with firmness in his voice, he whispered to me that he had a plan that would help us escape the camp. I was thrilled and terrified. And yet as he spoke, trying to ease my nervousness, I knew he had thought all of this through and it was worth the risk.

Looking back from the vantage point of time and age, my admiration and love for my father is stronger than ever. It must have taken an enormous leap of faith for him to lead us to freedom. But he did it anyway. I wonder now if he had a premonition of death if we stayed, if he feared for his own health, thinking he was getting weaker and worrying what would happen to us if he died. Did he ever think we would soon die after him? I don't know. He never talked about that night or our journey to freedom again. I asked a few times, but he refused. Was the pain too much? While watching Papa fighting for breath at the University of California Medical Center in the intensive care unit, I mastered the courage to ask him, "Papa, do you remember how you led our family on a dangerous journey across the border into Vietnam? Do you know you saved all of our lives?"

He stared at me with his frail soft eyes and struggled to find the right words, "It was my responsibility."

I choked back tears as I replied, "Papa, I am so grateful for what you did for us."

Shortly after our brief conversation, my father passed away, taking many painful memories with him, and I hope a few proud ones as well.

Other than a few photographs, our memories of him are all we have left of him.

Our escape to the border of Vietnam was terrifying but we trusted implicitly in my father. For days and nights, we snuck through the jungle. He was fearless. Eventually, we met with a group of Vietnamese, farmers and fishermen and fled along with them heading toward Vietnam.

How can I describe the conflicting feelings of excitement having escaped the Khmer Rouge but also being forced to leave our beloved Cambodia? On top of that I was worried that there might be Khmer Rouge soldiers waiting for us somewhere on the road. Maybe they would shoot us right then. Or capture us and torture us? I felt worried for no reason. But constant anxiety kept me alert and on edge all the time. By the grace of God, my father chose the right time to flee our terrified homeland.

Finally, we reached the border Tay Ninh, where we were fortunate to be welcomed by the Vietnamese soldiers. As soon as we were allowed to stride into the land of Vietnam, Mama burst into tears as she turned and looked back, waving her hand in the air, saying goodbye to Cambodia.

The night of our arrival at the border of new world, we slept under a big tree, which seemed like paradise to us. The next morning the sun shone bright. Birds were singing in the trees. I saw kids my own age laughing. The new environment gave us a sense about how our new lives were going to unfold. Most important of all, we now felt safe. We were relieved. We had survived, after all.

❀❀❀❀❀

After escaping the hell that reigned in my beloved Cambodia under the genocidal regime of the Khmer Rouge, we lived in Vietnam for five years. In 1981, two years after the Vietnamese Army finally defeated the Khmer Rouge, we had a visit from my Mama's cousin. Aunt Pieng traveled from Cambodia, with a friend of hers, Aunt Duon, to pay us a visit for a couple of days in our tiny apartment in Ho Chi Minh City.

Over a cup of tea and some Vietnamese sweets, Aunt Pieng told us she had lost her husband and her young son, and that many of our relatives were starving to death. Her friend, a tiny woman in her mid-fifties, was a very sweet and friendly woman with short gray hair. She spoke Cambodian and Vietnamese fluently. Aunt Pieng bought reams of colored fabric and clothing to resell back in Cambodia, and began to make enough money from her business to warrant a few return trips to Vietnam.

We all adored Aunt Pieng, but Aunt Duon was the mysterious one who captured our attention. She drove a mini motorbike throughout the city, speaking in a whisper when ever she met any of her "contacts." Sometimes she would ask me to accompany her on her motorbike as she met her various business associates. She would tell me to wait outside of their offices or homes while she conducted her affairs, often for quite a long time. Everything seemed secretive, providing no clue as to what she did or talked about inside.

I often worried that a Vietnamese security guard would one day stop and interrogate us. But the problem never arose. Aunt Duon had a way of stealthily sneaking in and out of the premises while remaining undetected. At the end of her mysterious visitations, she often treated me to a street stall for a nice meal of either grilled lemongrass pork chops or Bun Bo Hue, a spicy beef noodle soup. I admired her tireless energy and her having what seemed to be enough money to spend on anything she liked. The unknown source of her money and purpose of her visitations left me intrigued.

In the meantime, rumors were spreading, as they always do in times of war, through the neighborhood that the Vietnamese government was rounding up all Cambodian refugees and locking them in a confined camp somewhere in the countryside. As rumors escalated, tensions worsened throughout Ho Chi Minh City, which was already strained by its own years of constant warfare. The living situation of Cambodian refugees had become so worrisome and gloomy that many became fearful.

One morning just before dawn, we awoke uneasily to the tremor of big pickup trucks rumbling noisily through the neighborhood. People were running about, shouting and crying. As Papa, Mama, my siblings, and I peeked through our apartment window, we caught sight of Vietnamese security guards lining up several Cambodian families and roughly guiding them into a giant military truck. Shortly after, they all disappeared into the darkness. The whole district resumed its early morning silence, as if nothing had happened. Later, we heard that many Cambodian refugees had been taken to Song Be, a refugee camp about one hundred and twenty kilometers into the countryside, the same place where my cousin Chea Heng was previously taken.

With all this going on, I could no longer contain my curiosity. One evening, right after Aunt Duon visited one of her friends, I cautiously approached her.

"Aunt Duon, it's been really fun to go with you around town. I'm sorry if this sounds rude but I'm getting nervous. Cambodians like us are disappearing every day. So … you don't have to treat me to dinner today, but, please, I am getting scared. With respect, can I ask you to tell me what your business visits around the city are all about?"

Laughing dismissively, she replied, "Young man, you're not ready to know. When the time comes, I'll tell you. Let's go to dinner."

Disappointed by her refusal to answer, I was even insulted a little bit. I hated it when adults talked down to me. It also seemed like she was definitely hiding something, but as a kid there wasn't much that I could do, so I seethed with anger and hope that she wasn't dragging our whole family into her possibly dangerous business deals.

A few days later, I became even more intrigued when she revealed to me that she had to leave Cambodia on an urgent business matter.

"Young man, I'll be gone for three or four weeks. Once I return, I'll come to look for you."

Her sudden announcement threw me into an inner conflict. I was angry at her for endangering me and my family, but also enjoyed the sense of intrigue and adventure.

"Aunt Duon, why do you have to be away for so long?"

She smiled and gave me a mysterious look, and then silently left the building.

Rumors continued to spread in the city, which drove more and more people to escape west across the border. One of our neighbors broke down sobbing like a child when she heard that her family had fled by boat and was now reported missing in the ocean. Those who remained were afraid to sleep at their own home, for fear they would be caught at night and sent to the refugee camp, like others they knew. So, they left their homes in the evening and hid themselves at night at their friends' or neighbors' places, forced to once again face what they had experienced in Cambodia under the Khmer Rouge.

After several months of turmoil and uncertainty, one afternoon after lunch I gathered enough courage to approach Mama and confront her.

"Mama, I have made up my mind. I have to leave. I need to go west."

Stunned by my announcement, she stared at me in disbelief. Then she broke down and wept bitterly, tears streaming down her cheeks.

"I knew this was going to happen sooner or later," she sobbed.

Seeing the shock that my announcement had caused her, I tried to assuage my own feelings of guilt by soothing her.

"But Mama, this is the only chance to make sure I have a good future. If I can get away, it won't be just for me. There is no future for me here, but there may be a future for me there. If there is, it will be good for all of us."

I pleaded with her to accept my decision, but she skipped dinner and sobbed throughout the night. She wasn't the only one hit hard. Grandpa was also visibly concerned, even though he tried to support and understand me. We had been going through so many tough times together, but now I chose to leave everyone behind. Deep inside I suddenly felt sad, selfish, and ashamed but tried to stay calm and show no emotion.

Astonishingly, Aunt Duon showed up at our apartment the very next day, her face flush with excitement. She grabbed my arm, pulled me aside, and echoed what I had told my mother the night before. "Your life can be a lot better if you go west, young man. Everybody is going in that direction, to enter a Thai refugee camp, a port to resettlement in a free country where you can restart your new life. We must leave tomorrow."

That evening, I experienced an amazing rush of energy. Mama discussed the whole situation with Aunt Duon and agreed to pay her two *taels* of gold for helping me escape. Aunt

Doun assured Mama that she knew the road to the refugee camp very well and would be in charge of guiding me safely to the Thai border. Her obvious confidence persuaded Mama that she was the right person to help me.

During the discussion, Aunt Duon wrote down the address on a small piece of paper and handed it to me. "This is where we are going to meet tomorrow, exactly at 3:00 a.m., before daybreak. You must be there on time. Not a minute later." Aunt Duon looked at me sternly and warned me not to say a word to anyone, or else we would be caught and sent to jail.

That evening, Mama cooked a special dinner with a lot of meat and made sure I ate a lot of it. "You have to eat a lot to keep yourself strong. You will not have food on the road or in the jungle."

Even though I was too nervous to even think about food, I tried to eat to make her happy. It was already near midnight and yet everyone was still awake, though silent, and nervous. Looking at my sister, Mei Juang, and my brother, Sok, I realized how time had passed—they were now both teenagers and I wondered how their future was going to be, staying here in Vietnam.

Sometime during the night, Mei Juang approached me privately in the kitchen. "I wish you the best on your journey," she told me. "I know you will find your way safely. Someday when you are free, don't forget us."

I was reluctant to talk about the matter, lest I break down. I faked a smile and kissed her on her forehead. "Be a good person and everything is going to be fine," I assured her.

That night, Mama gave me some cash to ensure I had money to buy food on the road. She inserted twenty dollars into my pocket while insisting that I also hide two small pieces of gold in my clothing. Aunt Doun advised that I dress to blend in with local people who buy and sell goods at the border. I put on an old dark-red shirt and a pair of old blue jeans.

Then it was time to leave home. It hurt to say goodbye to everyone in the family. Shakily, Grandpa Kaing Hak Yi crawled out from his mosquito net and slowly tried to stand up. I hugged his frail little body and promised him that someday I would take good care of him.

With hope and confidence, he uttered, "Good luck, young man. I wish everything to go smoothly in your life."

At that moment, I knew that this was his final goodbye to me. My heart was never ready to leave Grandpa Kaing Hak Yi. I treasured his friendship, his wisdom and insight, his ability to judge correctly with knowledge and understanding. I always considered him a spiritual leader.

Mama began to cry again, but this time I avoided looking at her. With a sudden surge of resolve, I grabbed my little bag, which contained some boiled eggs and bread she had packed for me the night before. I turned my back and quietly walked straight down the balcony. Grandpa Kaing Hak Yi and Mama stood by the door. As I stepped forward, I heard Grandpa sigh deeply. I felt conflicted. I was leaving everyone I loved behind. I looked back and waved to their shadows in the darkness. I knew I would never see Grandpa Kaing Hak Yi again.

❦❦❦❦❦

The night was pitch black, the silence broken only by motorcycles occasionally passing by. Some street vendors had already begun preparing for the day, setting up their food stalls by the light of kerosene lamps. I could hear the distant sound of dogs barking.

I took a cyclo to the address where Aunt Duon had arranged to meet. When I arrived, she was already standing on the street waiting for me. She said I needed to have a Cambodian name. "I am going to call you Sok Kha from now on, and you are going to call me Mac (Mom), so people will think you are my son and therefore Cambodian. They will then not suspect that you are Vietnamese."

We rode a *xe om* (a motorbike-taxi) on a dusty and rough road for around four hours, from Cau Chu Y toward the City of My Tho. Along the way, Aunt Duon anxiously kept warning me to not talk or say anything to the riders. She cautioned me that they could be spying on us, collecting information on our activities that could get us in big trouble. We stopped a couple of times on the way, so as not to attract the attention of security guards by being in too much of a rush. So, we did not arrive at the City of My Tho until early morning.

In My Tho, we found ourselves in a totally new and strange environment. The appearance of both the land and the people were dramatically different from anything I had previously experienced. The dusty streets were busy with motorized cyclos roaring up and down the streets. Throngs of people rushed about, while the aroma of cooking spices from innumerable vendors wafted down the street.

Aunt Duon and I cautiously wove through the busy crowd, and soon spotted two security guards wearing red armbands, each holding a firearm. Standing in the middle of the road, one looked around for any suspicious activities while the other stopped a man and searched his backpack. Aunt Duon and I continued working our way through the crush of foodstall ladies, who were busily waving their hands to draw customers. Aunt Duon anxiously whispered to me, "Don't be nervous—just act normal." Luckily, the security guards did not stop us.

As we headed forward, Aunt Duon softly warned me, "Be careful, there's a checkpoint ahead of us."

Right then I grew awkward and uneasy, as I noticed people here and there curiously turning around to look at me. Aunt Duon suddenly scratched my hand, drawing my attention to a security guard walking toward us. She abruptly gripped my right arm, tugging me down into a chair at one of the nearby tiny food stalls. Even in my anxiety, I could not help but notice the enticing aroma of the barbecue sausage curling up from its smoky flamed grill. The saleslady at the food stall greeted us with friendly surprise, smiling straight at me.

"Young man," she asked, "are you from another town? You seem to have very light skin." The woman's curiosity made me edgy. Quickly, Aunt Duon cut in and ordered barbecued pork over rice, one for me and one for herself. At that moment, a flood of thoughts surged through my mind about what would happen if we were caught. Like anyone else trying to flee Vietnam, we would be thrown in jail.

I was chewing a mouthful of street food when Aunt Duon noted the guard's absence. "There's no security guard at the checkpoint. Leave now! You just keep walking straight. We'll find each other later."

Without hesitating, I left the food stall, managed to sneak through the checkpoint, and continued walking down the road without looking back.

✿✿✿✿✿

About an hour later, Aunt Duon and I found each other again. It was already around two o'clock on a bright and hot afternoon. Aunt Duon bargained with two men on a motorbike for a good price to add her and me on the back. Before I knew it, we were both lurching through the town of My Tho, and after a few hours we arrived at the port of Chau Doc, on the Mekong River. It was a little before sunset. Clearly distressed, Aunt Duon roughly ordered me, "You stay right here and wait for me. I have to run an errand. Don't go anywhere!"

As I watched her shadow gradually disappear in the dark, I turned to the crowded and noisy scene along the riverbank. Many boatmen began to light little oil lamps, and I watched them load their boats with fruits and vegetables and quickly paddle back and forth across the river. Bicyclists arrived with baskets filled with fresh produce, supplying the boatmen and the other vendors along the river. Some also sold livestock and all that activity created an almost festive scene, with the lights bobbing up and down on the river and the daylight slowly fading into a chilly dusk. Strong tidal currents began to wash up on the shore, constantly slamming into the riverbank and rocking the boathouses back and forth.

Meanwhile, I stood at the riverbank waiting impatiently for Aunt Duon to return.

By the time Aunt Duon returned from her errand, the sky had grown dark. She handed me a piece of pork sandwich and a small plastic bag of iced tea. I was not hungry, until I saw the food. She eagerly spoke to me in a whisper. "Sok Kha, I've arranged a boat to pick you up within one or two hours. It depends on the situation." She then led me to a tiny wooden house on the bank of the river. "The boatman is going to get some gas," she told me. "He will be here anytime now to pick you up. I won't be able to get onto the same boat with you, since it's overloaded and there's only room for one more. I will see you at the transfer station before arriving in Phnom Penh. Okay? Promise me you'll be on time."

I nodded.

"I have to go," she said, and she quickly left the area.

I was so exhausted that I could not care much about what she said. A lady in the wooden house greeted me in Vietnamese with a Cambodian accent. I leaned against the wall near the entrance and saw she was busy with her cooking. As I was about to fall asleep, a very short man with a bony face startled me at the doorway. "Are you Sok Kha?" he asked.

I nodded, assuming he was the boatman I was waiting for.

"You can call me Anh Ba," he said. Smart and energetic, he warned me that the whole area was under curfew and immediately rushed me along, explaining, "A boat is waiting for you."

Except for the sound of the flowing river, the whole area had turned deathly quiet. Anh Ba and I quickly found a small boat with a young woman who quietly pushed us across the river with a long bamboo stick. A few minutes later, she transferred us into an engine boat about three-and-a-half meters long, and full of hundreds of sugarcane stalks. Two men seated on the hard stalks stared at me as Anh Ba instructed me to crawl down into the cabin. He warned me not to drink or eat anything, so I wouldn't have to relieve myself.

As soon as I stepped into the boat, I became uncomfortable. Flies buzzed annoyingly around my ears and the odor of cigarette smoke fouled the air. The cabin was dark and piled with hundreds of green bananas that left me no space to stretch and no air to breathe. Anh Ba ordered me to squat down against a cabin wall and sit still, leaving me alone in the dark. I suddenly became fearful of getting stuck inside this tightly enclosed space. Abruptly, a light flashed and a man appeared— sitting in front of me, he had struck a match to light his cigarette. For a second, the flare illuminated the entire area, revealing several other people hiding in the cabin. At least I wasn't alone.

As time dragged slowly by, the muscles of my legs and back began to ache, and the stifling surroundings became unbearable. My head dripping with sweat. I tried to lean my face against a tiny square window covered with a tightly knitted metal screen, but there was no relief. After what seemed like forever, with a burst of speed the engine boat finally began to move. A moment later, Anh Ba shouted to the two passengers on the top level, "Everybody get down to the cabin! We're now getting ready to pass the Vietnamese security checkpoint."

As the boat sped up, there erupted a sharp staccato of bullets from across the river. Everyone in the cabin scrambled back and forth to avoid the gunfire, bumping into each other and rocking the boat. Anh Ba barked angrily, "Stop moving, stay calm, or else the boat is going to flip over!" Increasing daylight revealed water leaking through the tiny window, causing the person sitting next to me to scream, "Oh no, we're all going to die!" Two other passengers panicked and stampeded for the exit. Anh Ba's assistant shouted, "Mother fuckers, come back and sit still! You don't want to get shot! We're being attacked." As the boat rocked unsteadily from side to side, more water poured into the side of the boat.

Over and over, Anh Ba shouted, "Scoop the water out of the boat, mother fuckers!"

The water at the bottom of the boat kept rising, even as all of us took turns bailing the water out of the boat. Losing control, Anh Ba shocked me as he screamed fiercely, "Oh God, mother fucker, they got us! They got the boat this time! Don't stop! Keep scooping!" I became frantic, terrified that the boat was sinking, and we were all going to die, trapped in the cabin. That was when I spotted the water rushing in from the bottom of the boat. Anh Ba's assistant yelled to his partner, who was crawling to the deck, "Cut the rope! Let go of the sugarcane!"

As the boat churned through the swift rapids of the Mekong River, the sounds of bullets slowly died down. Daylight gradually appeared. While we continued struggling to bail out the water, Anh Ba finally announced, in a voice both exhausted and relieved, that we were now on the Cambodian side of the river. Later, I overheard that the police fired at us because our boat hadn't stopped at the patrol checkpoint for inspection.

As the boat pushed onto the riverbank at the transit, we were inundated by the noise from nearby houseboats. The sun blinded my eyes as I disembarked. My knees were stiff and sore from squatting all day long.

"Sok kha!" I heard Aunt Duon's voice out of nowhere. Then in Cambodian, "Are you okay? What's wrong? Let's go. We need to catch up to a boat leaving for Takeo province."

I unsteadily tugged along after her, still trying to recover from the dreadful trip. Aunt Duon passed me a blue *krama* patterned with white squares. "Wrap your head with this," she whispered, "so no one will notice where you come from. Remember, this is Cambodia—you cannot speak Vietnamese."

We walked along the river for about a kilometer and arrived at another port, where we were disappointed to see a dreadfully long line waiting to buy boarding tickets. We waited for about an hour for our tickets to Takeo province. The air was dusty, hot, and I felt smothered by the humidity. Children and seniors in tattered clothes held out baskets of fruits or trays of trinkets for sale. Security guards scoured the riverbank for suspicious activity. The sound of people talking in my native language suddenly assailed my memory, provoking long-forgotten scenes from my childhood.

Finally, we boarded a light green boat, approximately six meters long. We were crammed into a large, windowless, hot, and stuffy cabin next to the engine room. Everyone was still and quiet—no one seemed comfortable engaging in conversation with anyone else, so whenever Aunt Duon and I chatted they gazed at us steadily.

Before the boat started moving, a controller came and announced that the security guard was now aboard to inspect our documents and belongings to make sure no one was carrying anything illegal. I spotted a few security guards walking around randomly checking people's belongings. One guard with a long rifle approached a young lady sitting across from us. He spoke to her in Cambodian, instructing her to open her backpack. The young lady appeared to be very nervous and her eyes filled with tears. Her voice trembling, she pleaded with the guard, "These are all my personal belongings. I have not done anything against the law." After a quick search, the guard ordered her to the attic to have her backpack thoroughly inspected.

Just as one of the young guards came up to Aunt Duon to search her belongings, she handed me a loaf of bread, loudly announcing, "Here is your lunch, Sok Kha. Eat it. You must be hungry, my son." Feeling strange and a little confused, I noticed something unusual about the bread as I bit into it. While the guard searched Aunt Duon's belongings, my stomach was in knots. He then began to search our bodies, telling Aunt Duon to unfasten the safety pin in the pockets of her secret vest. When he failed to find anything, he ordered us to sit down. Unexpectedly, Aunt Duon spoke angrily to the guard in Cambodian, "Let me alone. My son and I are very hungry. Please let us eat our lunch. We have had a long day."

The guard ignored her and left to search another person. As soon as he stepped away, Aunt Duon snatched the bread from me, gesturing that she had something hidden inside it. The bell rang shortly thereafter, and the boat slowly began to move toward Takeo province.

❀❀❀❀❀

Before reaching Takeo, the controller came into the cabin again and announced in Cambodian, "The boat is going to take a break before going through the checkpoint. Whoever is not a Cambodian citizen will be required to disembark." Stunned and bewildered by the announcement, everyone anxiously stared at one another in confusion. Aunt Duon whispered to me, "You should leave the boat and just keep walking along the river. You will find your way. We will meet each other at the port in Phnom Penh." She then commanded me to memorize her address, in case I got lost.

Once I climbed out of the boat and onto the muddy river bank, I felt disoriented. About fifteen passengers immediately rushed out and followed me. Among them were three worried-looking females who seemed to be in their mid-thirties. As we walked together along the bank, no one said a word. "Where are you going?" I finally asked the woman walking next to me. Smiling politely, she nodded her head. I turned around and asked another man behind me in Cambodian, "Where are you from?" The man smiled at me but said nothing.

This was bizarre! My gut instinct was telling me that something was wrong. No one said anything, but they all continued to follow me.

As we continued along the shady, unpaved country road, I tried to calm my increasing anxiety. We passed by many Cambodian houses made of palm leaves and bamboo frames and I kept wondering if I was headed in the right direction. I decided to stop a middle-aged Cambodian lady who walked toward me from the opposite direction.

"Aunty," I said, "may I ask if this is the right direction to Phnom Penh?"

Glancing at me curiously, she turned her eyes to the group of people behind me. Hesitating briefly, she replied, "It would take one-and-a-half hours by motorbike to get to Phnom Penh." She then warned, "There is a police patrol checkpoint up ahead. The officer may randomly stop any suspicious pedestrian."

Thanking her for the information, I slowly headed forward. However, her warning worried me greatly, especially since I was already concerned about why these people kept following me without saying anything. I turned around and warned, "Listen, I am not going anywhere with you. I feel like you are following me. I want to walk alone by myself. So, stop following me." Giving me a perplexed look, they kept walking. At that moment, I spotted one of the ladies among the group with a red *krama* wrapped around her face, waddling slowly and clumsily. I inched toward her and asked, "What's going on?"

She smiled timidly and trembled. Finally, she anxiously answered me in Vietnamese. "Young brother, I am Thuy. I don't speak Cambodian. I am Vietnamese. I need to go to Phnom Penh. Please help me."

I was shocked, realizing that this group of people did not speak a word of Cambodian. I responded to her in Vietnamese, warning her of possible danger at the check-point. Later, they became more comfortable and began conversing with me in Vietnamese. Frustrated and confused, I didn't know what I was supposed to do. I kept asking myself if it was my responsibility to help them. I felt conflicted. I could break from the group for my own safety, but what would happen to them if I left them? Would my action affect their lives? My head throbbed and I began to worry about how everybody was going to get through the patrol checkpoint in the next few minutes.

After I related to them what the Cambodian woman had just told me, some of them were terrified, trembling as if they had already been taken into custody. Others were upset and began murmuring among themselves in despair. I immediately advised everyone to stay calm, assuring them that I would try my best to help them and find a practical solution.

I tried to speak calmly, saying, "Listen to me, I want to help you. But you must help yourselves by staying calm. We can't walk through the checkpoint the way you're acting."

At that precise moment, two *lamork* (a motorcycle connected to a trailer with two wheels) drove past us. I quickly waved for them to stop, and then negotiated a price for driving all of us to the dock in Phnom Penh. We split into two groups. A group of seven sat in one *lamork* and six in the other. I had the sickly-looking lady, Thuy, sit next to me, since she was the one I was mostly worried about. As we were getting into the trailers, I reminded them all to smile and pretend that were having a good time. In reality, of course, I was consumed with thoughts of what would happen if we were all caught at the checkpoint. I might be arrested and accused of helping people to escape Vietnam.

While motoring down the rustic road, I sought to engage the driver in friendly conversation, in order to distract him from anyone's suspicious behavior. As we were about to speed through the checkpoint, I noticed two patrol officers standing over on the side of the road, searching a group of pedestrians. Abruptly shouting in Cambodian to those in the other trailer, I tried to make it appear we were all a group of Cambodians traveling together and having a good time. I casually cried out, "Hey guys, I told you it would be hot and sunny today and wouldn't rain. Now you all believe what I said." They all burst out laughing, pretending to understand what I said. When we passed through the checkpoint, I felt incredible relief.

✿✿✿✿✿

By the time we reached the dock at Phnom Penh, the rays of
the setting sun cast a golden glow on the Royal Palace across
the river. Again, the familiar scenery provoked vivid childhood
memories from a lifetime ago. I could see Papa taking me and
Brother Chen on his motorbike and driving us across the bridge
to Chhrouy Chanva Park, where we would do our morning
exercises and watch the mystery of the sunrise over the river in
front of the Royal Palace. The bustling activity along the riverside awakened me from my reveries. Laborers loaded cargo
onto the boats while their supervisors shouted at them. Many
homeless people were pitching their tents for the night alongside the riverbed.

Finally, we departed from the *lamorks*. Everyone's kind
words of gratefulness deeply touched me, surprised by how
bonded I felt to people whom I had known only a short while.
After we said goodbye and wished one another luck, I
immediately started walking around the riverbank, trying to
find Aunt Duon. Not knowing where to look, I wandered along
the streets near the dock of Phnom Penh for a long time, until
the sun slowly sunk below the horizon and the area became
deserted.

Unexpectedly, I again ran into the sick lady, Thuy. I became very worried about her. She looked extremely weak and
tired, quietly sitting alone at the sidewalk, her knees pulled up
against her belly.

"What's wrong?" I asked her. "What are you doing here?
Are you not going anywhere?"

"I just had a miscarriage two days before I left Vietnam,"
she replied. "I still have some bleeding, abdominal pain, and
dizziness."

I told her, "You look very sick. You need a place to rest.
Do you have any relatives in Cambodia?"

She shook her head no. Looking me in the eyes, she
explained, "I'm not afraid to tell you, young brother, I am

finding my way west. But I don't know what I am going to do."
She angrily continued, "At first, I planned to leave Vietnam
with my fiancé. But a week before, I found out that he had
cheated on me. I fled without telling him." Tears came to her
eyes.

I interrupted her, as I thought of Aunt Duon. "Listen, I
know a person who may be willing to help you, but I can't
promise anything yet. Let me get back to you by tomorrow."
We promised to meet at the same spot the next morning.

I took a cyclo to the address that Aunt Duon previously
had me memorize. On the way, I wondered whether I did the
right thing, offering to help this lady when I had enough to
worry about with my own situation. The moment I made it to
Aunt Duon's residence, she stood at the door and started
yapping at me, "Where did you go? I was so worried about
you! I thought you already knew how to get here. Come in and
take a shower first and eat your dinner."

As soon as I stepped through the door, I saw several young
people about my age sitting in the living room. They were
loudly singing an old Cambodian song. The smell of cigarettes
and alcohol was strong. Aunt Duon led me straight toward the
darkness at the back of the house and to an alley where there
was a water faucet. I could hardly find my way, with only the
light of kerosene lanterns from windows and doorways pen-
etrating the darkness. She pointed to the water faucet. "There,
wash yourself and hurry up. You must be hungry."

I took a gulp from the faucet and splashed some of the
water on my face while Aunt Duon headed back inside the
house. I called out to her with mixed feelings about what I was
going to say next. "Mac!"

As soon as she heard me calling, she reappeared. "What's
wrong? Are you scared of the darkness?"

I hesitated a bit, "No, Mac, I have something important
to tell you."

She stared at me impatiently. "What?"

I continued, "I met a woman on the way here and she really ..."

She cut in sharply, "So you're telling me you're in love with a woman, right?"

"No Mac, I met a woman on the way this afternoon. She is very sick and she really needs help. We have to help her. She doesn't know anybody in this country. She said she wants to go west. Maybe we can do something for her."

Aunt Duon fixed her eyes on me. "No!" she shouted fiercely. "You mother fucker, you don't even know how to clean up your own situation and you're telling me you want to clean up others'? You and I could go to jail, young man!" Aunt Duon was so upset I thought she was going to faint. "It may turn out to be more of a burden than you want to take on. She could be a spy!" she said angrily.

Thinking Aunt Duon was being paranoid, I persisted, hoping to make her understand, "Mac, fine. Stop yelling. When I see her tomorrow, I'll tell her that we can't help her. It's that simple."

But Aunt Duon was really stirred up. "No, not tomorrow. I'm not involved with this. You are not going back to see her again. You have nothing to do with her. And stop making me worry about this."

Right after dinner, I went straight to bed without saying a word to anybody. I lay down in the middle of the floor, on an old dirty sticky pallet crowded with several other people. I tossed and turned, anxiously trying to fall asleep. Thoughts crowded my mind and I realized that I desperately missed Grandpa Kaing Hak Yi and everybody back home.

❀❀❀❀❀

I woke the next morning before the sun rose. While everybody was still asleep, I snuck out through the back door. Walking quickly to the riverbank, I found Thuy sitting at the same place where I left her on the sidewalk. The sun was rising along the riverside. At first, she was glad to see me, her pale face smiling wanly at me. Deeply torn by our situation, I told her that I could not help her, that it was not my decision to make.

She listened, silent and dejected. I put some cash in her hand and called her "sister Thuy" out of respect. "Please take this money with you and buy something to eat." I did not know what else to say. "I wish you luck."

She expressed her gratitude, telling me she would never forget my generosity. Taking a deep breath, I pulled myself upright and walked away from the riverbank. Filled with sadness for her, I wished I could have done more for her.

❀❀❀❀❀

After being gone for six years, it was hard to believe that I was back home again in Phnom Penh and trying to start life all over. While I had been staying with Aunt Duon at her home on the sixth day, we were eating lunch when there was a knock on the door. She opened the door to reveal a dark, skinny man with short, curly hair who talked softly with her for a few minutes. She then invited the man in and introduced him to me as Uncle Meah. Nervously, he shook my hand, turned around, and hastily left.

For a few minutes we resumed our lunch in silence. She then peered at me and anxiously uttered, "Sok Kha, it is time to go west."

I was a bit stunned and excited by the news.

Breathing deep and doubling down on her resolve, Aunt Duon went on, "We are going to leave Phnom Penh tomorrow before dawn, but because of the dangers that are still plaguing the roads we must travel separately."

Aunt Duon handed me a piece of light-brown paper with a red stamp, then instructed me, "Here is a document. It is forged. This is the only way. You must hold onto it and be extra careful not to lose it. If you are stopped or questioned by the guards, you must tell them that you came to Phnom Penh to visit your aunt, who is very sick, and now you are returning back to Sisophon, which is a small town in the north. You must say exactly what is on the document."

I was disturbed by the arrangement, knowing what would happen to anyone who was caught with forged documents.

Aunt Duon continued, "The man you just met was here at great danger to his own life. He told me that the road to Battambang province has become perilous. He notified me that many people have already been arrested by the army and security guards. We expect the worst for them."

These words instantly caused me great anxiety.

Freedom was within my grasp, but for me to earn it, a long journey was ahead that would require courage and vision and faith. That evening, I couldn't fall asleep. I was overwhelmed with anxiety as I wondered about what kind of life was waiting for me the next day on the road to the Cambodia-Thailand border. And then I tried to imagine what was beyond the border, the new world that I had to make for myself.

Finally, near dawn, it came to me, the word that encompassed all the hope and relief, pain and sorrow, relief and redemption: *freedom*.

Freedom is what I had been constantly struggling for since we were forced out of our home seven years ago, and that is what I vowed I would continue to fight for for the rest of my life.

Freedom.

Mama ' s cousin Aunt Pieng, taken in 1981 after surviving
the Khmer Rouge Genocide

Uncle Bun Hua, taken in 1986 after surviving the
Khmer Rouge Genocide

Acknowledgments

First, I would like to acknowledge my grandparents for their influence, and their legacy of love and pearls of wisdom. I would also like to thank my father for his courage and bravery in leading us across the border into the land of Vietnam, and my beloved mother for enduring everything just for me and my siblings, always wearing your warm, beautiful smile no matter how hard life was. I continue to owe you for my existence. I want to thank my beloved second mother, Dr. May Fung Mei Tam, for your sapience, rock-solid integrity, love, and great faith in me, and finally your courage to stand out against bigotry. Your history enriched me. For as long as I live, you are always in my heart. I also need to thank my beloved Eldest Uncle Phan and Aunt Kien for loving me and watching over me; to Aunt Pieng and Aunt Kim for loving me and revealing to me your courage and surviving strength; and to my brother, Dr. Vuong Lam, who once took good care of me and my family even though you lost your life to the brutal reign of Khmer Rouge with many other relatives. You all are always missed and never forgotten. Thanks are also due to my beloved Brother Chen, Sister Mei Juang, and Brother Sok, for their mutual courage and for sharing your bitter memories. And I would like to acknowledge my children—Udam, William, Hedan, and Samantha—for your support, contribution, and love during the very difficult time in my life. And to Uncle George and Aunt Amy Do's family" and all of my dear cousins, nephews, and nieces, for all of you to remember the story of our ancestors.

I cannot ever thank enough those individuals who helped make my dream come true. My soul brother, Christopher Rose, for your intelligence, brilliant insight, and brotherly love. Martine Bourquin, the International Red Cross delegate, for holding me accountable so I could achieve this project. Lt. Rob Guzman for your astute vision support and always being there throughout this journey. Sister Grace Su for your acumen, unconditional support, and labor of love. Ethel Newlin for your remarkable sharpness of mind and guidance. Cynthia Alexis, for lifting me up when I was falling; your discernment inspired me. Laurel Pallock, you have cheered me on all the way. Karin Shaw, you have surprised me with your creative spirit and gifted skills. Maria Alfaro Miguel for your encouragement and kind words. My jogging partner, Jason Colum, for pushing me to run and making sure I stay healthy. Anh Le Chi Quy with memories of all the love for watching me in the refugee camp. Audrey Moy, I value and respect your opinion. To Daren Wang and all of my friends whose names I may have forgotten to mention. And to all of my special fellow members of Viet-namese Land Refugees, I thank you all for being there for me and for helping me start this project; there will be more to come.

I would also like to acknowledge my great sympathy for all of my Cambodian fellow survivors, who had to endure the brutality of the Khmer Rouge. I salute every one of you for your courage in what you lived through. I must take this opportunity to remember my native innocent friend Karim, Tang Su-Kwong, who saved me when I was drowning in the river when we were exiled, and my friend Tang Liang, who was beaten to death after being accused of stealing. My heartfelt condolences go to all those who lost lives during this era. And to those brave souls who took the guts to write their stories: *There will never be the right words to recount our pain.*

For their help and guidance in the actual writing, editing, and production of this book, I would like to acknowledge Bob Cooper for his careful copy edit of the final draft of this book. Special thanks go out to graphic designer Jim Shubin of The Book Alchemist for his beautiful guidance in creating such a memorable and respectful cover and interior design, and for his help in getting the final book ready for printing at Ingram Spark in Berkeley, California. I would like to thank Phil Cousineau for his patient, careful, and respectful editorial guidance in shaping this book. You have been a great mentor. To have found someone who has visited Cambodia and deeply respects the culture has been fortuitous for me. And I would also like to express my gratitude to Gary Schouborg and Di Finch, who performed some early copy editing chores on this book, and Randy Rosenthal.

I can hardly express the width and depth of my thanks to Father Thomas Dunleavy, who befriended me at the Thai-Cambodia border refugee camp, and who for many years has been encouraging me to tell my story. My deep gratitude goes to Dr. Gilles Germain, Dr. Hali Hammer, Dr. Peter H. Hwang, Dr. David Tran, Alameda County Administrator Carlos Sanchez, Adjunct Professor Gayle Tang, and my dear friend Heidi Li Esq. for their generous support and endorse-ment of this project in its early stages.

Finally, I would like to express my gratitude to Dr. Nang Du for his support when I began this memoir for the way he encouraged me to keep going in the belief that my story might help to heal those who read it.

✿

The Author

During Sieu Sean Do's idyllic early years, he was immersed in the ancient rural Cambodian traditions practiced in the Kampong Speu province. His family then moved to Phnom Penh, where he adapted to the bustling city life of the capital until he was twelve. But that is when the Khmer Rouge seized control of the country to begin their awful reign of terror. City dwellers spared execution, including his family, were forced to relocate to the countryside and subjected to violence, brutality, and starvation.

After surviving a year in a labor camp in the Cambodian jungle, Sieu Sean and his family escaped and fled across the border into Vietnam. After six years, however, he realized that Vietnam offered refuge but no future. Cambodian refugees in camps in Thailand received resettlement offers to Europe, the US, or the British Commonwealth. So once again he risked his life and traveled back across northwestern Cambodia to a refugee camp on the Cambodia-Thai border.

Due to his fluency and aptitude for languages—Khmer, Vietnamese, Mandarin, Cantonese, Chew chow, French, and English—the American Refugee Committee trained him as a camp physician's assistant. He also supported the Inter-national Red Cross and Doctors Without Borders as a volunteer serving thousands of refugees in crisis.

A Cloak of Good Fortune, Sieu Sean Do's first book covers the portion of his life that concludes with his arrival in the Thai refugee camp. He is now working on a second book, focused on his life in the camp, which will document the little-known, life-and-death secrets that affected the desperate refugees he encountered there. These refugees struggled to adapt while enduring crowded confinement in a foreign land as they recuperated from trauma before figuring out their next moves toward freedom.

If you've enjoyed this book, please join my mailing list at sieu@sieuseando.com and I will send you an excerpt from the next book in my two-volume memoir.

CPSIA information can be obtained
at www.ICGtesting.com
Printed in the USA
BVHW040356140421
604820BV00005B/398